ROCKY MOUNTAIN
BOOM TOWN

ROCKY MOUNTAIN BOOM TOWN

A History of Durango, Colorado

By
Duane A. Smith

University Press of Colorado

Copyright © 1980, 1986, 1992 by Duane A. Smith

978.8
Smith

Published by the University Press of Colorado
P.O. Box 849
Niwot, Colorado 80544

9 8 7 6 5 4 3 2 1

The University Press of Colorado is a cooperative publishing enterprise supported, in part, by Adams State College, Colorado State University, Fort Lewis College, Mesa State College, Metropolitan State College of Denver, University of Colorado, University of Northern Colorado, University of Southern Colorado, and Western State College.

Library of Congress Cataloging-in-Publication Data

Smith, Duane A.
  Rocky Mountain boom town.
  Bibliography: p.
  Includes indexes.
  1. Durango (Colo.) — History.   I. Title.
F784.D9S64   1986   978.8'29   86-5071
ISBN: 0-87081-257-2

The paper used in this publication meets the minimum requirements of the American National Standard for Information Sciences—Permanence of Paper for Printed Library Materials. ANSI Z39.48–1984
∞

Cover photograph courtesy of Dana Helvey, Pennington Aerial Services, Durango, Colorado.

For Gay

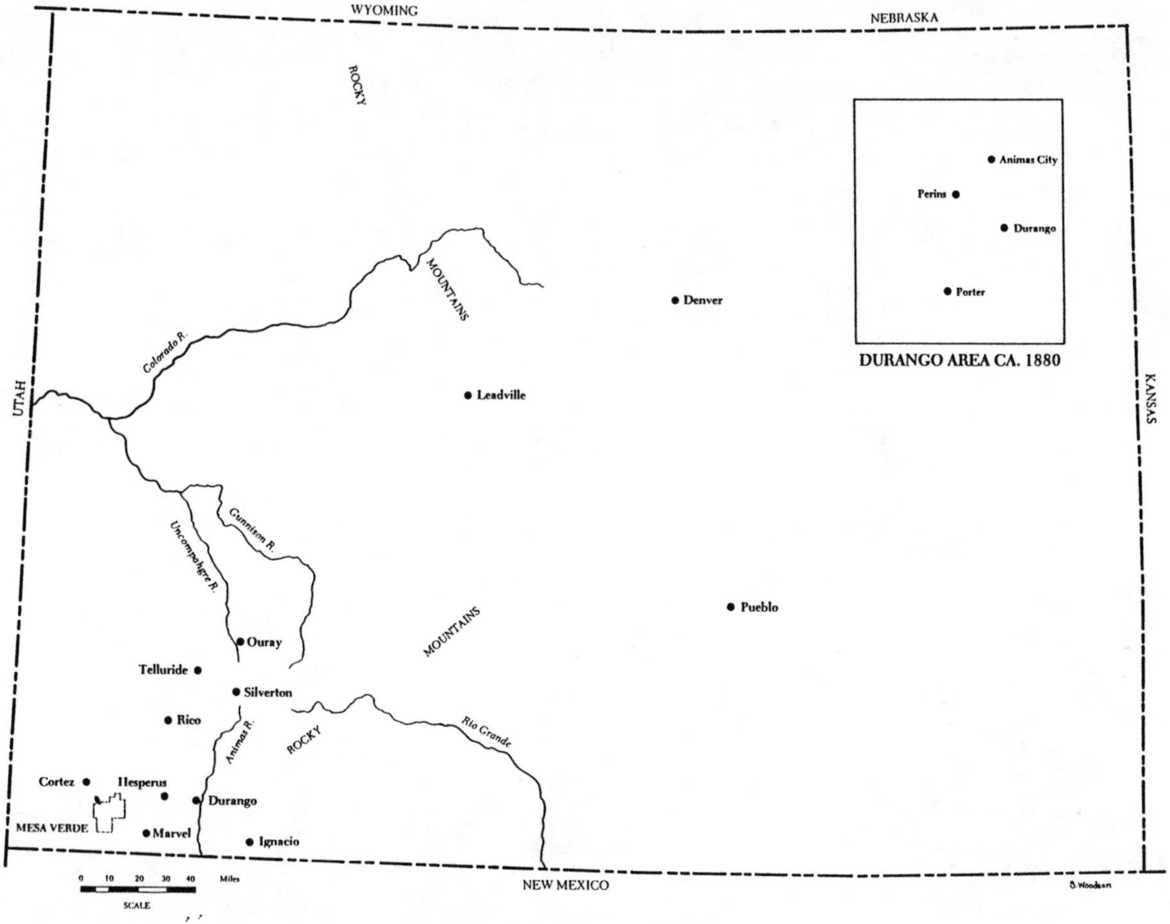

DURANGO AREA CA. 1880

- Animas City
- Perins
- Durango
- Porter

KANSAS

NEBRASKA

WYOMING

ROCKY

MOUNTAINS

- Denver
- Leadville

- Pueblo

Colorado R.

Gunnison R.

Uncompahgre R.

- Ouray
- Telluride
- Rico
- Silverton

ROCKY

MOUNTAINS

Animas R.

Rio Grande

- Cortez
- Hesperus
- Durango
- Ignacio
- Marvel

MESA VERDE

UTAH

NEW MEXICO

SCALE

0   10   20   30   40   Miles

SOUTHWESTERN COLORADO

S. Wooden

Contents

Tables

Preface

December 7, 1991, was a day for Americans to remember events of fifty years earlier, when World War II came crashing in on the United States with the bombing of Pearl Harbor. Durango, Colorado, has changed immensely during the five decades sine then, but no more subtly or significantly than in the past five years.

The economy of Durango has rebounded from the doldrums of the mid-1980s as tourism has increased, the college (Ft. Lewis) has grown, and business has improved. Once again Durango has managed to avoid the extreme highs and lows of a fluctuating U.S. economy. By steering a less turbulent course, it bucked a national trend. The same was true when durango maintained the viability of its downtown business district against the treat of shopping malls.

Tourists visiting Durango have begun traveling in new ways — coming earlier and staying later. No longer is Main Avenue crowded only during the summer months; today the tourist season stretches from early May to late October. Families continue to predominate throughout the traditional vacation months, while senior citizens and others without children prevail during the extended season. The narrow-gauge train, Mesa Verde, and the scenery have maintained their positions as the premier attractions. Though Purgatory ski area has endured some difficult seasons in recent years, as have the majority of Colorado ski resorts, early snows in 1991 promise better days.

La Plata County and Durango find themselves at loggerheads on a variety of issues in early 1992, including home rule for the county and the fate of its Main Avenue–ensconced fairgrounds. Durango)population 12,430 in the 1990 census) constitutes the core of the increasingly urbanized northern section of the county; these "suburbs" have experienced most of the growth of the eighties. As a result, the purely rural areas have dropped further behind in economic importance and political clout, a local example of what is happening throughout Colorado. These changes have only intensified already strong opinions and emotions. As the nineties move along, debate continues to center on two controversies: establishment of county home rule, designed to lessen the power of the commissioners, and the relocation of the fairgrounds, creating the need for another decision about what to do with the old site. A resolution of these issues may come in 1992, but the underlying differences of parties on both sides will no doubt live on.

One relic of the past disappeared when, in 1991, the Environmental Protection Agency finally completed removal of uranium tailings from the old smelter site on the banks of the Animas River. Now the disposition of the land at the foot of Smelter Mountain has become an issue for debate. The Animas–La Plata Project took a few more twists and turns during this same time and seems to be nearing the start of construction in the spring of 1992.

Meanwhile, for a variety of reasons, Durango is being "discovered" by people seeking a haven from traffic congestion, crowded conditions, and many other drawbacks associated with large metropolitan areas. These individuals want a "family mountain town," not an Aspen or a Vail's "Peter Pan Wonderland." The result has been an improved real estate market, rising prices, a population influx, and, for better or worse, growing popularity. The small-town Durango of 1941, with its rural hinterland, has faded into oblivion.

Though their heritage has become only a memory, Durangoans are working valiantly to preserve it, evidenced by the approval of a preservation ordinance and the creation of a board to oversee its implementation. As part of the town's quality of life and attractiveness to tourists, the importance of Durango's Victorian and early twentieth-century history cannot be underestimated. Nor does a better way exist for newcomers to put down roots than to understand their community's past and then to involve themselves in its present and its plans for the future.

Durangoans have come to appreciate their role as stewards of their heritage. No one else can fill that role. With the past looking over their shoulders and the future in their own hands, they look forward to the nineties with a faith and optimism that would have made their 1890 forebears proud.

Duane A. Smith
December 1991

Preface to the First Edition

Durango! The name rings of the frontier West, a legendary land and time. The town's location—a river valley oasis in a semidesert, mountainous region—could hardly be more beautiful or more typically western. The reader is certainly justified, though, if he questions whether this supplies enough basis for writing a book.

The answer is yes and no. Inescapably, Durango's history provides a fascinating subject. It stands, as Walter Prescott Webb once said of the West, at the end of an era and the beginning of a legend. Many legendary strands have been woven into Durango's story, creating a myth that never was, yet always will be. Part of the fun of this research was probing and weighing the facts, trying to match Sherlock Holmes's expertise in separating them from the fiction.

Another significant reason for writing this book was to recall some interesting people before they vanished into history. Civil War historian David Donald called history books "the limbo of lost souls." It is my sincere hope that the engaging charm and richness of the human story that is Durango comes through clearly in the pages that follow. History is people; Durango is people. An appreciation of them and their times produces a better awareness of the present and the future's challenges.

Colorado Senator Gary Hart perhaps expressed it best when he said of Durango, "This town, this part of the state represents everything that Colorado is all about. And Colorado represents everything that this country is all about." It is difficult to know one city well, but this book is intended to give the reader an understanding of the extent to which Durango is like other young American cities, and the extent to which it is unique, a product of its particular circumstances and situation.

Finally, the town is changing, rapidly and unabashedly. This is an attempt to document some of its spirit and its past before it is no more. Louis Newell, in a March 9, 1977, editorial in the *Herald*, caught the mood of change: "On second and third glance, on better acquaintance Durango doesn't look so much like the tranquil city for the golden age, but more and more like quarreling Mesa County, fractious Pitkin County. . . ."

Durango is growing; La Plata County is growing. "Bound to Boom," crowed the *Southwest* in a long-forgotten issue (December 1880). The newspaper soon migrated to the raw settlement from its doomed neighbor, Animas City. A doubled population by century's end is not an unreasonable assumption; an exponential growth rate of 3 percent would produce nearly that. As one person commented, "Durango of tomorrow can be seen in Los Angeles today." Studies indicate that when the population reaches 15,000, the interrelationship of social, economic, and political life changes, most noticeably with the decline of participation by community members. Durango is fast approaching this divide in its history. And always there remains the warning that the English poet Samuel Coleridge, among others, left to posterity, "If men could learn from history, what lessons it might teach us!"

For reasons now lost, no complete history of Durango has ever been written, although as early as the 1880s plans for one were discussed, and in 1915 Colorado Congressman Edward Taylor challenged the high school's senior class to do it. It should have been written before the pioneers were gone, an irredeemable oversight. My fifteen-year residency does not qualify me as an expert; an old-timer warned me, however, when I first came, "You'd better leave before the valley takes hold and you can't escape." His words were prophetic—Durango has taken hold; it is my home. I realize that this raises a serious question about the objectivity of this study. So be it.

Durango's history could not have been written without the interest and support of many friends. If someone remains unnamed, it is not because of lack of appreciation. It is simply that too much time has gone into the study to remember all the help given over the years. Ken Periman, Fred Kroeger, William Eakes, and Lyle Dorsett read chapters and offered constructive suggestions. City Clerk Lyle Fields proved most generous in helping find Durango records, as did retired County Clerk Avis Harris. Jackson Clark, Mac Randall, Earl Barker, Jr., Lloyd Gladson, and Sam Maynes helped in many ways; so did Maxine Peterson, W. G. and William Goodman, Ralph Downey, Marion Jarvis, Jim Sheppard, Linda Mannas, Richard Gilbert, David Martinez, and Eldon Koontz. Beverly Darmour, Patsy Tregoning, Jan Crandall, and Roma Sylvester transcribed interviews, as did Cathy Conrad, who also typed and endured a lot of friendly harassment along the road. Milford Shields graciously donated a poem, and many people allowed me to pry into their lives and their memories of Durango. Words cannot fully express my thanks.

Once again, my dear Texas buddy Marjorie Morey found Durango photographs in the Amon Carter Museum, and Lee Scamehorn provided assistance in several sticky matters. Marguerite Norton of the Center of Southwest Studies was particularly helpful, and a tip of the hat goes to Roberta Schilling for all those interlibrary loans, and to the rest of the Fort Lewis College library staff for their help. A prime motivator in igniting this project was the encouragement of Elsie Neff and Frances McCarthy and the Durango Public Library staff, who were also most helpful during the research, and my friends in the La Plata County Historical Society. As they have for so many years, the Colorado Historical Society and Denver Public Library could not have been more helpful. My sincere thanks to one and all.

Two people, above all, made the publication of this volume possible, Beth Gard and my wife. Beth encouraged, kept the faith, and shepherded the manuscript through publication. Gay has shared and enriched the beauty of our Durango years and proved a most patient, perceptive, and erudite editor and proficient typist. Without her, *Rocky Mountain Boom Town* would not have seen the light of day, and to her it is dedicated.

ROCKY MOUNTAIN
BOOM TOWN

Prologue

El Río de las Ánimas Perdidas, the Spanish named it: "the river of lost souls." It starts high in the San Juan Mountains, the silvery San Juans of legend, before rushing down a narrow, rocky canyon to burst out into a long, lovely valley. Then it stretches southward into the desert, there to join the San Juan River on its way to the sea, via the Colorado River. Not a long river, nor noted for the importance of its drainage lands, the Animas is still significant in its own right.

The river carves its course through mountains, some of which have reached the hoary age, geologists tell us, of over a billion years. Volcanoes once disgorged here, depositing the substances miners later came to dig. Glaciers gouged the opening for the water and deposited a terminal moraine in future Durango, to the dismay of later soil tillers. The water naturally followed this readymade route out of the mountains into the valley. Before reaching this point, however, the glaciers and river exposed a geology textbook.

Once gaining the valley floor, the Animas slows its pace between its companion reddish-brown cliffs. The valley broadens and, like a free spirit, the river has changed course at whim in the wide expanse known as the floodplain (before man put a stop to such inconvenience). At Durango the mountains crowd the river a bit, then widen the aperture to allow it to continue its southward journey.

Thanks to the Animas River, the valley became an oasis in a mostly semiarid land. In the well-watered valley grew grasses and trees, which attracted animals, as they would later humans.

For all its spectacular beauty, a majestic solitude prevailed over the valley, a lonely land. Isolated by deserts, mesas, and mountains, the Animas rolled unimpeded on its journey with no one to chronicle its story or that of its valley. A short time ago in its geologic history, about seventy-five generations removed by man's reckoning, Indians walked in, gathering berries along the way, hunting, and eventually huddling in caves for homes. Finally, then, the first tentative scratches were made on parchment, and they began the history of the valley and the river of lost souls.

PART ONE

Land of Milk and Honey
1870-1892

*[I Have come] . . . to bring them up out of that land
unto a good land and a large, unto a land flowing
with milk and honey; . . .*

Exodus 3:8

1. Planters of Empire

Peering through his transit, the surveyor signaled approval and a hammer's stroke planted the stake into the ground. Thus, on a late summer day in September 1880, a railroad's sleight of hand gave birth to Durango.

The busy surveying crew could not have realized the significance of their act. For centuries the natural beauty of the curving valley of the Animas River had rested undisturbed by man. Now it would never again be the same. Urban development had come to stay.

They surveyed and staked a pretty little bend in the valley. An early visitor wrote, "The whole place was covered with sage brush, sunflowers and some lofty pine trees." To the north the already snow-dusted San Juans glimmered; to the west scrub oak and pine-dotted mountains cut off the view, one particularly impressive peak looming like a ship's prow breaking a wave. The river oxbowed where they worked, giving birth to a rolling meadow stretching eastward until choked off by a steep-sided mesa.

Soon all the survey lines were drawn, the stakes driven. Where nature had held unchallenged sway, streets and blocks took shape. The progenitor of this flurry of activity, otherwise known as the Durango Trust, saw to it that certain lots were reserved for "preferred parties," the rest thrown open for public sale. Make way for the rush; Durango, "City of the Silver San Juan," had been born.

Durango might never have seen the light of day had not the ambitious Denver and Rio Grande Railroad clashed with a stubborn Animas City. The railroad's management planned to build through the valley and along the Animas Canyon to tap the rich mining district in the heart of the San Juan Mountains at Silverton. To do so, it had to go right past the small farming and ranching community of Animas City, two miles north of future Durango. The Rio Grande was willing to develop Animas City into a railroad center for a price and on its terms. Animas City would not stoop to either demand.

Those Animas City people displayed justifiable pride in what they had accomplished in the past few years. Overcoming all kinds of obstacles, they made Animas City the region's trading center. Animas City's determination was much like the early-day local rancher whose six children came down with scarlet fever, whose wife took sick, and who himself fell off the roof, breaking his arm. He thought for a few moments before deciding that he "might have to send for a doctor." The story is probably apocryphal, but the determination is not.

Animas City's origins remain hazy; settlers came into the valley in the early 1870s, responding to the high-priced agricultural market opening in the San Juan mining camps. Ranches and farms were compatible with the milder climate and longer growing season than those of the mountains. The river provided the water for this oasis in semiarid southwestern Colorado. Miners needed everything from oats to butter, and transportation costs effectively priced out much competition. Blessed by this monopoly and a growing demand, settlers took up homesteads in the valley so recently ceded to the United States by the Ute Indians.

Animas City was one of several towns that optimistic developers planned to promote in the valley. Elbert City and Hermosa shared a common fate—neither survived for long, after a short spurt of activity. Nor did they make their founder-promoters rich and famous. Animas City lasted longer. In January 1874, John Smails wrote a friend that he intended to go to Animas City to secure a few good lots and also a ranch. Whether he actually did so is not known, but he referred to Animas City as a going concern. It seems likely that he had in mind this Animas City, not an earlier, similarly named community. (Animas City No. 1, located northward up the valley near today's Baker's Bridge, lasted two years, 1860–61. It was part of the first mining rush into the San Juans.) In August 1876, the townsite was officially surveyed, and two years later residents voted to incorporate. The founding date is of little significance now. Backers of the town, the Animas City Town Site Company, dreamed of a fortune that never materialized.

As farming communities are apt to do, Animas City grew slowly. The 1880 census taker found 286 residents of solidly American stock, a large percentage of them married couples. The small business district encompassed a hotel, livery stable, lumber dealer, saloon, butcher, and a couple of general merchants—enough to satisfy the local clientele. Unusual for a community of this size, Animas City also possessed a newspaper, the *Southwest*.

This was no mining camp of sudden birth and unpredictable "boom-and-bust" fluctuations. It evinced more of a midwestern rural flavor than a mining camp atmosphere. The seasons came and went without much change, except during the winter, when miners moved down from the mountains to enjoy the milder weather. Although Animas City offered few amusements, it had an abundance of farm products and a nearby hot springs for hungry and bone-weary miners.

Church services and a school enhanced the village's appearance. The well-known Presbyterian minister George Darley reached here in 1877 to organize a congregation. A year later one of his colleagues ran into difficulties and sadly concluded, "Many do not wish to give up dancing." They seemed to want to construct the church building, he observed, "just to get a church building here as an addition in building up a town, and now when I insist on membership first they have lost all interest." Further visions of grandeur appeared in attempts to wrest the county seat from Animas City's only rival, the mining camp of Parrott City, located to the west at the mouth of La Plata Canyon.

The measure of this rival was taken by 1880, and Animas City would have won the prize had fate proved kinder.

By 1879 ranching and farming had matured to the point that a flour mill, fruit trees, dairy cattle, and sufficient crops satisfied home demand and helped supply the San Juan market. A sawmill turned out lumber, and frame construction replaced earlier log structures. Animas City was putting on airs. Simply by backing a wagon up and taking a winter's supply, local residents launched a new industry, coal mining. Then an ambitious little company tapped the outcroppings and offered coal for sale. Exploitation had arrived. Some gold mining was even carried on in nearby Junction and Lightner creeks. To show its growing stature, Animas City went all out for the July 4 celebration in 1879. A blacksmith's "Anvil Chorus" rang in the patriotic dawn, followed by a day full of speeches, music by the ladies, lemonade, "pop-crackers," races, and a "hop" in the evening. Beer and whiskey undoubtedly lubricated some celebrants' enthusiasm, but the correspondent politely refrained from commenting on the fact.

Eleven companies of cavalry and infantry garrisoned Camp Animas during the uneasy aftermath of the killing of the Ute agent Nathan Meeker in the so-called Meeker Massacre, September 29, 1879. With them came fifty-six-year-old Major Alfred Hough, who saw the Animas Valley as a good place for a town. Of Animas City he wrote, "There are not more than 20 houses in this city but it has true Yankee enterprise— churches, a school & newspaper." Before he and the troops departed in January 1880, a shooting brought about the death of a cowboy, and the town marshal and the mayor fled to the camp for protection.

Season followed season, each seeming to be a little more promising. A door opened into Animas City's insular world in the winter of 1879–80, when Colorado's "baby railroad," the Denver and Rio Grande, announced plans to lay track up the Animas Valley on its way to Silverton. This was no new idea; at least six earlier schemes had proposed the same thing. The D&RG proved to be more tenacious than the others and actually appeared on the scene. Such a railroad connection would convert Animas City into a thriving regional trade center and gain for it the coveted county seat designation.

Alas, the smooth courtship turned rocky when the Denver and Rio Grande demanded a dowry. Exactly what it was is unknown, but if past examples held true, they wanted land for a depot or right-of-way, purchase of company stock, help in grading, or a combination of these. If such aid failed to be forthcoming, the railroad threatened to establish a rival community, a pattern already practiced at Trinidad and Pueblo. Misjudging its own significance and failing to read history, Animas City stood pat; haggling produced no compromise.

Following the failure of negotiations, the Rio Grande's William Bell and Alexander Hunt selected a site for the rival community. A physician with a bad case of railroad fever, Englishman Bell, long-time friend of the Rio Grande's founder, William Palmer, became one of Durango's principal early promoters. A master of municipal organization, Bell had traveled this path before for the Rio Grande. Former territorial Governor Hunt probably selected the name Durango because of the location's similarity to Durango, Mexico, where he had just traveled on railroad business.

As early as January 1881, Hunt was credited with suggesting the name; by the previous September, however, a Durango Mine in the vicinity already had a forty-foot-long tunnel, which must have resulted from a season or two of work. Whether the mine suggested the town name or vice versa will never be known. It does indicate that the name already may have been in use in the area. The meaning of the word Durango has also aroused burning controversy among antiquarians. Included in the various claimants are "meeting of the way," "enduring," "watertown," and "waterville."

By April 1880, businesses were planning to open in "the new town of Durango on the Rio Animas" when the D&RG reached the locality. On April 14, Bell purchased 160 acres for $500; the D&RG was ready. Still, the boosters of Animas City stood firm, either from ignorance of Palmer's technique of building almost to an established town and then throttling it, or because they feared no danger from upstart Durango. The *Southwest* hurled defiance in its May 1, 1880, issue: "What the 'new town of Durango' is to be or not to be, God and the D&RG Railroad only know." God claimed no part in the transaction; the latter took sole responsibility.

What might have been merely a bluff to force Animas City concessions became a serious proposition when they were not forthcoming. Spring mellowed into summer with little Durango activity. As one writer expressed it, "floating loose and had been for months, at first it [Durango] was just ready to drop down on Animas City, then it was scudding around between the head of the valley and the coal banks. . . ."

The lack of activity on the site did not mean Bell and Hunt had been resting. At the close of 1879, a number of persons, primarily Denver and Rio Grande people, had organized what they called the Durango Trust to purchase coal land and townsite property in new districts being opened by the railroad's extension. They subscribed $105,000 to underwrite the venture. Hunt fronted for the Trust in acquiring the townsite and also some twenty-three hundred acres of coal and agricultural land in the immediate vicinity. Bell officially became trustee in July 1880, and thereafter management of the Trust's affairs fell to him. Not wishing to put all their chips on one hand, they diversified, purchasing more coal lands near Crested Butte and shares in the Buena Vista and Crested Butte town companies.

The Animas City–D&RG impasse was broken unilaterally on September 13, when the Trust started surveying its site. Civil engineer Charles Perin, who would give his name to the towering peak across the river and to coal lands beyond, surveyed the townsite and sales began. The Trust hoped to make money from town sales, but probably held greater expectations for its coal and agricultural lands, which stood to appreciate in value once settlement flourished.

Plans had been carefully drawn for Durango. According to twenty-nine-year-old Cincinnati native Alfred P. Camp, who came down from Animas City in September to investigate what was happening, he had been told by the town agent, James Luttrell, that Main Avenue would be the "wholesale street," Second Avenue the "retail business," and future Third Avenue the residential boulevard, with "rows of trees down the middle like Colorado Springs." This would put the business streets along the first bench parallel to the Animas, and the residences, churches, and schools on the elevated table land away from noise and traffic dust and with a "fine mountain view." Brisk sales in September and October confirmed the Trust's faith in Durango. So good were they that Bell, who made only partial calls on pledged subscriptions in 1880, proudly declared the Trust's first dividend on March 15, 1881. Poor Animas City never paid any dividends to its founders. The Durango hubbub encouraged expectations there, but they died aborning when many of its merchants, including cautious banker Camp, cast their futures with its rival. Even its once ardent defender, the *Southwest,* packed press and pen and departed. Animas City became merely a railroad stop on the Rio Grande line to Silverton, a sort of nineteenth-century version of the "bedroom" community for Durango.

It was a shame that Animas City suffered such a fate. Its site would have been as easy to develop, albeit not as profitable for the Trust. The agriculture, coal, and nearby hardrock mining that Durango developed into a prosperous economy were nurtured by Animas City. Durango built upon Animas City's pioneering, offering no reward and little appreciation. Even the Parrott City and Animas City toll road, which the famous San Juan toll road and railroad builder Otto Mears purchased, went to Durango. Never had the Rio Grande's plan for rival town development worked so well in its behalf.

No time for tears or regrets—Durango boomed. Dubbed the "Denver of southern Colorado," the "magic city" took shape before one's very eyes. Money was to be made; lots once framed only by sagebrush sold for $200, then $300, and finally, choice corner spots, for $1,000. Homes and buildings needed to be built. Even with six sawmills working to the limit, lumber continued to be scarce, and local brickyards could not keep up with demand. The Trust at first planned to restrict construction to brick or stone buildings in the business portion; regrettably, this wise precaution was abandoned in the construction crush. Recently arrived Louisa Weinig remembered the sounds and sights:

> I shall never forget the excitement and noise going on as we entered the town where we were to make our home for so many years [November 1880]. Very few houses and stores were yet completed, but the noise made by wagons and teams and men, and by the saws and hammers of the builders proved that houses would soon take the place of tents, which were living and business quarters at that time.

The *Southwest,* just before decamping for Durango, said the "embryo city" was already assuming "metropolitan airs." Initial success spawned pride, optimism, and cockiness.

Durango cornered its share of the promotion market, far more than Animas City ever achieved. The *Denver Tribune* ran a one-and-a-half-column story on October 13, and news items appeared in papers throughout the state, particularly in nearby Rico and Silverton. "She is bound to boom," crowed the *Southwest* in December. Such success was equally bound to arouse jealousy. Already Silverton's press took some swipes at this upstart, and Denver was about ready to do the same.

Silverton had cause to be perturbed: Durango had stolen its smelter, a feat engineered by John Porter. The thirty-year-old Connecticut-born metallurgist and smelterman had ridden into the San Juans in the mid-1870s, then gone to Eureka, Nevada, before being lured back to Silverton as manager of the smelter. Realizing that Silverton did not provide the best locale for a smelter, he recommended the move.

Undoubtedly he was influenced by the railroad's plans; perhaps the two cooperated because the smelter would provide a tremendous market for the Rio Grande. By October 1880, construction was started, and on October 16 Silverton's *La Plata Miner* could only forecast simply that removal was not "fraught with [the] injury and disaster" many feared:

> The great cost of fuel, which is at best a poor material, and the disadvantages attending the operation of the smelter during the winter months, render it imperative, in the opinion of those interested to move the works to a point lower down, and further south, where cheap fuel, cheap labor, and a good climate will make smelting operations less expensive.

Without much effort, Durango acquired a significant industry, one that grew into a regional smelting center under Porter's skilled guidance. Porter's catholic interests led him into coal mining. Mines lay within hailing distance of the smelter, crowded on the Animas's west banks under what became known as Smelter Mountain, a mountain whose vegetation soon would be seared by fumes from that plant. Ambitious and driving, Porter quickly constructed kilns and had a quarry dug on the grounds to provide building material. Durango's first entrepreneur found plenty to occupy his time.

Meanwhile, back across the river, men with similar ideas worked just as feverishly. By mid-November, Durango's business district had seven hotels and restaurants, two blacksmith shops, two bakeries, eleven saloons, dance halls, meat markets, general stores, and a variety of other businesses. Bruce Hunt, son of Alexander, was on the scene early with a stock of goods to sell. The Trust knew a good thing when it saw one. Instant organization, however, also produced instant problems, such as poor sanitation, lawlessness, and a jerry-built, riff-raff slum along the river. The Trust had not anticipated building between its land and the Animas, but squatters did just that. Already a reported 2,000 people had crowded into Durango, and a forecast of 5,000 within two years did not seem unbelievable. A few of the more enthusiastic boosters placed the figure at 10,000.

Some wanted to rename the town Palmer City to honor the Denver and Rio Grande's visionary founder. That idea died in infancy, as did some other Palmer railroad dreams. Other Durangoans wished to incorporate, an idea whose need, but not its time, had come. Not unexpectedly, Durango was becoming somewhat unruly. The Rio Grande's construction crew and the "drifting crowd" always present at the birth of a new western community combined to cause the ruckus. Tough and efficient James Sullivan, acting deputy sheriff, found his hands full, with the nearest jail in Animas City. Consequently, the only thing he could do to maintain peace and order was to "knock down and drag out" the culprits, an art Sullivan "does successfully." Municipal law enforcement remained months away.

Permanency was assured by the time winter settled a cold grip on this youthful metropolis. "Old-timers" said there was not a "pleasanter place" to spend the winter in Colorado than Durango. Indeed, Durango displayed characteristics that charted its development for the next century: boosterism, a grow-or-die philosophy, real estate speculation, determination to become the queen city of southwestern Colorado and the San Juan Basin, and the aggressiveness to carry out its dreams. Such traits certainly were not unusual for late nineteenth-century urban America—every successful town had its Porters and Bells. The end would justify the means; already Animas City suffered from those means.

A few days into the new year, Caroline Romney, editor of the *Durango Record*, praised her town and the people who established it. She eulogized Durango as "the new city in the wilderness, . . . another monument to the energy, pluck and perseverance of that portion of the American people who constitute the planters of empire." "Planters of Empire" was what they hoped to be.

2. "One More River to Cross"

Durango—the name had a magnetism in 1881 that drew all kinds of people to the "richest part" of Colorado. In January, Durango was racing to fulfill the promises made for it. Few cared anymore about the fate of Animas City.

The community was well on its way, but just where was it going? The boosters' ballyhoo pictured an "already flourishing city" with many substantial buildings that would be "creditable to Denver," or any other city of thirty to forty thousand people. William Palmer glowingly described the area's coal potential, smelting works, and "mild and salubrious" climate to railroad stockholders in his April report. Durango's progress, he said, "is strong evidence of the faith of the people of Colorado in the immediate and future output of the San Juan silver mines."

On the other hand, its newness and other attractions assured it a tumultuous, somewhat wild, youth. Even before there was a Durango, the region had been infected with disputes over cattle and range land. One persistent feud involved two groups of adversaries, one based in Colorado, the other in Farmington, New Mexico. Complicating these problems was the fact that the raw settlement appealed to the typical "drifting crowd"; one person described them as "degenerates" looking for a fast buck or a temporary haven. Add to them the motley railroad crew, and it became inevitable that the fuse would burn toward an explosion. Making matters even worse was the absence of local government to keep things under control. Unincorporated, the town flourished, and La Plata County commissioners did not have the experience, finances, or power to govern it. In January 1879, for instance, they approved two liquor licenses for the whole county; in January 1881, twenty saloon bonds were approved for Durango and eight more returned for additional surety. The harassed, overworked deputy sheriff was more a symbol of concern than a deterrent to crime. So new was the numerically stronger, law-abiding populace that they had not congealed into a cohesive body to support law enforcement.

Initially, the press winked at the disorder. The *Durango Record*, January 29, called the first holdup a "sure sign of a booming town." Such newsprint logic belied the fact that crime was on the increase. Lawlessness increased in February, from public nuisances and petty crime to burglary. In March a cold-blooded murder resulted in the killer's lynching outside town. Even such drastic action failed to curb "the boys." The Coliseum "theater," of dubious reputation, attempted to contain rowdiness by requiring that weapons be checked at the bar. Nothing provided a lasting deterrent.

Finally, during Easter week in April, the dam broke. Lawlessness rampaged and citizens reacted. An early Sunday morning killing resulted in the lynching of the murderer, Henry Moorman, shortly after eleven that evening. To the twenty-three-year-old dentist, William Folsom, who had just ridden into town on a stage driven by Moorman, it was a sight to be remembered. "He was hung on a pine tree across the street from my office. . . . This was a hard country then." Editor Romney, in her account in the *Record*, swam in maudlin Victorian prose: "The pale moonlight glimmering through the rifted clouds clothed the ghastly face with a ghastlier pallor." A light wind swayed the body "to and fro" as a crowd gathered.

Then, on Monday morning, the two conflicting cattle gangs fought it out on the mesa directly east of town. Continuing the earlier dispute over rustling and control of the cattle range, the feud took on new meaning—supremacy in Durango. Isaac Stockton, the resident gunfighter and "western badman," led the local band. Riding and shooting like characters in a dime novel, they battled it out. Shots were sprayed over Durango, fortunately injuring no townspeople and doing little damage to the participants; only two were slightly wounded. Silverton's *La Plata Miner*, April 16, covered the battle with barely hidden glee:

> The Farmington light cavalry brigade under General Cox, advanced up the Animas on Sunday last, and arrived at Durango just about the time the entertainment given by the committee of safety was at its height and in view of the fact of the large number of people on the streets, General Cox's command did not attack the forces under General Stockton. . . .

> The troops on both sides conducted themselves with astonishing bravery under fire, and their movements gave evidence of the superior military skill of their respective commanders.

All this hullabaloo aroused residents to hold a meeting on Monday afternoon to devise ways to protect themselves and their city. Pleas to kick every disreputable character out of town immediately were overruled by calmer heads, who gave the undesirables until Tuesday noon! Returning from the wars, the Stockton crowd became incensed at the abrogation of their rights and threatened mayhem. Both sides cooled off, and A. P. Camp commented that all the uproar and disorder necessitated a vigilance committee because of the notorious "bad men crowded into town who wanted to run the place."

At the heart of the problem was more than just lawlessness—who *was* going to "run the place"? The merchants and others vehemently emphasized it would not be Stockton and his ilk. That April week marked the high-water line for the kinds of shenanigans that later became the favorite themes for television and Hollywood westerns. Triumph of the "good guys" was foreordained, if Durango hoped to mature into that cherished "city."

A situation obviously out of hand had begun to improve as the citizenry rallied. City government and law enforcement could offer immediate answers. Out of the noisy uproar of those turbulent months came the initiative for incorporation proceedings in March, and city elections in May. A typical frontier urban pattern emerged, somewhat accelerated by the times. The thought of those unfilled offices aroused political instincts, and three tickets advanced their candidates, the Liberal ticket winning.

Pioneer druggist John Taylor triumphed in the mayoralty race, joined by a recorder and four trustees, a businessman-controlled body, most of whom had signed the incorporation petition. These founding fathers set about to create a government. During the month following their May 16 installation, they were battered by a whirlwind of issues and problems, from creating ordinances to dealing with day-to-day nuisances. No local precedents could serve as guides. An eye toward long-range development, and a firm conviction as to what the future of Durango should be, guided the discussions. Most likely, the group was more active during this month than any similar group in Durango has been since. Those unsung men were the real pioneer stalwarts, not the Stockton breed, who received far more attention.

The young city's first crisis required that something be done quickly, and the response amazed even the dubious. By May 30, eleven ordinances had been written and approved, including appointment of city officers and regulation of their duties, definition of misdemeanors and nuisances, establishment of business licenses, and regulation of the sale of intoxicating liquors. A strongly worded fire ordinance and provision for a police department and police judges showed they meant business. Indicative of the urgency of the problems was the fact that all council actions were a response to immediate needs. Within two weeks the framework of government and law was established, and a source of revenue had been found to pay for it. Legitimate businesses paid lower license fees than their more unsavory neighbors (billiard halls, shooting galleries, hucksters, and the like). In the midst of all this activity, the city fathers also found time to pass an ordinance (#7) prohibiting dogs running at large (it proved ineffective). Among his other duties, the marshal was instructed to kill any bitch in heat found loose in the town.

The city council met eight times in May, four in June, and seven in July, as it hastened to defuse inflammatory issues. It instituted meeting procedures, appointed permanent committees (four), and elected or appointed town officials. As one of its first efforts, it selected a town marshal and two policemen, a number soon increased. Bids were advertised to feed the city prisoners a spartan offering of bread, meat, and coffee or water. The economy was attractive to those not incarcerated; the lowest bidder offered twenty-one meals for $3.25. The street commissioner was directed to clean the streets, which he did, hauling 202 loads of rubbish outside the city limits. Nineteenth-century Durangoans were prone to litter!

All these things cost money, and by June 6, $354 had been collected in business licenses and fines. The city collected, but not without protest from the contributors. The liquor interests, unhappy with their $400 annual fee, protested mightily and petitioned the council for redress on June 10, the first of many such confrontations between the two groups over the years. The trustees responded in typical fashion by appointing a committee to look into the matter, and there it rested until the city got tough in September and demanded payment of the full fee. By September, over $5,500 had come into the city coffers.

The municipal honeymoon was interrupted by occasional problems, one of them being the inability to keep a police force. By the end of July one member of the force had been fired (reasons unspecified) and others had resigned. The council and marshal persevered. Durango eventually calmed down, and the city government emerged with the power and backing to govern.

Marshal Robert Dwyer and his force had their hands full mopping up the aftermath of Durango's eight months of negligence. He remembered:

> A typical instance of trouble-making was of the tough cowboy who had been painting the town red; he rode his horse right into a saloon, twirling a revolver in each hand. I started forward to arrest him, when Mike Moran, the bartender, exclaimed, "For God's sake, Bob, don't interfere or he will shoot up the place!"

Seeing thirty-six-year-old Bob Dwyer in action was impressive. Years later George Doughty recalled, "Bob Dwyer had plenty of nerve and was the coolest man I ever saw." Dwyer served for a little over a year, until a deputy making an arrest accidentally shot his boss. The wound proved so serious that Dwyer went east to have the bullet removed from against his jugular vein. His career as marshal had ended and this Irishman turned to ranching.

Symbolically, the end of the lawless period came in September with the death of Ike Stockton, who was mortally wounded while resisting arrest. Durango's "gunfighter" was consigned to the Animas City cemetery, almost unmourned. All this provided grist for the local press mill, and the *Durango Herald* rose to the occasion on September 22:

> They were both [Stockton and companion Bud Galbreth] known to be desperate characters with rewards on their heads, and are about the last of a gang of hard citizens who have caused a world of trouble in Southwestern Colorado and Northern New Mexico. Pity for the innocent wives and children is universal, but there are few to mourn over the fate of the men.

Durango's newspapers had come of age. Five made their debut within a year of the town's birth. The *Herald*, through several rises and falls, would prove to be the most long-lived, but the *Record* had the most immediate impact. The latter had its editor, Mrs. Caroline Westcott Romney, to thank for its prominence. In a day of freewheeling journalism, she had mastered her trade. An outstanding editor, the energetic Romney brought her press down from Leadville in December 1880, hustling to be Durango's first daily paper. Cheerful even under the worst of conditions, she reportedly sang the old gospel song "One More River to Cross" to encourage her freighters as they struggled through the winter's snow. They crossed one river thirty times, by Mrs. Romney's count, and another sixteen, with no bridges.

She did not stop battling once she reached Durango. The slightly plump (it was fashionable), "very pretty" little lady feared nothing, and her sharp pen jabbed at everything, from Denver to Ike Stockton. She even refused to retract a statement in the face of a Stockton threat. Before the year ran out, she and her rivals were deeply immersed in local politics, newspaper jealousies, the boosting of Durango, and innumerable individual issues. Mrs. Romney, upon arrival, had promised to devote herself first and foremost to Durango, "the new wonder in the Southwest," then to southwestern Colorado, "a land not only 'flowing with milk and honey' but seamed with silver and gold and floored with coal." She supported women's rights, advocated Sunday closings for business, attacked patent medicine advertisers who wanted too much space at too low rates, and encouraged girls to come and tame the masculine world. "The only lack of resources is those potent civilizers of their pioneer brothers—the girls."

Caroline also took the Denver press to task for "conspiring" against Durango's reputation with its lurid coverage of the town's lawlessness. Like many others, she chose to shift most of the blame for outlawry to the Farmington crowd, a convenient scapegoat. Already jealousy between Denver and Durango had surfaced, most of it undoubtedly reflecting the insecurity of a youthful Durango. Nicknamed the "Denver of the Southwest," which sounded just fine to local ears, the young city brooked no threats or challenges to its supremacy. Denver, Colorado's leading city, was worth emulating. Some basis for comparison actually existed: Durango was a natural gateway to the San Juan mining region, had a "charming climate," controlled potentially rich agricultural and mining territory, and was growing into an important business center.

However, Denver journalists' demeaning description of Durango as a "town to which hell itself is a paradise" cooled a budding relationship. Romney urged a retaliatory vote against Denver in the election of 1881 to decide the location of the state capital. She and others continued to call for a "square deal" for the city and region, sounding a challenge that echoed down to the next century. On Durango's part, jealousy, fear, and envy of the big city fueled the feud, which was pretty much one-sided since Denver generally ignored the upstart, thereby rubbing salt into the sore.

Similar, less heated squabbles involved nearby towns, including Silverton, whose newspaper audaciously charged, "Durango is a modest town with modest editors, modest aspirations but great expectations," and concluded by saying that Durango offered little inducement for immigration. Only Rico seemed to be compatible with its neighbor, perhaps because neither saw the other as a rival, but rather as a complement to one another. The pecking order needed to be established, the measure of the rival taken.

The newspapers also chronicled Durango's first political year. In one of the less important local issues, Mrs. Romney's call to punish Denver failed when Durangoans voted overwhelmingly to retain it as the capital. Two chauvinist diehards voted for Durango, 676 for Denver, and 143 for Pueblo. Durango was politically a man's world; women could vote only in school elections, which they did in May. By the November general election, the press spat partisan venom, with charges such as "vile slander," "conceived in iniquity and born in sin," and "prostitute" inciting the reader. Durango had come of age politically as well.

The most momentous local contest was the fight for location of the county seat, a prize worth attaining. La Plata County then included all of southwestern Colorado, with the county seat located in the small, isolated, declining mining camp of Parrott City. Serving as the county seat guaranteed increased business (court sessions offered a fine time to trade), jobs, permanence, and community prestige. Durango coveted the honor, and what it wanted, it got. Almost from the driving of the first survey stake, its residents had schemed to win the designation. It took more than plotting—a two-thirds county vote was needed to approve the shift. In July 1881, the county commissioners were presented with a petition calling for an election, which they set for November. With the support of Durango businessmen, press, and ordinary citizens, there was little question of the outcome. Parrott City was doomed from the start. As the *Record* blithely argued, "Parrott City people don't want to live there in the winter anyway. Let them vote for Durango, where they will spend at least half of the year." The Durango Trust sweetened the pot by setting aside half a block of land for county purposes, offering more if needed.

Parrott City disregarded Mrs. Romney's appeal, voting 71–1 to retain the county seat. Already Durango's political clout dominated the county, as the town voted 605–9 to secure it. Even Animas City, which had ample reason to take revenge on its neighbor, voted 101–5 in favor of Durango. The *Herald* proclaimed on November 10:

> The choice of Durango for the future county seat of La Plata County is an excellent thing for this city and will result in good to the entire county. Even Parrott City will suffer no injury from the removal. Parrott would be poor, indeed, if its future depended upon the holding of the county-seat.

Poor Parrott City—the young giant on the Animas had trampled its second victim. Neither Animas City nor Parrott City ever recovered; the latter declined to the point of near abandonment within a decade. The building of the "magic metropolis" produced its less noble aspects, but Durangoans had no time to bemoan the fate of Parrott City and its like. The strong would survive and evolve; had it not been foretold in this age of Darwinism?

The Durango Trust, meanwhile, had been busy in ways other than donating land for the county seat. A half block went for a school and two lots for a city hall. The brisk sale of lots bestowed the first 10 percent dividend on jubilant stockholders, and a second one was announced before 1881 ended; the other profits went into purchasing more land. Durango, Bell wrote an investor, "is assuming the proportions of a city." The Trust encouraged anything that would improve it: churches (with a free lot), newspapers, and businesses. The Trust had faith—its energetic agent, James Luttrell, was supervising construction of a two-story brick and sandstone building for the Hunts.

The trustees also watched with interest the construction of the smelter across the Animas and the coming of the Denver and Rio Grande. All were interrelated—the smelter, railroad, and town. As the *Engineering and Mining Journal,* July 2, 1881, reported, three directors of the D&RG served on the directory of the smelting company. Porter and mining engineer J. H. Ernest Waters, construction superintendent, vigorously pushed the building of the smelter. From the start the company put its smelter in the hands of a well-trained staff, a wise procedure that paid dividends. The plant was not completely operational by the end of the year, awaiting the completion of the railroad to Silverton.

The train assured success, because it was "easier for the ores to reach Durango by downhill grade, than it was for coal to reach Silverton by an uphill grade." As soon as spring weather permitted, the D&RG pushed on toward a town that awaited its arrival with an eagerness born of visions of profits. A summer slump was expected to lift once the train arrived. With great rejoicing and proper celebration, Durangoans greeted the official first train on August 5. The railroad, not allowing the tumult of the celebration to go to its head, promptly notified firms with buildings overlapping the railroad right-of-way on Railroad Street to move. Twelve businesses reluctantly did so, and the Rio Grande raced on toward Silverton. The company also unearthed some serious payroll discrepancies in the San Juan division, and the guilty superintendent was arrested. Winter closed in before the tracks conquered the Animas Canyon. Silverton had to await the coming of another year.

The marriage between the railroad and its town began smoothly enough, except for those squatting merchants. Both parties believed only blessings and bounty lay ahead. Durango was depending on the railroad to make it the region's dominant community by lowering the cost of living, providing year-round transportation, and stimulating the local economy. The Rio Grande envisioned a growing market, multiplying passenger and freight revenues, and a community guided by its leadership.

Durango's future truly rested with transportation. It could not hope to reach the promised millennium with horses, stagecoach, and wagon. The Sanderson Stage Line had arrived in 1880. And soon after, there was the local Pioneer Stage Line running to Silverton, Parrott City, Fort Lewis, Rico, and elsewhere. Horace Tabor, Colorado's great silver-mining entrepreneur, purchased the firm, renamed it the H. A. W. Tabor Pioneer Stage and Express Line (it operated even after the arrival of the train), and ran stages to the outlying settlements. Even Tabor's millions could not cushion the trip to Durango, and Mrs. Romney's "One More River to Cross" was probably echoed by many. Dentist Folsom remembered the trip over very muddy roads, on a stage that hit a stump just outside Pagosa, turning over and throwing the passengers into the river. One broken arm and a thoroughly soaked, depressed group of passengers were the casualties of the accident.

The visitor's impression of Durango was not always the one the hometown folks hoped to convey. Young Eva Pearson, coming from Elgin, Illinois, "stepped off into the sage-brush," and asked her father, "Is this Durango?" It was, and it did not seem like any town she had ever known. More to the residents' liking would have been the impression of Laura Laurenson, who first saw Durango from a stagecoach window in the early morning hours. Though it was past midnight, the well-lighted streets buzzed with activity, and the sound of voices and laughter could be heard over it all. On her way to Fort Lewis to be married, she stayed at the Grand Central Hotel, locally considered a fine establishment, where thin board partitions muffled no sound, much to Miss Laurenson's disgust.

Was it to be a "sagebrush metropolis" or a thriving community? Its residents were determined to see that the latter impression prevailed. They agreed with Horace Tabor's favorable opinion of Durango and his evaluation that southwestern Colorado was "destined" to be one of the "richest and most prospering" portions of the state. They hoped others would follow the investment instincts of Colorado's best known business and mining magnate. It pleased them when the state and eastern press puffed their community, and they became outspokenly defensive when it did not. When in February 1881 Denver's *Rocky Mountain News* praised the region for having the state's best agricultural land, beautiful scenery, and a wonderful, though little developed, mining potential, the local elation was evident. Pride almost burst all bounds when the respected *Engineering and Mining Journal* described Durango as an unusually attractive community with a class of buildings doing credit to any new town. It was frosting on the cake when *Frank Leslie's Illustrated Newspaper* (May 28) called it "the yellowpine metropolis of the San Juan," with an outlook in "every way hopeful and encouraging." Even that favorite of the barber shop and saloon, the risqué *National Police Gazette*, carried a story in praise of Durango.

This was a place to make money, a town with a future. Come to Durango! The young, the middle-aged with the spark of adventure, the ones to make something of themselves—those were the kinds who were wanted. It was, one old-timer declared, "too exciting for his declining years." Durango was a town to grow with.

In their haste to settle and build a community, Durangoans ignored the seamier side of the town. Refuse desecrated the site and beyond. The county commissioners protested the dumping of "garbage and offal" along the banks of the Animas by residents and/or the city. The 202 wagonloads of trash and those that followed had to be put somewhere! Crowded between railroad and river grew the well-named "poverty flat." Beyond the Trust's property, people squatted in tents, shacks, or whatever they could afford. Here also the red-light district staked its claim, along with saloons, variety theaters, gambling houses, and dance halls. "This section has a considerable sprinkling of honest businesses," a visitor noted, "but is in places a little off color." The city's first slum thus began.

The red-light district's location resulted from natural selection, part of it a zoning by rejection. The city fathers at first virtuously prohibited bawdy houses and gambling. But virtue soon gave way to practicality and profits. The "games and women" provided a good source of revenue ($235 by September 1); every month they were fined and permitted to continue unmolested. Victorian sensibilities would not even allow them to be called prostitutes in the press; "erring sisters" and "soiled doves" were the preferred genteel euphemisms. Although a veil of secrecy was drawn over the red-light district, it attracted business to town by providing needed services.

Only occasionally was that veil drawn back, as when "Maud Austin" died. Mrs. Romney penned an editorial about that "remarkably good looking woman," who lived a "life of shame, and here we drop the veil of charity." A rumpus involving the ladies of the line might make the paper, as would an unusual show in the Coliseum, such as a fight between two men of "color." Nor was Durango pleased when Silverton, in a temporary burst of piety, drove the gamblers and harlots out; most of them simply shifted their base to Durango. Finally, in response to pressure from a growing minority, the city government resolved in December to confine all houses of prostitution to the area west of Railroad Street, a nineteenth-century form of zoning.

Durangoans received a shock in September, when an opium "dive," doing a "very good business," was discovered. The call went out for the authorities to close it down. Promptly blamed on the Chinese, the whole affair raised doubts about whether they should be allowed to take up residence. The question had come up before in the spring, when their arrival provoked some harassment. Chin Hock, a naturalized American who was given a week to leave, called his oppressors' bluff and asked for protection by law officers. The Chinese had come to stay and, though they got off to a bad start, generally found town residents congenial.

When not concerned with sordid exposés, the newspapers lavished praise on a multitude of community "firsts," not all of which merited so much attention. The first marriage, robbery, death, church meetings, school, theater, stock growers' organization, dancing club, and Masonic installation naturally caught reporters' attentions. The first baby, Una Pearson, received a rousing welcome, including a lot from the Trust, a dog, a bag of gold dust, and a feature article in the *National Police Gazette*. The papers also announced "The Durango" (a "boss cigar"), carried the advertisement of a violin teacher, mentioned a small orchestra ("first class music"), described the memorial services for President James Garfield, and related the purchase of a fire engine. The papers described with pride the building of the school (Longfellow), which, to the relief of the children, was not completed until 1882, and recorded the July 4, Thanksgiving, and Christmas celebrations. A fledgling sports page brought the results of the Durango nine's games; the national pastime had come to southwestern Colorado.

"DURANGO AT FEVER HEAT. GOLD! GOLD! GOLD!" screamed the *Record* on April 30, during Durango's only local gold excitement in 1881. Although claims were staked along the entire river bottom at the big bend, none of them panned out. Nor did coal create much interest, even with the local product already on the market.

Development of Peter Fassbinder's addition, just north of K Street (current Twelfth Street) to the river, was watched with pride. Lots ranged in price from $75 to $250, with easy terms and plenty of water. German-born Fassbinder became a small-town entrepreneur; after homesteading land with a spring on it, he piped the water over the river, barreled it, and sold it in town. He also built the first bridge across the Animas, primarily to help sell his lots in another addition over there, then watched it wash away during high water in April. Nothing daunted him; at forty-six he was just starting his Durango career.

The first subdivision appeared early, in January 1881, but the Trust did not seem concerned. Its agent, Luttrell, was busy selling the company's lots, and he controlled the Trust's local activities for Bell and the others. Indeed, the *Rocky Mountain News* patted him on the back for helping to locate the community. There was land and lot speculation enough for the Trust, for Fassbinder, and anyone else who dared to dabble. During the first few years prices rose and fell against an upward curve. Those who failed to get in on the ground floor might suffer the misfortune of Harry Jackson, pioneer hardware merchant. He turned down a chance to buy two lots for $1,000 and had to pay $4,000 for them a couple of years later.

As the town grew, so did its business district, which by March included a reported 134 business houses, although the permanence of some of them was questionable. Twelve lawyers hung out their shingles, only to find that an epidemic of lawsuits did not always accompany the boom of a western community; ten dealers in real estate and mines had also opened offices—the plague had arrived.

As 1881 drew to a close, Durangoans could look back on an exciting, rewarding year. No other Colorado community could boast of having secured railroad connections, the county seat, five newspapers, and the biggest building boom in its history within twelve months. And it was not over. The depot and the Methodist Church were nearly completed, and the Presbyterians were building. They had all helped make it possible, those diverse Durango pioneers—William Bell, Maud Austin, Peter Fassbinder, John Porter, Ike Stockton, John Taylor, Bob Dwyer, Caroline Romney, Chin Hock, Una Pearson, and the silent corps of others now forgotten. All of them were "planters of empire," to use Mrs. Romney's words.

Under their guidance Durango had changed dramatically; never would there be another period like the past sixteen months. Perhaps those days look more adventuresome now that the passage of years has mellowed the scene. It seems reasonable to assume, though, that those early residents thought of themselves as adventuresome pioneers. They built well—their achievement not individual, but total; their vision not past, but present and future.

Young Alfred Camp in 1876 or 1877, just after a season in the San Juans and about to take up banking in Del Norte. He eventually migrated to Animas City, then to Durango, where he established a banking dynasty. Married in 1883, he established one of the first families of Durango, one whose influence continued up to the 1960s. *Center of Southwest Studies*

Nearly sixty, Caroline Romney still looked as determined as when she edited Durango's best pioneer newspaper. Lively, cheerful, and attractive, Caroline kept her readers interested and the town alert. Little escaped her eye and pen. Few women have matched her influence in the years since. *Denver Republican, July 28, 1901*

No one did more to establish Durango on a firm foundation than John Porter. The smelter, coal mines, the trolley — the list goes on and on — owed their existence to him. So fleet is fame the by the mid-twentieth century he had been nearly forgotten, but Durango owes a great debt to this man. *Colorado Historical Society*

Thomas Graden, shown here in later life, was one of the most popular men in early Durango, and also one of the most energetic. He had his hand in many enterprises, including one store still in business. It was said of him that he did not like copper coins; thus his cashier threw out any pennies found in the till at the close of business. *Helen S. Daniels*

Richard McCloud, lawyer and author, promoted Durango continually. Born in Dublin County, Ireland, McCloud practiced law in Silverton before casting his lot with the rival downstream on the Animas. *Duane A. Smith*

23

In the late 1880s and during the hard times of the 1890s, Ernest Amy managed the San Juan smelter. Active in Durango, his most enduring monument is the fine mansion on Third Avenue, now the Hood Mortuary. *Duane A. Smith*

Colorado Senator Charles Newman, if you please. The pioneer druggist and Rico mine owner represented the Nineteenth District in the 1890s. His building on Main Avenue represented the best of local architecture, and Newman symbolized Durango's power elite. *Denver Public Library, Western History Department*

Dave Day and friend enjoying a leisurely afternoon. Dave was not considered a "turkey" by his contemporaries; one wonders what the one on his lap thought of this man. Whatever, Day kept the Durango pot stirred up with his satire and practical jokes. *Western Historical Collections, University of Colorado*

3. "Until Durango Has a Population of 100,000"

The decade of the eighties saw the dream of the Durango Trust realized. The town it had midwifed and nurtured grew into a strapping youth. As a dutiful parent, the Trust had times of anxiety and moments of pride; unlike some parents, however, it planned to make a profit from its offspring, and it did. By 1884, 840 of the original 1,780 lots had been sold for a gross of $127,563, or about $160 per lot. Not entirely materialistic, the Trust donated 21 lots for schools and churches.

William Bell continued to chart the Trust's course; and when he proposed to convert the Trust into a company, the stockholders concurred. On September 1, 1884, all the Trust's property was "purchased" by the Durango Land and Coal Company with Bell continuing to superintend affairs. In the Trust's last report, Bell wrote with pride and practicality: "Leadville excepted, no town in Colorado had such a 'boom' as Durango, during the first two years of its existence. After this the demand for lots gradually lessened until it practically, for the time being, has come to an end." He warned stockholders not to expect another selling spree until the town built up and the population expanded.

From the Colorado Springs office the company watched Durango's development. Unhappily for it, the move was northward into the Fassbinder Addition, where no profit was to be made. The originators of the scheme bemoaned the fact that the townsite they had developed offered so little land "well adapted" for additions. Then in 1889 prospects brightened with a southern swing; even so, lot sales stagnated. All this provided little to cheer President William J. Palmer, Vice-president John Porter, and Bell, but they did not lose faith. That faith was soon rewarded, because in 1891 and 1892 Durango boomed again. Never willing to say it was down, the company opened the Mountain View Addition on its original property and developed the Sunnyside Addition north of Fassbinder. It also joined with "farseeing and influential" citizens to purchase 330 shares of the Durango Railway and Realty Company, which owned the horse-drawn Main Avenue Railway and former city marshal Robert Dwyer's homestead. The rail line was extended to their property and eventually into Animas City and converted from horsepower to electricity. Durango prospered, so why not plunge again?

It was not Bell, Palmer, and the other absentee owners who pulled the strings behind the scenes. John Porter, on the scene, shouldered the biggest load. A large stockholder in the Durango Railway and Realty, he was probably the most influential man in town. With the backing of Palmer and Bell, Porter could hardly not have done well, but this talented businessman carved out his own empire.

The major local industry, smelting, was Porter's brainchild. And Durango proudly wore its title, "Smelter City." One of its incurable boosters, Richard McCloud, gushed that ores came to the smelters as "naturally as the river seeks the ocean," because "God so ordained it by placing around it [Durango] on every side, coal fields of the best quality, and almost inexhaustible in quantity; also by placing close at hand lime rock and bog iron for fluxing." Whether or not God ordained it, Porter saw the opportunity and seized it.

Under Porter's guidance the smelter opened for business in August 1882, at the same time the Denver and Rio Grande reached Silverton. In the years following, the plant proved a qualified success, frustrated by isolation, severe winters, and the retarded development of regional transportation. Porter, never one to stand still, made improvements and by 1887 smelted over a million dollars' worth of silver, lead, gold, and copper, making his the ninth ranked Colorado smelter and the San Juans' largest. By the end of the decade Durango emerged as a potential regional smelter center (a logical development, according to the well-known mining engineer Thomas Rickard), because of its railroad connections and natural advantages. It had surpassed all nearby rivals—not without jealousy and bitterness, since nearly every mining district coveted a smelter of its own.

A hint of underlying troubles surfaced in April 1888, when the San Juan Smelting and Mining Company assumed control of the San Juan and New York Mining and Smelting Company. This reorganization brought new faces and fresh financial blood into the concern. Retaining his interest, Porter continued for a while as manager, until Ernest Amy, a Columbia School of Mines graduate and son of the company's president, New York banker Henry Amy, learned the tricks of the trade. Porter then became the executive advisor (1891). In the early 1890s the company confronted a serious problem when Silverton mining declined in the wake of falling silver prices. Nor did it help when it was discovered that the "late" auditor had been systematically defrauding the company. Undaunted, Porter and Amy recommended plant improvements to allow them to compete successfully with Denver and Pueblo, whose smelters, even with the added transportation expenses, offered cheaper reduction rates. When eastern stockholders hesitated to invest more, Porter persisted. The improvements helped, as did the opening of the Rio Grande Southern Railroad, which gave the plant access to many more mines. Outside factors played a role, too; Denver and Pueblo smelters raised their rates, making Durango competitive. By the end of 1892 the smelter was "doing splendidly," Porter reported to William Bell, whose Land and Coal Company still retained its stock.

Porter, always concerned about competition, tried to defeat any potential rivals by modernizing and modifying his operations. Though expensive, the practice had succeeded in the 1880s in preventing any serious inroads. There had been rivals. For a while Animas City hoped that a copper-based smelter would make it equal to Durango.

Treatment of copper ores from Red Mountain had been one of Porter's weaknesses. The Animas City smelter, blown in in 1885, struggled for several years before failing; it was sent to an early demise by the Durango smelter's improved ability to handle copper ores. Its Indiana and Ohio backers emerged poorer and, it is hoped, wiser, while Animas City's ambition turned sour.

A more serious rival challenged in 1892, when the Standard Smelter opened about a half mile south of the San Juan Smelter. Devoted especially to the treatment of copper ores, and with better financial backing, management, and process, it threatened its older rival's dominance. Whether there would be enough ore and profit for all was the immediate question. Durango could ill afford a disastrous smelter war. The Standard Smelter planned to employ over 150 men, while the San Juan employed 300 with a $30,000 monthly payroll. The purchases the companies made in town, their taxes, their regional promotion, and the coal mines they owned or nearly subsidized through purchases made their economic impact considerable. Durango had indeed become a "smelter city" of regional significance. None of the San Juan mining districts—Silverton, Red Mountain, Ouray, Rico, and Telluride—could compete; and all fell into its orbit, with the possible exception of Ouray.

Without coal there would have been no smelter. An old mining proverb referred to coal: "God made the coal, then hid it. Then some fool found it and we've been in trouble ever since." Durango exemplified the point. Discovery of coal, the black diamond of Durango's first generation, antedated the town's birth. Porter himself liked to relate the story of his coming to the Animas Valley in 1875 with two saddlebags full of coal to use in assaying, only to find huge outcroppings as he rode down Horse Gulch. Dismounting, he threw his coal into the arroyo in disgust. A June 1878 report in the *Engineering and Mining Journal* described La Plata County's coal field as "remarkable," predicting the beds to be "practically inexhaustible." With foresight, the author, mining engineer Joshua Clayton, warned that its "value must be measured by local demands," it being too far from the seaboard to make it of "great commercial importance."

Excited residents would not agree with killjoy Clayton. After all, the Denver and Rio Grande and the Trust had patented all the land they could, and fast-acting locals had beat them to some spots. The Durango Coal Company was operating as early as January 1881, when it closed to finish a tramway down the hill for easier loading of its coal. Newspapers periodically puffed local coal deposits and mines with a great deal of ballyhoo, predicting great things to come. "When you come down to plain facts it is the necessary that is going to make Durango famous for the San Juan" (*Southwest*, Feb. 2, 1884).

Men of vision, like John Porter, saw in these coal deposits a promising future, particularly since the Denver and Rio Grande ran past the doorstep. Such pioneers as merchant Thomas Graden (one of Palmer's young men), civil engineer and surveyor Charles Perin, and erstwhile constable and mayoral candidate John Pennington owned or leased coal mines. The Land and Coal Company, meanwhile, was having its problems. The initial effort had been at the Carboneria Mine south of town, whose coal proved too dirty and ashy and the mine dangerously gassy. Its second effort, the Porter Mine in Wildcat Canyon, in which the company owned a quarter share, suffered because of wagon freighting difficulties to Durango and the railroad. These freighting problems were overcome, however, and the mine proved to be a good one, although for most of the 1880s it remained leased.

The first coal mining efforts were small operations to supply local consumption, with some outside shipments to Silverton. Miner Frank Lake remembered one Horse Gulch mine owner, an inveterate gambler, who was consistently unable to meet the payroll. He told the men he would try to win the money; if he did they got paid, if not they had to wait. While these small, one-horse operations were poor reflections of Pennsylvania's great operations of the day, they were similar to the rest of Colorado's. The state's first coal-mining inspector, John McNeil, reported in 1884, "The coal mines of this State, as a rule, have hitherto been worked in a rude, miserable and even reckless, manner." Providentially, no deaths and very few accidents were reported in La Plata County during these years.

Fortunately, the local bituminous coal proved excellent for coking, a fact Porter quickly apprehended and developed. Twelve ovens along Lightner Creek soon glowed in the night sky, furnishing the needs of the smelter, with a small surplus left for the local market.

By 1890, when the pioneering years had passed, coal's future rested more on fact and less on vision. Production had risen from 12,000 tons seven years before to 33,000 tons, not a large amount by coal production standards, which ranked the district a distant tenth in the state. Yet the mines had survived, and with the building of the Rio Grande Southern a whole new market opened. Ninety-seven miners were employed, making this Durango's second most important industry. The *Durango Herald* surveyed the field and found seven mines actively working and a smaller group either inactive at the moment or spasmodically operating.

The largest mine was the Porter, with a 2,000-foot tunnel, a budding settlement around the mine, and 80 percent of the district's production. The building of the Rio Grande Southern right past the mine's portal resolved its only problem—transportation. Porter, who shrewdly backed Otto Mears's efforts to establish the railroad and whose hand is evident behind the scenes in its early history, promptly organized the Porter Fuel Company (with Bell as vice-president) in August 1890. Discreetly, he purchased more coal land along the road's right-of-way near future Hesperus and set about developing both properties. Porter wrote his partner Bell in February 1892, "Our coal business is doing splendidly." To the stockholders he noted in the First Annual Report that, despite the cost of land purchases and development, the future looked bright and production had reached 250 tons daily. They sat back to await those cherished profits.

Porter provided just the needed spark for the local coal field. He introduced corporate development. Few Durango coal mine owners possessed the necessary wherewithal (construction of a boarding house cost $1,750, steam boilers $2,000, and so forth) or the financial reputation to back the development of that indispensable second railroad. Porter's days of active, on-the-scene involvement waned now. His multitude of interests, including Telluride's famous Smuggler Union Mine, took more and more of his time, and bachelor Porter shifted his home with ease. His Durango ties never were severed, and he would come back for weeks at a time to check on his various investments and for summer vacations. He left behind a namesake mine and a small community around it, initially called Porter Station, then simply Porter, the first of Durango's satellite coal mining camps and a good example of how key men and enterprises interlocked.

The vision of more railroad connections was not Porter's alone; a large segment of the business community shared it. Part of this desire grew from the realization that the Denver and Rio Grande could be a hard taskmaster as well as a beneficiary. A railroad with a monopoly over a community and region held an enviable hand, one very manipulable for corporation profit. Mutterings soon arose about discriminatory freight rates, and the *Durango Weekly Tribune*, May 25, 1891, finally exploded: "The Rio Grande system of express charges is a system of highway robbery."

Richard McCloud pinpointed what was needed; always the diplomat, he expressed gratitude for the railroads but emphasized that a little competition would do wonders. One of the earliest schemes advocated a railroad to the south, an outlet to Albuquerque and the west coast. Some businessmen, including Charles Perin and Robert Dwyer, went so far as to incorporate the Durango Southern Railway Company, which hoped to reach Guaymas, Mexico. The railway, but not the dream, died on the planning board. Even Porter, with his close ties to the D&RG, expected to see the day when that dream became rails and right-of-way.

While disappointment met attempts to the south, the railroad builder of the San Juans, Otto Mears, was planning the Rio Grande Southern. Completed in 1891, the road ran from Durango to Ridgway across 172 miles of spectacular mountain country. An engineering feat, Mears's line traversed four mountain passes and 142 bridges and trestles. Connecting with the Denver and Rio Grande at both ends, it tapped the railroad-starved mining districts of Rico, Ophir, and Telluride. For Durango it meant a second line, although one hardly free of the Rio Grande's influence. As Porter and Mears envisioned, it stimulated coal business, increased smelting, and provided a new market for local agricultural products. Nor could new jobs, from laborer to engineer, be overlooked. The business community found an expanded market as well. Striving to become a real "metropolis" of the southwest, Durango had immeasurably strengthened her position. Thanks to Mears and the Rio Grande, the town now had direct connections with every major San Juan mining district, except Creede and Lake City, and could tap a wide agricultural area.

As Durango's youthful period drew to a close in 1892, she could boast several major achievements. The emergence of the regional smelting center, the development of coal mining, and the construction of the Rio Grande Southern shouted to all that here was not just another soon-to-fade western wonder.

Much of the credit for what took place must be given to the young aggressive leadership. Some of these were Palmer's boys—Porter, Bruce Hunt, Robert Sloan, and Thomas Graden. Graden was typical. The friendly, lanky, quick-witted Civil War veteran did not turn forty until 1886 and never abandoned bachelorhood. He joined with Sloan in the lumber business, then constructed a flour mill, and eventually organized the Graden Mercantile Company. He found time to promote and superintend the Durango Railway and Realty Company, dabble in coal mining, and serve a term as mayor. The railroad brought others, such as Thomas Wigglesworth, surveyor for both Palmer and Mears.

Most arrived on their own, attracted by the opportunities. Already balding Alfred Camp was 30 when he moved to Durango, after correctly gauging what its future would be. Few men would have a greater impact on the community than this studious, observant Ohioan, who fell in love with his adopted home and forged his bank into its premier financial institution. Peter Fassbinder's early efforts have already been chronicled, and he hardly slowed down. German emigrant Isaac Kruschke operated a store for nearly forty years in Durango, one of a continuing line of distinguished Jewish merchants. And there was Alexander L. Harris, San Juan mine owner, who served two terms as mayor, slightly older, at sixty, when he came to Durango in 1881. Already his career extended back to being mayor of Kansas City in the mid-1860s and pioneering in the San Juans in 1876.

Another merchant who invested in mining was industrious Charles Newman. A solid claim can be made for his opening Durango's first business, certainly the first drug store. At one time he and his partners operated a chain of six drug stores, but Bostonian Newman, who loved the mountains, caught mining fever, made a fortune at Rico, and sold his business. Fergus Graham, graduate of the University of Virginia law school, abandoned his books to develop a hardware business into a chain of four stores in the major San Juan mining towns. Among his partners was former governor Alva Adams. Not all of these men stayed. Big, genial restaurateur John Elitch briefly sojourned here before going on to Denver and Elitch Gardens. And banker Charles Williams left in 1889 to settle in Colorado Springs, after a career that included real estate, banking, and promoting electrical power. For them and others Durango had been only a way-stop in search of their elusive promised land.

These, then, were examples of the pioneering leaders. Almost all were business-men, young, and from the Midwest or East. They held in common a conviction that Durango would prosper, and that they would grow with it. Consequently, they promoted their community, not without self-interest, obviously, and were determined to guide its destiny. Ambitious, touched with a bit of speculativeness, they willingly took chances, confident of Durango's and southwest Colorado's destiny. They and their key industries interlocked, increasing stability and conserving limited financial resources, a fact that increased their power and prestige.

Preferring to work behind the scenes, they only occasionally ran for public office, though businessmen dominated city government throughout these years. Candidates for office were carefully chosen from a fairly select group. For instance, an investigator for a New York banking house that was considering handling Durango municipal water bonds reported in 1882 that the town officers were "all wealthy or well to do" intelligent gentlemen.

Most likely, city dwellers observed these men working through Durango's Board of Trade, which, though active in the 1880s, died and was resurrected in 1892. Here existed an organization near and dear to all hearts. Porter, who served two terms as president in the mid-1880s, stated clearly the aspirations of the Board and its members in his year-end summarizing speech in March 1886. Optimism and faith in the future permeated every paragraph; prospects for agriculture, Durango, and mining never looked so good. He urged upon the membership a railroad to Rico and a bridge across the San Juan River to secure the wool trade of northern New Mexico and of the Navajos. A desire for Navajo business did not keep Porter from advocating removal of the Utes to open up their rich and valuable reservation land. The members concurred; if it was good for Durango, it was good for everybody.

Reestablished in 1892, the Board stated that its objectives were to advertise the city and promote its interests by disseminating information related to commercial, financial, and industrial affairs. Lawyer and former registrar of the U.S. Land Office Richard McCloud served as its secretary and unofficial spokesman. Graden, Kruschke, Camp, Newman, and Ernest Amy were among its officers and directors, and hotelman Henry Strater was president. A true son of Erin, McCloud wrote and published *Durango As It Is*, a promotional pamphlet, before the year was out. In December Daniel W. Ayres was to see that Durango secured space for a coal and coke exhibit at the upcoming Chicago World's Fair, and the membership as a whole was discussing how to develop the best route to the newly discovered San Juan River gold fields. Such activities showed these men at their best—promotive, aggressive, and confident. "Its members," wrote McCloud, were "the live business and professional men of Durango, and they do not intend to stop work until Durango has a population of 100,000." Durango was fortunate to have gained leaders of their caliber; no other nearby community had such luck. Much to their dismay, no doubt, not all of their contemporaries caught the vision; and in December 1892, twenty-three names were read of members already in arrears with Board dues.

A prime objective of these men was to carve out an economic empire, increasingly referred to as the San Juan Basin. These urban pioneers, to a large measure, preceded the rural pioneers who settled in the outlands, and they were determined to use Durango as their advance base for economic occupation of the hinterlands. This economic imperialism disregarded such man-made distinctions as state boundaries and looked to natural watersheds for urban allegiance and control; hence the interest in the San Juan River bridge and the southern outlet.

Steadily they increased their zone of influence, based upon the advantages Durango held in banking, accessibility, location, businesses, and natural resources (coal, water, land). Local leadership perceived opportunities and exploited them to the fullest, which allowed them to parlay a headstart into dominance.

Animas City was the first to fall under Durango's dominance, becoming by default a suburb of its larger neighbor. Along the Rio Grande's northward line, the resort of Trimble Springs and the tiny village of Rockwood suffered a similar fate. To the west Parrott City and its more thriving rival, new La Plata City, came into Durango's economic orbit, as did the ranching hamlet of Mancos. Fort Lewis, the region's military bastion, served Durango more as a market and an employer than as a protector from Indians, who were now defeated and powerless. But let the government even hint of abandoning this post and the howls could be heard on Main. The Boulevard cried, too; Nettie Haggard recalled the handsome young Fort Lewis officers at Durango social affairs and the post band and orchestra. Also, to the south and east along the Rio Grande tracks lay a potential market that Durango strove mightily to dominate, with varying success at this particular time.

Silverton, larger and more economically independent than any other San Juan Basin community still succumbed to Durango because of the railroad and smelter. Vocal in its opposition to submission, Silverton, nevertheless, could not escape its ambitious, aggressive neighbor. The Rio Grande Southern opened up the Dolores River Valley, Rico, Ophir, and Telluride, although the farther one got from Durango the weaker her hold. After all, the other end of the line opened a shorter route to Denver, via Gunnison, and the agricultural lands around Grand Junction and Montrose.

As agriculture spread through Colorado and the San Juan Basin, farming and ranching communities made their appearance. A potential rival arose with Cortez in 1886. It grew slowly, as did the whole area, without a railroad connection; this handicap did not doom the "Metropolis of the Great Montezuma Valley." Durango was none too happy with a movement in the late 1880s to carve Montezuma County out of La Plata to serve better the needs of that far corner of Colorado. The *Durango Herald*, February 22, 1889, blamed Cortez, complaining that its promoters planned to usurp two-thirds of La Plata County to "gratify their greed." When someone else tried what Durango had already done, the shoe hurt. Complaints had no effect, and the busy 1889 legislative assembly created thirteen counties, Montezuma among them.

A natural rivalry was born with the creation of Montezuma County and the designation of Cortez as its county seat. Agricultural Cortez, however, entered the lists a decided underdog to larger, more urbane Durango, a fact unlikely to deter its boosters.

Speaking of agriculture, Durango's leaders did not slight it in their move to strengthen the community and create a balanced economy. Farmers and ranchers needed a shopping, shipping, and marketing center, and Durango met all of these requirements. From the small start in the Animas Valley, ranching and farming spread along the river valleys, inhibited somewhat by the large expanse of Ute reservation across the southern end of the county.

Frank Leslie's Illustrated Newspaper, in May 1881, had correctly predicted what Durango meant to agriculture: "A short time ago the produce from these valley ranches [Pine and Florida rivers] went begging for a market, but now they can scarcely supply the constantly increasing demand. Durango has made the whole country 'boom.'" A local agreed, saying "Rome was built upon seven hills. Durango's future is built upon seven agricultural valleys." Beyond them was the San Juan mining district. "A constantly increasing mining interest is a sure guarantee of an ever ready market for all that can be produced," wrote agricultural expert William Pabor in 1883. Pabor hit the proverbial nail on the head. The railroad not only opened these markets but, as eastern writer Ernest Ingersoll noted while touring the San Juans in 1882, caused farm property of the Animas Valley to double in appraised valuation over twelve months, with good land selling for as high as $100 per acre. Certainly the Rio Grande opened the area to outside competition, which caused little concern at the moment; local ranchers and farmers were competing with ease.

Not about to let such an opportunity pass, Durango lauded its agriculture. The rich river valley soil, plus abundant water for irrigation, got agriculture off to a promising start. As one 1891 visitor said, "In all the West there is no lovelier agricultural section than this." In these days of the horse and buggy little country stores dotted many a crossroad, each dependent on Durango for supplies. The community gained from all quarters as her agricultural hinterland matured.

What was true for agriculture can also be applied to the lumbering industry. The high demands of 1880 and 1881 made the business unsurpassed for profit, as Graden, Porter, and Sloan, among others, quickly found out. Local demand lessened as the years passed and the weaker mills failed; however, with abundant forests to tap, easily accessible to the railroad, lumber eventually was shipped throughout Colorado. The importance of this industry to Durango's growth and the development of a regional economy cannot be overestimated.

Lest the reader think that the Durango leadership simply emerged as a provincial, materialistic elite, narrowly confining its interests to those that benefited only its members, it should be pointed out that these men held larger visions. To be sure, a dose of self-interest would always be evident—pure altruism is a rare commodity. But they joined with their Western Slope neighbors for a series of annual meetings, called the Western Slope Congress, to consider common concerns. Durango served as host to the 1892 meeting. This coalition passed resolutions pertaining to removal of the Utes, opposing legislation against railroads (not all the Slope had connections yet), advocating a just and equitable state assessment law, and, interestingly, asking that no national park or timber reserve be established in any part of Western Colorado. As strange as this might seem, in light of what later happened, it was typical for that day—the Westerner did not want any infringement upon his right to exploit natural resources. The Western Slope, even at this early date, found itself playing second fiddle politically to Eastern Slope interests, centered around urbane and powerful Denver. Durango extended a hearty greeting to the delegates that November, entertained them royally, and bade them goodbye with the admonition that the "spirit of unity is the hope for organization" (*Great Southwest*, November 19, 1892). Everyone seemed to have had a good time, and the economic windfall from all those visitors did not go unappreciated.

Those great boosters of their city and western Colorado, the Durango newspapers, weathered a period of trial. They fought each other, nearby rivals, and Denver with equal ferocity. Five expectant newcomers joined the ranks; cruel fate, however, made no distinction between old-timers and upstarts. Seven merged or folded, including Mrs. Romney's *Record*. Only the *Durango Herald* and Ouray's once famous *Solid Muldoon*, now transplanted to Durango, survived.

The one-sided contest with Denver continued. The "magic metropolis" brooked no rivals, as expressed in 1883 in the flowery, promotional pamphlet *Durango:* "[It is] surrounded by more varied natural beauty and grandeur than any other town in the State can boast." No superior was acknowledged. When the occasion warranted, Denver got a lashing for trying to keep the San Juan towns "mere hamlets" and using its influence against Durango. Such shortsightedness, it was claimed, would not keep Durango from becoming the center of the Southwest, "as water is to run down hill." Denver, hardly nettled by such huffing, far outstripped its upstart challenger in the 1880s with an amazing spurt of growth backed by Leadville silver.

Denver's indifference did not long miff Durangoans, who were now too busy with their own projects. Convinced that local mines were nothing short of miraculous, they went so far as to organize a mining stock exchange in 1882 to list "worthy" local properties and protect investors against misrepresentation. After the exposé of the Leadville mining manipulations during the past two years, Colorado needed to move warily in this field.

No need to fret; not many investors came to plunge in local gold and silver mines. No potentially profitable mines had grabbed the headlines to attract them. La Plata Canyon offered the best possibilities, albeit supported by a record of spotty production, small development, and misspent dreams. La Plata, a new camp established in 1882 nearer the heart of the district, challenged rapidly declining Parrott City. It finally gave the *coup de grâce* to the one-time county seat but did not enhance local mining fortunes. La Plata miners awaited a railroad spur from the mainline of the Southern and a mill to handle ore so low-grade that it was not worth the freight charge to the smelter. Twenty years after their start, the La Platas, in 1892, were still nourished by pipe dreams rather than production.

Nearer Durango, the Junction and Lightner Creek areas were prospected; what they needed were better roads and decent ore values. Small mining operations working faintly promising veins repeated an oft-told tale. To the north the Needle Mountains offered potential, if a good road could reach the district and investors would bankroll development. Consequently, local papers boomed the San Juans and emphasized how close Durango was to that significant mining region.

Durangoans invested heavily in local gold and silver properties without possessing the resources for promoting, developing, or selling them. An 1883 listing of investors in La Plata mines tallied numerous residents, but none of those who have been identified as the leaders. They apparently steered clear of this high risk investment, or did as Porter did—put their money in better known and richer districts.

A hint of the future came with the announcement in the *Southwest*, January 19, 1884, that "we are in a petroleum region." Oil seepage and something described as oil shale had been discovered, and the reporter exuded optimism. All Durango needed were a producing well and a refinery; visions of an oil boom danced in the heads of the opportunists. A producing well was a long way off, but someone was on the right track.

Of more practical importance, the Main Avenue business district was growing steadily in the 1880s and early 1890s. A little padded, perhaps, was a report of the Board of Trade in 1892, which stated that annual sales topped $3,000,000—not bad for a twelve-year-old community. Durango at that moment was catching its second wind, enjoying prosperity almost equal to 1880–82. The economic climate had not always been that balmy. The years 1883–84 were termed "not so lively," 1885 "slow," and 1888–90 "depressing." Though these trends did not affect all businesses equally, they were evident in land sales of the Land and Coal Company, as well as in complaints from those emblems of prosperity, the saloons, which in slow times demanded lower license fees. No one who saw the situation realistically expected Durango to maintain the pace of those early months.

But progress continued inexorably, if not always dramatically. The town came to be the regional banking center, led by the First National Bank. Its designation as county seat proved as profitable as its supporters had foreseen, and the elaborate county courthouse, jail, and office building dominated Second Avenue. Securing the United States Land Office in 1882 also refined Durango's image, which was further strengthened by the establishment of a district court. Even at this early date, federal agencies helped bankroll a part of the economy.

Local industry grew right along with business. Graden's Flour Mill was an example, as were the cigar factory, brick company, foundry and iron works, and the brewing company. This last enterprise had languished, swamped by competition from Pabst, Anheuser-Busch, and other larger brewing companies, until local capital rode to the rescue in 1892. "[It] will not be long before the thousands of dollars annually sent East for beer will remain at home, where it belongs." Home, indeed! Keeping that money at home was a primary occupation of Durangoans, who, consequently, listed over sixty-five other occupations in the 1885 census. One enterprising blacksmith, Al Andrews, shod 19,138 animals in four years. Money could be made by the ambitious.

Governing this growing, changing community were the city fathers, men who built upon the 1881 foundation, while confronting new problems of their own. They worked nearly as hard in 1882 as in 1881, passing twenty-two ordinances, compared to thirty-one the previous year. Haste did produce some waste, evidenced by the time spent amending and revising previous ordinances. With the stabilization of government and community, the mayor and trustees dealt with issues more common to a late-nineteenth-century western community. Hearing citizen requests for additional sidewalks or complaints about maintenance of those already worn by service consumed many a meeting. On at least three occasions the city was sued for damages when people fell off or through a wooden sidewalk. The water works and water supply ran a close second for instigating annoying problems.

The ordinances passed after the initial flurry were typical. Some dealt with "sin," outlawing "opium joints," and prohibiting any male under twenty-one or female under eighteen (girls were tempted less!) from being in or about a saloon, billiard hall, gambling house, or house of ill fame. The city leaders fell victim to that favorite Victorian pastime of legislating morals and denounced drunkenness, nudity, lewd behavior, gambling, profane language, and bawdy houses. The business license system was continued, and, in fact, expanded. A number of ordinances related to Durango's quality of life were approved, which will be discussed in the next chapter. And finally, the city granted franchises for a streetcar company, electric company, and Western Union, and established Greenmount Cemetery in 1887. The result was that governmental expenses jumped from $17,000 in 1882 to $35,000 ten years later.

The Trustees hustled to find revenue sources that met the age-old American requirement of being painless. They legislatively prohibited girls and gambling, then collected fines from each regularly (in October 1888, thirteen girls paid $5 each), displaying their practical nature in the matter of morals. Over repeated protests, saloon licenses remained high. A system of town taxes was instituted, based on a mil-per-dollar ratio. Alfred Camp, serving a term as town treasurer in 1883–84, reported the following receipts: liquor licenses, $6,900; town taxes, $6,352; water main fee, $1,427; police court collections, $1,394; licenses, $922; and a few other miscellaneous items. Durango was coming of age financially, since the healthiest share of this revenue was collected from permanent sources.

What did Durangoans think of their ever more costly city government? One predictable response was a clamor to reduce expenses. One local complained in 1885 that the people of Durango had grown tired of lame-duck councilmen fixing up jobs for themselves or friends. "Abolish and cut down the expenses of Durango's government" was his solution. Apathy, more than action, seems to have been the typical response to most complaints, unless some pressing issue motivated voters to bombard the ballot box. If petitions reflect interest in government, residents were decidedly involved. The petitions, however, often appeared to embody self-interest, such as a sidewalk or a business license, rather than some vital community problem. On the other hand, there were those who called for more expenditures. "Durango has reached that period of its life [1891] when there is no question of permanency to justify two-for-a-quarter statesmen in delaying public improvements."

Only one major scandal blotted the municipal government record. In late August 1891, and for several weeks thereafter, Durangoans talked of little else. Police magistrate Robert Carter was accused of "enjoying," maintaining, and shielding a prostitute (after illegally forcing the lady's "husband" to leave town); the city attorney of failing to perform his duties; and the clerk of being incompetent, failing to collect water fees, and "padding" his payroll. The whole episode smacked of political intrigue. Three council members, Ernest Amy one of them, heatedly protested the "monstrous outrage being perpetrated" by the majority. Rival council factions fell to arguing and filibustering, and city government braked to a halt. Charges of "gang rule" and "gross abuses" charged the atmosphere. When all was said and done, the mayor, street commissioner, police magistrate, marshal, city attorney, and clerk resigned or were removed from office. Regrettably, newspapers are missing for most of these weeks and the council records soon fell silent.

Such deviations aside, Durango's leaders, who could be called a power elite, were able to look back with satisfaction over the formative years of their community. It survived and, in a day and time when growth equaled success, it had done very well. These men could, with a forgivable touch of pride, point to their own significant contributions. Their personal concerns and ambitions coincided nicely with those of their town. They provided the drive, leadership, vision, and, many times, the resources to carry out their schemes, with benefits accruing to both individuals and town.

Urbanization had compressed extensive transformation into little more than a decade. The rapid growth was reflected in agriculture, transportation, settlement patterns, and regional interests. Durango's determination to dominate the area dictated its reactions to local and regional issues and molded its development. The reader need only consider the slower growth of a typically agricultural area (Animas City) or the boom-bust cycle of mining districts (Silverton) to understand the difference.

Durango's permanence was now assured. Where it might go from there hung on an unknown destiny and the ability of community leadership to foresee and master what lay ahead. The foundation had been solidly built.

4. Manifesting Its Destiny

Durango's turbulent birth pangs receded, giving residents time to contemplate the "quality of life," to use a modern phrase. To attempt to define this term retroactively is perhaps presumptuous. Obviously, it suggested ideas in 1887 that are different from those of the present. In each generation, however, certain common themes emerge when one endeavors to interpret quality of life.

The 1880s and early 1890s emphasized materialism. The town had leapt from the log-cabin stage to frame-and-brick construction in virtually a fortnight. Material comforts and opportunities were naturally emphasized, and "substantial" brick and stone buildings were pointed to with pride. The growing commercial district impressed resident and visitor equally as a symbol of prosperity and eminence. Durango could pride itself on having "no pioneer cabins for corporations," wrote the noted historical writer Hubert Howe Bancroft in praise of the work of Hunt and the Trust in the early eighties.

Beyond these concerns, interest centered on easing and modernizing the lifestyle—electricity, telephones (private lines, no public exchange yet), water works, and the like. Nor would residents allow their religious, educational, and medical facilities to take second place to any town of comparable size, or even larger. From its commencement Durango possessed unusually good medical facilities and doctors; in 1892 McCloud listed eleven physicians and surgeons, including two women. There was an inconsistency, however; Durango acknowledged no "superior anywhere" for a healthful climate!

Perhaps these medical people were attracted by the natural beauty and "picturesque situation," early recognized as one of the primary ingredients for quality of life. Natural resources—coal, gold and silver, water, lumber, agricultural and grazing land—were also esteemed as present or potential contributors. But these busy pioneers were not stopped from despoiling them in the rush for profit. The riches were placed there by God, according to current reasoning, for men "whose strong arms and steady purpose will reach out and develop the resources of this rich and beautiful land, and with patience work out their own and the country's way to wealth and greatness."

This statement defines better than any other the fact that quality of life, in this particular time, equaled "wealth and greatness." That the natural resources might not prove limitless or the natural beauty unspoilable rarely crossed anyone's mind. Pollution had already fouled Durango's air. Coal and wood smoke from homes and businesses, potentially choking under normal conditions, multiplied sharply during the cold months when chimneys belched and temperature inversions trapped the smoky haze. Little could be done to avert such pollution; people had to heat their homes. The smelter, though, was another matter. Acid smoke from the blast furnaces and roasters seared Smelter Mountain's vegetation and wafted across town. The "smelter city" gloried in its title, and no one dared attack the major industry. That great booster and defender Richard McCloud proclaimed boldly that the smelter's smoke did not affect residents, that currents of air swept it away from the city. The problem was already bothersome or he would not have felt compelled even to mention this rather disturbing topic. One factor outweighed another, and nature and clean air lost out. Here the late nineteenth century reflected a generations-old American attitude.

Implicit in Durangoans' thinking, and their contemporaries', was growth. They craved it. The *Durango City Directory* of 1892 put it this way: "The fact remains that no one ever stayed and found reason to regret his so doing." Growth undergirded the basic ingredients that threatened quality of life, something people refused to concede. If Durango planned to grow, it had to present the best possible civic image to the public. No more of that "bad, wicked Durango" that a Leadville visitor had expected to see on arrival in October 1882. Nor did town boosters appreciate the eastern image of western mining camps as "perfect hot-beds of crime and lawlessness" and their populations as "gangs of murderous ruffians."

Durangoans, however, did not look upon their city as a mining camp. They worked to overcome the frontier image, which detracted from the very nature of what they sought to achieve. As yet they had not recognized the tourist bonanza they were living through. With a bit of pride they read what that same Leadville visitor went on to say, "Durango has either greatly reformed or else she has been most miserably misrepresented for to a Leadvillian the town appears most woefully dead." That last sentiment proffered a backhanded compliment; unruffled locals liked to think of it as a reflection of Leadville's jealousy. By the late 1880s Durango had "materialized its manifest destiny" and emerged with a metropolitan character, at least in the eyes of its residents.

Optimism and a confidence born of youth and success permeated these years. Even a tragic setback failed to dampen them. On Monday afternoon, July 1, 1889, a disastrous fire swept away seven blocks of the business and residential center of town. Young Neil Camp, son of A. P., remembered that "big fire" seventy years later: "I was just engaged in making some very good mud pies when the fire broke out." His mother hurried him out of harm's way, as did all the other mothers with their children. Over half a million dollars' worth of property and buildings went up in flames, a staggering blow to the young city. Valiant efforts by the firemen and desperation measures, including dynamiting buildings in the fire's path, failed to slow the fiery onslaught. Panicked residents fled to the mesa, carrying items grabbed in haste. In horror they watched a "terrific" west wind push the fire from Main Avenue over to the Boulevard—stores, saloons, churches, homes fell to the flames. Sinners and saints alike saw their property go up in smoke.

By nightfall, the worst past, armed men patrolled the streets under a city government martial law decree. A cavalry troop rode in from Fort Lewis to provide further protection. The strong suspicion of a "fire fiend" (never proven) heated passions as residents returned to their smoldering, smoky city. Fortunately no one had been killed.

Not down yet! The next morning the situation was evaluated; less than half the loss was covered by insurance. A mass meeting, held in the afternoon, raised twelve hundred dollars within an hour to help the poor and destitute. The community politely declined immediate offers of assistance from outside sources, announcing:

> Our citizens are not disheartened by the disaster. The burnt district will soon be rebuilt, a number of businessmen having announced their intention of erecting substantial brick structures to replace the old frame ones destroyed. There is a feeling that in spite of everything the calamity was a blessing in disguise and marks a new era in the progress of our fair city.

They were as good as their word; within days, phoenixlike, the town arose from its ashes. And they were right; Main Avenue took on a new appearance, as did neighboring Second Avenue.

Harper's Weekly, July 13, provided national coverage of the catastrophe that had struck one "of the most promising younger cities of the far west." The article's author concluded that perhaps the calamity might prove a blessing, because the buildings destroyed, for the most part, were ordinary wooden frontier structures and now the business district could be rebuilt, "equal in size and appearance" to Denver's and Pueblo's. Those were words Durango loved to hear, especially in the depths of despair.

The July 26 *Durango Herald* lavishly praised stalwart citizens for their progress since the "disastrous conflagration." The rubbish had been carted off, business resumed, plans made, and building started. Pride in this case proved justified; Durango rebounded with fortitude from one of the most destructive Colorado fires to that date and the worst in the city's history. It was too late to second guess, but one cannot help wondering why the Trust's original idea of constructing only substantial stone and brick buildings in the commercial district had been ignored. Had the idea been carried out, the fire might have been easily contained, since this type of construction provided an excellent firebreak, besides giving the air of permanence and prosperity.

Durango rebuilt. A year later the town's appearance had changed markedly. Main now displayed brick and stone, and its appearance has not changed radically to this day. As the *Herald* asserted on January 1, 1890, "nothing can possibly keep her back." After a slight derailment, Durango resumed its course toward becoming the "commercial capital of the big Southwest," the "magic metropolis." The next two prosperous years confirmed that the disaster had been a blessing in disguise. John Porter wrote Bell in February 1892, that "everything in Durango is booming." And Otto Mears ventured to predict that within a few years the community would be the third largest city in Colorado, with a population of 25,000.

Both before and after the fire, residents sought diligently to present a respectable image to visitors. Physically, this meant erecting an elaborate county courthouse and churches with steeples stretching to the sky. But to the Victorians, as materialistic as they might seem, it meant more. There needed to be substance under the shell of civilization. Durango, eastern visitor Ernest Ingersoll remarked, aspired to be an intellectual center.

Durango epitomized the proverb "actions speak louder than words." After a slow start, a good public school system evolved (two schools and a third one, Central, under construction in 1892); the census taker found 681 scholars from ages five to twenty enrolled. Women teachers predominated, as did the "Three R's"—no frills allowed. The Catholic Church conducted its own schools, a grade school and St. Mary's Academy operated by the Sisters of Mercy. God, too, had come to Durango, though some thought otherwise, and churches took hold. The Boulevard, destined to be more than just the fanciest residential area, also became the "church street," with those main-line Protestants—Methodists, Presbyterians, Episcopalians, and Baptists—calling it home. In North Durango the Catholics raised St. Columba Church as part of their complex, which included the schools, convent, and the Sisters of Mercy Hospital, this last the only one in southwestern Colorado.

The schools and churches did much to refine Durango's image, particularly because they represented agencies in which women took an active part. In this mostly masculine world, women found few outlets, and none was better than the church. School elections were all the political voice they exercised until 1893. The church's impact was felt at this particular time by the larger community, not just by each individual congregation, more than at any later day, when other diversions arose to challenge its influence. Choirs, church groups, Sunday schools, bazaars, suppers, musical festivals, Sunday worship, picnics, and a variety of programs offered to families and unmarried alike acceptable social activities and feminine leadership opportunities unmatched elsewhere in town. Middle- and upper-income ladies responded energetically; seldom was an unchurched woman found. Church women agitated for reforms, such as Sunday closing (as late as 1891 businessmen opposed this attempt to curtail profits) and organization of the WCTU. They determinedly backed improvement of the schools, clean city government, and abolition of the red-light district. Durango lived up to its title "city of churches," another McCloud-coined caption.

Speaking of titles, Durango yearned to become a musical center and actually received plaudits as the "most musical town in southern Colorado." According to local legend, the first piano accidentally rolled down a mountainside (without breaking a string) before finally reaching its destination. Such a favorable omen could not be ignored, and by 1887 the "choral union" presented the popular *Mikado*. Fort Lewis's regimental band and a post orchestra further augmented the musical offerings. At least two churches had organs, and many homes, pianos. In its first decade, however, Durango failed to attain that apex of nineteenth-century musical/cultural aspirations, the opera house. The *Durango Weekly Tribune* scolded the town for this shortcoming and for its inferior public amusement; Durango was "entitled" to the best.

Women certainly agreed that their town deserved the best, and they fought to secure it. Initially few (Mrs. Estelle Camp recalled seeing a "scarcity of women on the streets" when she arrived in 1883), their numbers increased steadily and sufficiently enough for them to play a significant role behind the scenes in maintaining churches and schools and pushing for civic improvement. For them no greater goal existed than to make Durango a fit place to live and to raise their children. They organized a "Ladies Athletic Club" to enjoy "regularly such exercises as they most need for their physical development," and fought against the "drunken husband" evil. Sara Scott Trew showed what an energetic, talented woman could do in this day before women were permitted generally to vote or hold elective office. This beloved school teacher found time to help start the Methodist Church and the WCTU, and her administrative ability and "ardent zeal" served each well. She held offices in both. When she died in February 1889, it was said of her, "Never has the truth been illustrated more forcibly that the Christian life is good to live by and die by. . . ." Sara Scott Trew stands for them all, the wives, mothers, sisters, and daughters of Durango.

A variety of public entertainment, most of it failing to meet contemporary middle-class standards, was available. As in the mining camps to the north, it catered to men. Masculine dominance, however, ebbed faster here than it did in Silverton and, by the early 1890s, families were gaining the upper hand. What kept the red-light district bright was the ride- or walk-in trade, when miners and cowboys came to town.

Main Avenue's saloon block stretched from the First National Bank north to Tenth Street. Respectable ladies did not walk on the west side of that block. From there the district rambled west toward the Animas, the "soiled doves" being limited by law to that area. A "Fat Alice" or May Porter only created news if she ran afoul of the law or attempted suicide. Victorian Durango tolerated the sporting element, though only barely. Scandals always erupted; for instance, the *Record*, 1882, found another opium den, and Mrs. Romney took out after that "degrading dissipation." Not until late 1883, after yet another exposé and the subsequent passage of an ordinance, did the furor subside. The Clipper, a "theater" gambling hall, provided a longer-lasting sinful attraction. It changed owners, who tried to attain a better image but were never able to achieve Victorian respectability. The district supplied gambling, girls, drinking, and entertainment, all for a price. The customers seldom got the best of the games. One old-timer remembered: "The sucker never made any money on those games. He wasn't supposed to."

Many people learned of such activities only through periodic newspaper revelations, inspiring a fleeting moment of community righteousness. Sentimentalism still cloaked the "demi-mondes." When Clara Chase "passed from earth," the *Morning Durango Herald*, March 29, 1887, was moved to say, "Another gone wrong in life, over whose acts we draw the mantle of charity, hoping before Him who rules she may find the forgiveness for her fall on earth for which she prayed with her dying breath." That mantle fell many a time, without coming to grips with the real problems of the fair but frail. Victorian sensibilities were appalled in May 1891, when a "poor mortal" gave up a "position in society" to move across the railroad tracks to take up a "life of shame." So great was the shock that her name was never disclosed.

Other editors on other occasions mentioned drinking problems, lack of enforcement of the habitual drunkard law, and the fact that Durango had fifteen thriving saloons but only six uncrowded churches. Perhaps *The Idea*, April 10, 1886, summed it up for all who opposed the district:

> The time will come for Durango when a lady can pass through the streets without seeing prostitutes and their companions in infamy. When there will not be half a dozen low gambling dives filled with greasy old gambling tables. When men . . . find something better and higher to do than keeping dens of infamy and perpetrating disgrace upon the community. When good order will prevail . . . .

That time had not come. As long as the district maintained a semblance of order, the city government, police, and citizens tolerated it for the profit it generated, and because it served a need.

It created business and raised revenue, and not until the 1890s did the overdue challenge come. In May and June 1891, the *Durango Weekly Tribune* criticized that "policy of doubtful character," the collection of monthly fines (ten dollars each) from the girls. From a "condition of shame" Durango derived revenue: "Do you believe it is right to hold up these poor wretches for such a rent and such an amount? Turn them loose or shut them out entirely, and give Durango a clean skirt to flirt in. [June 1]." The sporting element lived on, sub rosa, backed by the businessmen; the red-light district clearly enhanced Main Avenue business.

Self-righteous bigots liked to blame the red-light evils on the "foreign" element. With a then common attitude, the *Herald*, November 22, 1883, had this to say about Jim Lee, operator of a Chinese laundry found to be an "opium dive": "[a] typical representative of the meek, lowly, cunning, vicious, and depraved off-scourings of the Celestial empire." The facts do not support such a contention.

In both the state census of 1885 and the federal census of 1890, Durangoans overwhelmingly listed themselves as native-born, white, and married. Two-thirds of the immigrants who resided in the city and county came from Great Britain and Ireland, with Germany trailing far behind. As might be surmised, a larger percentage of the foreign-born settled in the county, in agriculture, than in town. Durango was not unique in these trends—it fit the regional pattern.

Mrs. Hubertine Pulvermiller, looking back on the eighties and nineties, described her contemporaries as "generally pretty friendly" and "blessed with good times." The agent who surveyed Durango for a water bond sale pictured residents as thrifty, enterprising, and people of "more than ordinary intelligence, prosperous and contented." Their common Anglo-Saxon, Protestant cultural background, with a strong midwestern flavor, no doubt contributed to this image. Taken all together, these characteristics fashioned a solid middle class, the cement of the community.

The morality, the ambition, the values of its middle class shaped Durango during these years. The results resembled other late-nineteenth-century communities, except perhaps in pace of development. In no small way, these people deserve the credit for the rapid passing of the rough frontier days. Most of them unknown today, they charted their city's future.

Others who did not blend so smoothly into the middle-class Victorian norms also resided here. Mexican Americans found themselves tacitly segregated across the tracks or in the south end of town. The few blacks, only thirty-four in the whole county in 1890, were trapped in menial occupations; the Strater Hotel for years employed black porters. The Chinese continued as laundrymen, gardeners, and cooks, with only one Chinese merchant. Durango remained off limits to the neighboring Utes, except for trading purposes.

Verily, a growing cry could be heard across the city, "The Utes Must Go." The reservation came within a few miles of town to the south, and "obviously" the Indians were squatting on excellent farm land that whites could put to much better use. This became one of the favorite long-term themes of the local press, one that found support on Main Avenue and Boulevard alike.

> Are we in Southwestern Colorado alone to be left at the mercy of the red-skins? Let the people move in this matter . . . to remove the Southern Utes.
>
> *Durango Record* (Daily), May 11, 1881

> The Utes must go! *Southwest,* February 9, 1884

> It now appears that throwing open a million acres of the Southern Ute reservation is only a question of a few months.
>
> *Durango Herald,* March 7, 1890

John Porter expressed Main Avenue sentiment in 1886, when he spoke as president of the Board of Trade. He did not want the Utes moved just a few miles away; he wanted them beyond Utah's Blue Mountains. Neither Porter's nor Durango's hope of a speedy solution materialized.

The time had passed when the government simply shipped Indians to some uninhabited western territory; none existed. Utah saw no reason it should take any more Utes; after all, that territory had acquired the Meeker Massacre removals. Back east the Indian Rights Association made noises on behalf of the Indians, something few diehard Westerners could grasp. Congressional removal bills died and there the matter rested.

Ute money in trade, on the other hand, was more than welcome. Local merchants regularly anticipated the day the Indians received their allotments. But accepting them as permanent neighbors was an entirely different matter. As long as a profit could be turned, people showed great interest in Indians, current and ancient. The latter offered great potential by encouraging tourists to visit the "Old Aztec People," as the ruins were often described. Amateur archaeologists had collected arrowheads, pots, and other relics almost from the time the first survey stake was driven. It did not take them long to capitalize on more general interest in the ruins. The *Southwest* struck a chord that echoed down the decades, when it advised locals in March 1882 to give the tourists a "warm and hearty welcome." Durango did, and would broaden the appeal to include recreation, health, and scenic attractions, "a great resort for pleasure and recreation generally."

The late eighties brought the discovery of the magnificent ruins at Mesa Verde, the full impact of which would not be recognized for several years. Mears and his Rio Grande Southern took advantage of the ruins and exhorted visitors to take their route to the "Homes of the Cliff Dwellers." Some of the early Mesa Verde relic collections passed through town and were exhibited there, but Durango had to yield to Mancos as the jumping-off point for the time being.

Durango could hold its own so far as health attractions were concerned. It had at its doorstep one of those favorites of the age, a hot springs resort. Trimble Springs, nine miles north of the city limits, advertised "curative qualities unsurpassed," and a fine bar and billiard rooms for the recovered. A splendid brick hotel, built in 1882, stood within walking distance of the D&RG tracks, and close enough to Durango to become a favorite buggy trip despite jarring county roads. Though beautifully located, Trimble Springs was dogged by misfortune, as frequent changes in management testify. Long a favorite of Silverton and Durango, it never caught on with the larger clientele of health seekers. It simply had too many fancier and better-advertised Colorado rivals. A couple of miles farther down the road, an even less developed Pinkerton Springs claimed that its soda springs rivaled Manitou's. Bottled, the water graced many a Durango table.

Durango was blessed with an abundance of good physicians, including two women who "paid particular attention to chronic diseases of ladies." It is hoped that few of them had to work under the conditions William Folsom faced. His newly opened dental office featured a kitchen chair (with a head rest attached) sitting on a packing box so the patient would be high enough to examine without a back-breaking stoop. A spittoon on the floor, more often missed than hit, completed the arrangement. For a while the community was actually "overstocked" with doctors, a problem that natural attrition soon resolved.

Area residents succumbed to the same illnesses, imagined and real, as other Coloradans, if patent medicine ads can serve as guides. "Disfigured skin," catarrh, "lazy liver," lumbago, headaches, and toothaches bedeviled their days and disturbed their nights. Some problems could be traced directly to "the awful effects of early vice." The Cook Remedy Company and Denver doctors Betts & Betts, advertising in local newspapers, promised to cure syphilis and gonorrhea, restore lost manhood and decayed faculties, and alleviate female weakness. There was, of course, no known cure for syphilis. As the Victorian saying went, "Thirty seconds with Venus, a lifetime of Mercury" (one of the "cures"). On a more positive note, a Keeley Institute opened in 1892, promising the "double chloride of Gold remedies" to cure liquor, opium, morphine, and tobacco diseases. One of sixty institutes in America, it claimed fifty cures within two months.

Physicians and others debated whether their community was unhealthy, not from natural causes but from man-created sources. The answer was an unequivocal yes, and the city administration could only partially solve the problem. Voters wanted low-cost government; sanitation and pure water were high-cost items. They got what they wanted—lower costs—yet with them came higher risks. The water works, complete with a reservoir on what henceforth was known as Reservoir Hill, pumped water from the Animas River, a polluted stream. Sewers were a more complex matter, and sanitary conditions literally stank. Winter's cold suppressed the smell, spring's warmth and rains brought it to full bloom—an "unbearable stench," testified one reporter's nose. Too shallow privies, littering, animal pollution, and general untidiness contributed to the contamination. The muck below reeked to the sky above, but the cost of sewer construction seemed so prohibitive that the situation was left to deteriorate.

The city fathers meanwhile worked legislatively to enhance the "quality of life." Numerous ordinances to improve sight, sound, and smell came from their deliberations, including limiting the speed of railroad trains to four miles an hour and prohibiting their stopping on street crossings for more than ten minutes. Animals at large were to be impounded, and a public pound was established, although it was only spasmodically maintained. Among city prohibitions were riding bicycles on sidewalks and from twilight on without a lighted lamp and alarm bell; shooting of fireworks within city limits; and riding by "fancy women" on horseback or in open carriages, or otherwise exhibiting or advertising their occupations on the streets. The council worried about cesspools and sewers but did not get around to doing anything about them. After public petition, a Sunday closing ordinance was passed. It failed to produce the promised millennium of life without drunkards, wider Sabbath observance, and increased morality. What it did was stir up a lot of discussion in the 1890s. When Victorian morality and business interests found themselves at odds, materialism won out.

The liquor interests triumphed this time; however, their foundation was shaky and they remained on the defensive. The WCTU and related groups were organized and active in Durango and elsewhere; early muckraker Benjamin Flower called the saloon "the modern inferno." Temperance could no longer fill the bill, but prohibition promised to end the evils of liquor for good.

One problem, lawlessness, had declined dramatically since the early years. The killing in December 1883 of the young merchant Bruce Hunt marred the record, however. Helping to foil an attempted robbery of the Bank of Durango, Hunt was shot, and for weeks afterward this robbery created front-page news. This outburst of violence brought an end to rampant lawlessness. The city marshal's reports in the years following showed more sins of the flesh than violence—drunkenness, fast driving, disturbing the peace, and gambling. The marshal spent much more time corralling stray animals, small boys, drunks, and dogs than he did assuming the "role" of a western peace officer. His efforts were not always appreciated. One evening some "mischievous party" let loose all the dogs the officer had worked so hard to impound the previous day. The July 1889 fire burned both the city hall and jail, so human criminals soon found themselves in new quarters.

By the 1890s Durango had taken on "metropolitan" and "cosmopolitan" airs, according to its boosters. They must be excused for a virulent case of overenthusiasm. But there was some substance to their argument. Their city had been one of the first in Colorado to adopt electric lighting; the local electric company began operating in January 1887, backed by Thomas Graden, James Luttrell, and John Porter, among others. Arc lights illuminated previously gas-lit streets, and business houses and residences glowed warmly after dusk. A few "bugs" needed to be worked out, but the Herald, September 26, 1888, proudly proclaimed, "Durango has electric lights for her workers, an advantage to the city's conveniences which is more than pleasing, and an advantage to such institutions as that of the San Juan Smelting and Mining Company which cannot be estimated."

The glow of the street lights revealed steadily improving residential streets. As befit the smelter's superintendent and son of the company's president, Ernest Amy built Durango's most imposing home, appropriately on the Boulevard. At a cost of nearly $50,000, Amy's "Elizabethan mansion" proved that Denver held no monopoly on fine houses. The Amys entertained lavishly and maintained an elegant household; Durango would see few of their kind. From the early eighties on, middle-class neighborhoods also were transformed. Fassbinder's addition took on a stable appearance, and east and south of the Boulevard more homes dotted the landscape. Having rebounded from an 1888 housing shortage and the 1889 fire damage, Durango looked quite refined. Richard McCloud could hardly restrain himself when viewing the scene: "To look down upon the residences, trees and green grass lawns from one of the many hills that surround Durango, is a sight never to be forgotten for grandeur."

Durango had become a "home of wealth." Many who made money in San Juan mining invested and/or settled here. The irrepressible McCloud wrote in 1892, "When they reap the fortune that comes to all mining men who stick to it, they spend their money in Durango in such a way as to pay a handsome income." From Rico, Silverton, Ouray, and other points they came. Charles Newman, for instance, although a local druggist, made a fortune in Rico, and in 1892 was underwriting construction of the handsome Newman Block on Main Avenue.

Already an upper class was emerging. Estelle Camp, A. P.'s wife, said that there were two extremes of social life. The mining engineers and managers, the smelter's official staff, and the army people from Fort Lewis joined with the Camps and other Durango well-to-do to form one group. She remembered them as a "cultured, well educated, traveled" class. The other extreme in Mrs. Camp's eyes was "wild and woolly."

Inhabitants and tourists alike acclaimed Durango's finest Victorian building, the Strater Hotel, "strictly first class in all appointments." The Strater, opened in August 1888, graced the southern end of Main, a block and a half from the depot. A fine hotel was the mark of a progressive city, and Durango had always prided itself on good ones. Now it offered the traveler a distinctive one. Henry Strater, backed by family money, built it and, no hotelman himself, promptly leased it. Lessee and lessor soon fell to quarreling, and in 1892 Strater was constructing an annex next door.

The social and cultural calendar was crowded every week of every season. From Shakespeare clubs to the town nine, there was something to appeal to everybody. When Silverton thumped the team 25-6, civic pride smarted. Unsportingly, though not uncommonly, the victors had imported a professional battery to strengthen their team. "Durango can afford to lose a game of baseball, but Durango cannot afford to win by questionable methods," moralized the *Herald,* July 19, 1892.

A history of the "early settlers" already was proposed by a local writer; then, for some unstated reason, the project was dropped. The holiday seasons were characteristically crowded with parades, balls, races, and other events. The Grand Army of the

Republic's Sedgwick Post No. 12 took a prominent role on the patriotic flag-waving days. Among the "boys in blue" marched such stalwarts as Robert Sloan, Thomas Graden, and Peter Fassbinder. The G.A.R. brought together urban and rural, banker and laborer, saloon keeper and rancher to reminisce about the fading days of the Civil War.

Those days are as far removed from us as those people were from George Washington's day. Yet life leaps from the faded photographs and newspaper pages. July 15, 1892, was just another summer day, but an attempt to relive it reveals what Durango was really like then. The Smelter City Brewing Company was promising to knock out eastern competition, a dance was planned at the Porter Coal Mine, and Kruschke's Dry Goods store headlined a sale of parasols for $1.60, just what a fashionable lady needed for that dance. The Rio Grande Southern carried tourists to within an easy ride of the "Cliff Dwellers," and Professor George Garlow, the "world's greatest specialist on diseases of the scalp," temporarily domiciled at the Strater, promised to "contract to produce hair on bald heads." No money need be paid until the hair reached one and a half inches in length! Ladies' low-necked sleeveless vests sold for 20¢ and choice lots on the Boulevard for $1,250. The parties dumping trash into Lightner Creek were threatened with prompt arrest, if caught—they happened to be polluting the smelter's drinking water. John Porter arrived in town on last night's Southern, down from his Telluride mines.

Gone, yes, as much as that warm July day and the people who stopped for a cool beer (a glass of lemonade for the WCTU'ers) to quench their thirst. A day faded into yesteryear. These people's hopes and dreams were not so different from yours and mine, and from them Durango took root.

DURANGO IN THE NINETEENTH CENTURY
A PICTORIAL REVIEW

From birth to age twenty, Durango lived a full life. Nostalgia tends to mellow a backward look at the scene but should not delude the viewer into yearning for the "good old days." Herein are pictured the people who helped build and maintain the community. They would probably be pleased to have us remember what they did and that they looked to the future.

One is reminded of a once-popular song, "Wait Till the Sun Shines, Nellie":

> Wait till the sun shines, Nellie,
> And the gray skies turn to blue,
> . . . .
> We'll face the years together
> Sweethearts, you and I, . . .

Durangoans saw more blue skies than gray during these years, except that some of the gray ones turned into a thundering storm. They and their town faced the years together and the marriage proved to be a happy one.

Durango, as the Trust envisioned the town in 1880. The Boulevard became Third Avenue and the other north-south streets became avenues. The east-west streets were renamed: A became Third Street; B, Fourth Street; and so on. The county block and north park were never developed, but south park is now Fanto Park. *State Historical Society of Colorado*

By mid-summer 1881 Durango was starting to settle down. On the "large pine tree" across from the post office, Henry Moorman was lynched the previous April. The European Hotel and its neighbors on Railroad Street would soon be moving, because they squatted on the D&RG right-of-way. Next to Goodrich et al. on Main was the Bank of Durango, and behind the bank on G Street (modern Ninth) were the post office, St. James Hotel, which promised "everything brand new," and other stores. *Center of Southwest Studies*

50

Forced to move, the European Hotel is dragged down Second Avenue sometime in late August or early September, 1881. Once advertising "meals at all hours," its fate remains a mystery. Elitch's Oyster House was operated by John Elitch of Denver's Elith Gardens fame. Oysters were not always available for genial John, and one drunken miner got chunks of tripe "cooked to a queen's taste" after threatening the proprietor's life for not having any oysters. *First National Bank*

George Woods, as the expression went, was "jerked to Jesus" in Durango's only legal hanging, June 23, 1882. Woods had gotten his man one month before to the day; justice was swift in those days. Note the children witnessing the execution and, it is hoped, learning that crime does not pay. *Center of Southwest Sudies*

51

Main Avenue in the mid-1880s was dusty in the summer, muddy after rains, and polluted by horses, burros, and mules. Ladies faced a challenge crossing it without besmirching their skirts, while also avoiding the unladylike behavior of raising them above the ankle! In the evening, gas lights gave the walker only dim help in dodging the piles and puddles. To the left is the saloon block, where no "lady" would walk and where "There'll be a hot time in the old town tonight" meant masculine fun. *Amon Carter Museum*

Trimble Springs was Durango's resort and health spa. This is the first hotel built in 1881–82. After it burned, an even larger and fancier structure rose, lacking "none of the modern conveniences of a first class hotel," even a skilled chef. *Eleanor Roberts*

Longfellow's smithy, Durango version. Three of the old-time businesses are seen, Naegelin's blacksmith shop, Durango Bottling Works, and an ad for Geo. Goodman's paint and wallpaper. A real pioneer, Naegelin worked at Parrott City and Animas City before coming to Durango. He died in 1934. *Durango Herald*

If the ballad "Mother was a Lady," which begins "Two drummers sat at dinner in a grand hotel one day," had had Durango for its setting, it would have been the Strater. "Strictly First Class," it had been a Durango landmark since 1888. The horsedrawn streetcar dates the photograph to 1891. It was advertisements such as those tacked onto the poles that aroused the council's ire, and the ill-repaired wooden sidewalks that antogonized their constituents. *Center of Southwest Studies*

53

Durango's two major smelters. The San Juan Smelter (above) was by far the more important; the Standard Smelter had a brief independent career before being consolidated with its rival. Work at both was hot, hard, and long. *Strater Hotel, Goodman's, Inc.*

Smelters were Durango's largest industry, as well as the major pollution contributor. In this turn-of-the-century photograph, smoke drifts over Durango. In the lower righthand corner is the Amy mansion, which set the pace for Third Avenue and all Durango; at lower left is Central School, the first high school. *Durango Herald*

North Durango was seldom photographed, but on both sides of the river were Durango's first subdivisions. St. Columba Church stands at the lower right, Whittier Elementary School just above it and to the left. A nickel-a-ride streetcar is near the bridge, partly obscured by the smokestack of the water works. *Durango Public Library*

"In the good old summer time" men wore straw hats and rode No. 5 as it passed the Newman Block, built by Charles Newman, using part of his Rico mining profits. In winter, sides replaced the curtains to keep passengers somewhat warmer. The banners indicate the knights of Pythias were having a celebration. *Center of Southwest Studies*

Patriotic school children passing the future site of the Newman building. No streetcar tracks are visible, which dates this about 1890. As there was no Columbian school, the parade probably honors Columbus on a beautiful fall day. *Goodman's, Inc.*

Durangoans welcomed the Utes at allotment time. The corner of Seventh and Main was reserved for their camping and gave the tourists at the Strater an extra attraction. The Indians' ponies look rather worse for wear in this early 1890s photograph. *Amon Carter Museum*

The ladies and gentlemen of the Durango Wheel Club enjoy an outing at Baker's Bridge, June 16, 1895. Near here, a generation before, stood Animas City (No. 1). Its founder, Charles Baker, also left his name at Baker's Park, site of Silverton. In June, 1895, two local stores advertised bicycles at prices ranging from $40 to $100. *Goodman's, Inc.*

The volunteer Hook & Ladder Company, a dedicated group of "fire laddies," served from 1881–1894. Number 4 was George Goodman, the last volunteer and first salaried chief. *Goodman's, Inc.*

Groups of workers, and probably managers, at the power plant about 1891. If the date is correct, the Durango Electric Company was the owner. Among its incorporators were Thomas Graden and John Porter. In 1890 four dynamos easily handled all of Durango's electrical needs. *Western Colorado Power Company Archives*

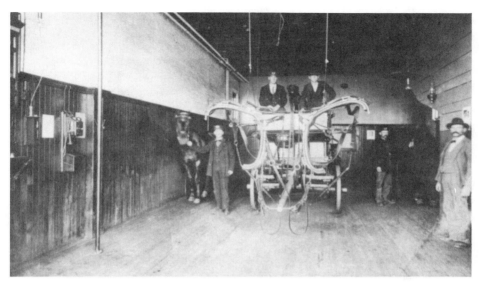

Tiger and Joe stand patiently awaiting the call in this mid-nineties view of the firehouse. Durango did not have a paid fire department until February, 1894; before that, four volunteer companies answered the alarm. City Hall shared this same building. The current City Hall and especially its parking lot occupy the site now. *Goodman's, Inc.*

Durango High School's first graduating class, all dressed in the styles of 1891. The future looked bright that year, but a depression lurked ahead. Durango's school system has always been one of its community strengths. *Center of Southwest Studies*

59

The boys of Company K drill in front of the county courthouse on Second Avenue. Either these lads or their contemporaries lost Durnago's first recorded football game. The courthouse was built in 1891–92 and was typical of the architecture of that era. *Center of Southwest Studies*

One of Durango's homegrown industries. Note the two doors, with one ramp going up, the other down. The carriages at the right were probably made here. This was the land for which Harry Jackson, by hesitating, ended up paying four times the original asking price of $1,000. *Jackson Clark*

60

Harry Jackson (at left) stands with his workers. Durango's "tin bucket brigade" was hailed as the greatest contributor to her nineteenth-century prosperity. Unheralded, these men and others provided the muscle that built the community. *Jackson Clark*

Waiting in line to claim land after the opening of the Ute Strip. May 4, 1899. Despite much ballyhoo, it did not match the Oklahoma rush. Homesteading south of town was anything but romantic. Many people simply gave up and drifted on, while a few Durangoans were caught trying to bend the residency requirements. When Uncle Sam told them to live on the claim or forfeit, they forfeited. *Duane A. Smith*

The Chinese overcame their neighbors' bigotry and proved every bit as respectable as citizens. Fong Tong and Fong Chang opened Bank of Durango accounts in 1881 along with such notables as Peter Fassbinder and Caroline Romney. S. King Ching, houseboy of the McNeil family, is pictured. *Center of Southwest Studies*

"She's only a bird in a gilded cage, a beautiful sight to see." We will never know for sure whether Lillian Lee was a "girl of the line." The photograph, dated April 22, 1897, was in the company of other material that pointed in that direction. Regardless, the mysterious Lillian was a beauty in the Victorian manner. *Western History Department, Denver Public Library*

PART TWO

Refiner's Fire
1893-1916

That the trial of your faith, being much more precious than of gold that perisheth, though it be tried with fire . . . .

I Peter 1:7

5. "Should Auld Acquaintance Be Forgot"

Hardly had the last strains of "Auld Lang Syne" faded away than Durangoans, with lofty expectations, plunged into 1893. Twelve years had passed since their town's birth, a generally prosperous time, despite a few slow years. They could not complain; Durango had been good to them and they expected better days ahead. Even the more persistent peculiarities of the frontier had now been polished by urbanization. The once isolated local economy was integrated into the Colorado mainstream by the railroad and outside investment. Now it was being integrated into the national economy. These recent pioneers surveyed the scene with a measure of pride; where the rate of urban mortality ran so high, they and their community thrived.

In the waning days of the winter of 1892–93, John Porter wrote his old friend William Bell that he expected to sell some of the remaining Land and Coal Company's Main Avenue lots for $10,000, certainly $9,000, and was holding Boulevard lots for $4,000. Porter was pleased the company invested in the Brookside Addition: "I think it will pay three or four fold, to say the least." Summer, he reasoned, would bring the very highest prices. That summer of prosperity never arrived.

Instead, the town, the state, and the whole nation were rocked by the century's worst depression. Debate over the causes centered on the world money and trade markets, excessive speculation and credit, an agricultural price slump, and, in Colorado, the emotional one of the Sherman Silver Purchase Act. The silver issue being strictly an academic debate to most of them, what Durangoans saw was only a violent financial storm battering the community in the last six months of 1893. Signs of trouble had been considerable but were met by blind eyes. Porter found many to join his chorus in praise of the "metropolis of an empire," the town of nearly "perpetual sunshine."

An already depressed agricultural condition was complicated by a long dry spell that carried into early summer. Even though Durango was building as "no other city in Colorado was building," the *Great Southwest*, on April 12, pointed out that there were three workers for every two jobs. When the whirlwind hit, some of the town's underpinnings were found to be weak.

Raw statistics show the magnitude of the depression, if not the individual emotional and traumatic depths of it. During July and August, 400 people lost their jobs, fifteen businesses failed; a Colorado Bureau of Labor Statistics survey called the situation "gloomy." That keystone of prosperity, the Rio Grande Southern, was rumored to be in trouble as early as April. And Mears's road was in jeopardy—Mears lost control of it in August. With traffic on the narrow gauge less than half what it had been at the start of the year, the Rio Grande Southern fell into receivership and eventually emerged under D&RG ownership.

The reason for the dwindling traffic was easily determined. One of the immediate effects of the depression and repeal of the Sherman Silver Purchase Act had been the collapse of the price of silver. If Durango was buffeted by the depression, consider Rico with thirty mines closed and 1,200 unemployed, Telluride with nine mines, 375 out of work, and Silverton with ten mines, 1,000 jobs lost. Facts like these doomed Mears's heavily mortgaged line and threatened the very heart of San Juan mining.

Obviously, Durango's major industry, smelting, could not weather such a storm for long. Chronically short of working capital, the San Juan firm had lived under financial pressure for years. Planned construction was first to be eliminated. Money borrowed to buy ore proved difficult to repay. Another unexpected sidelight, noted by Ernest Amy, came with the closing of the mines that supplied lead-silver ore (lead was needed as a flux and always seemed in short supply). The smelter was forced to go to Utah for lead, thereby raising expenses. Finally, in 1894, the smelter closed, throwing more men out of work. Losses mounted and the San Juan Smelter trembled on the brink of disaster. From the metallurgical point of view, operations were successful, but it was small consolation. "At no time in the history of the Company," Amy gloomily reported, "have we been compelled to face so many unforeseen difficulties in the way of conducting successful operations."

Nor did coal escape—the mines, railroad, and smelter had been its major purchasers. The Porter Fuel and its smaller competitors suffered accordingly and production slumped. A national coal strike in 1894 threatened Durango but actually caused only minor problems.

Porter's hoped-for real estate boom went by the boards as well, and all that could be said was that the company held its own. Times were hard everywhere. The *Southwest*, under attachment for unpaid notes, temporarily righted itself, but never recovered, and was gone before the depression loosened its grip. The *Herald* self-righteously announced that Durango was no field for two daily papers. Two years before, such a statement would have been considered unpatriotic. No business escaped unscathed; no businessman avoided the pinch. The Strater reduced room-and-board rates and made a determined effort to keep going "despite the stringency in money matters," but, alas, Strater lost both his original hotel and his just-completed annex.

The hard times took their toll. A despondent, unemployed Frank Burke blew off the top of his head with a shotgun blast. It was May 1894, and he left behind this note: "Good bye all friends. Times too hard. The Boys can have a wake. . . . Born in '58 Baltimore, Md. What I owe now I'll owe forever." Thirty-six years old, and for Burke there seemed no hope.

The "jobs wanted" column, which had previously contained mostly advertisements by women seeking employment in housework, chamber work, and cooking, soon included machinists, engineers, and men looking for any type of work. Problems bad enough at home were made worse by Durango's national ties. The United States had never before stepped into such a quagmire of difficulties: bank and business failures, bread lines, labor unrest, food shortages—all these and more. Escape from all of them was impossible for the ordinary person. No relief existed. Private resources soon failed, exhausted. In 1894, when the railroad unions struck against the Pullman Company, the Denver and Rio Grande temporarily terminated its run to Durango. The *Herald*, maintaining a "stiff upper lip," saw consolation in this: "Our outside creditors cannot reach us—for a few days." While the *Herald* forever prophesied improving times, they did not come.

The local impact of one crisis was made clear to Durango when its Colorado Guard, Company K, was ordered to Cripple Creek by Gov. Davis Waite on June 5, 1894, to help restore order during a miners' strike. Fifty of the guard boys dutifully rode off in a special car on the regular eastern train. Luckily for them, the 130-day strike ended June 10 without more violence.

The times spawned radicalism, or what passed for radicalism in the nineties. The *Southwest* called for public work projects as early as July 16, 1893. Durangoans read about the 1894 march of Coxey's Army on Washington to demand such a program; some sympathized, but no volunteers rushed off to join up. The state government was in no condition to respond to similar demands, and the federal government would not stoop to such socialism. Keep itself solvent and let the business community pull itself out of the depression was Uncle Sam's motto.

The community did join with the rest of Colorado to support the silver issue, Colorado's war cry. Briefly and simply described, overproduction and declining use in coinage forced down the international silver price. For twenty years silver interests had called for government help, which came in the form of federal purchases and the coining of silver dollars. Never would the government go so far as to guarantee the price, something ardently sought by silver miners. The Sherman Silver Purchase Act of 1890 had partially satisfied western demands. According to eastern financial experts, however, it had caused a financial drain on the treasury and loss of confidence in federal policies. President Grover Cleveland, in one of his initial actions in 1893, called a special session of Congress to repeal this act. This "foul deed" was accomplished over the heated protests of the western silver congressmen and their allies. The price of silver collapsed to 63¢ per ounce from an 1890 $1.05 average, and the San Juan silver mines found themselves in desperate straits.

Although it had no silver mines of its own, Durango rose in righteous anger to defend its mining interests and its primary railroad and smelting industries. Even the *Herald* and *Southwest* stopped feuding on this issue. In spite of an editorial uproar, nothing could be salvaged, and silver went down to defeat.

If they could not win in 1893, Durangoans would voice disapproval in other ways. They turned politically "radical" to support their interests. They became Populists, the new political party on the block. The Populists promised the free coinage of silver at a sixteen-to-one ratio (sixteen ounces of silver worth one ounce of gold), which would return silver's price to $1.25 per ounce. This was what Durango wanted. The political change had been coming since early in the decade, and in 1892 and 1894 Durango voted Populist. The voters could hardly wait for 1896, when they would get a chance to turn the rascals out of the White House with a silver landslide.

Those who lived through 1893–94 never forgot the experience. If they thought times were bad at home, they had only to pick up their daily paper to read about worse things—a miners' strike at Cripple Creek, the coal miners' strike in Pennsylvania, and the antics of Colorado Governor Davis Waite. Trouble erupted everywhere. The American dream had turned into a nightmare.

Yet through it all life went on, showing the resilient, optimistic natures of these people. In the depths of their despair, they cheered silver and read about its young champion, William J. Bryan. The sports-minded followed Gentleman Jim Corbett and his successful defense of the heavyweight championship. More than anything else, Durango events proved that, although adjustments were required, the business of living continued, nevertheless.

Without doubt, 1893 proved to be the worst year. It took a while for the shock to wear off; even then, however, there was a sprightliness. The "wheelmen" spent many pleasant Sunday afternoons riding out to Trimble Springs. With the safety-bike and better roads, bicycling came of age; there was talk of organizing a club. Probably no picture reinforces the image of the "Gay Nineties" more than a group pedaling out for a picnic at Trimble Springs on a warm summer day. But the 1890s were definitely not gay, even though popular legend has fixed this image in the public mind.

The town came of age in another way, reveling in the luxury of "artificial ice." Five carloads of ice machinery arrived in April for the Smelter City Brewing Association; as soon as it was put together, presto, ice for everyone. No more cutting ice on cold winter days and storing it covered with sawdust. Fresh ice was dispensed for the icebox, lemonade, and chilled beer. The saloons, too, matured, offering appropriate establishments for both the rough and the genteel in the 900 block of Main. As times toughened, these accompaniments of prosperity declined in number.

Newspaper readers were for a while intrigued by the discovery of the bones of a prehistoric creature (*Stegosaurus ungulatus*) west of town on Montezuma Creek. Although Durangoans like to think of it as their own (every town needs a 100-foot-long monster), it really belonged to rival Cortez.

The Durango Archaeological and Historical Society concerned itself more with Indians than with fossils. Organized in April 1893, it remained active throughout the decade. The members had hoped to buy one of the collections of relics being carted out of the Mesa Verde cliff dwellings; they could not have picked a more inauspicious time to raise the money. It was therefore suggested that members contribute items from their personal collections for the society's good. If all else failed, they planned to make collecting tours during the summer of 1893 to gather relics.

The high school, located in the Central Elementary building, had hardly graduated its first class before an alumni association was organized in the fall of 1893. Then, in December, came one of those monumental "events that alter and illuminate the times"—the first football game. At least it seems to have been the first, although Caroline Romney mentioned a football "kicked around" back in March 1882. The high school eleven defeated the men of Company K, 2–0, on a flying wedge safety. The event "stirred up interest" in the game, and within a week plans were afoot to organize a "crack" football city team to "mop up" all rivals. The doggedness of the depression doomed such athletic aspirations.

It did not dim interest in athletics, however; and Decoration Day, 1894, celebrated the grand opening of the Durango Athletic Park, just across Junction Creek and on the east side of the road that eventually became Main Avenue. It provided a baseball diamond, football field, dancing pavilion, and a bicycle track, six laps to the mile. The inaugural featured a rematch between the Company K boys (soon to march to Cripple Creek) and the high school, winner to claim $75, loser $25. So much for amateur athletics! Unfortunately, the next issues of the paper are missing, so the outcome is lost to posterity. Football never approached the popularity of baseball, though, and Durango fielded a crack nine that year. The July 4 celebration gave top billing to a three-game set with Ouray, which the Durango team won 26–18 and 25–15. The middle game, after a great deal of "kicking" about the umpiring, ended in a 21–19 Ouray victory.

The same park was host to the "party of the year" a few weeks later, a private affair that included society's elite. Dancing went on until 1:30 in the morning with breaks for refreshments. In August another group of the upper crust went for a ten-day "outing party" at Vallecito; a four-horse team conveyed tents, provender, and a cook. Depressions could be weathered easily if one happened to have enough money!

Most people were not that affluent, so they might go instead to Parsons Drug to listen to the phonograph, selecting from among the seventy vocal and instrumental numbers available. The telephone was here to stay and the novelty was wearing off. By March 1894, sixty-six phones were installed and sixteen applications lay in wait to be processed. The city fathers rose to the occasion and granted the Southwestern Telephone Company a twenty-year franchise. Bicycle riders were already causing trouble, and ordinances to curb some of their excesses were passed and enforced. Thus, one of Durango's young men found himself arrested for pedaling down Main at night without a lighted lamp. The latest bicycle model attracted attention, since few had money enough to buy a Temple Special with wooden rims.

On Arbor Day a group of school children hiked up Perin's Peak to study nature firsthand. And in the fall, before school started, the city and county teachers gathered at the new high school building for a "Teachers' Normal Institute." They went to work enlightened by sessions on pedagogy, orthoepy (speech), school management, and child development.

The major construction project of the year was designed to fulfill the burning desire for a "grand opera house" seating 500 people. McCloud and others had called for "one of [Durango's] Tabors" to build himself an enduring monument; now the day was at hand. Though built in 1894, it did not open until 1895. With hotel business way down, the Strater Annex was converted into the Durango Opera House earlier, in 1894. The opera cup suddenly overflowed. The Durango Opera House opened with a potpourri of entertainment. Sometimes slim attendance forced cancellation of performances, and on other occasions those who attended kicked themselves for doing so. Miss Howard, the spiritualist, gave a performance on Sunday, September 9, 1894, for example, "considerable of a fake," bemoaned a reviewer. Nonetheless Durango's theater aspirations now were fulfilled; it only remained to see if patrons would support two theaters. A depression did not seem a good time to find out. It was not, but the Durango Opera House survived.

The ladies in town had coveted respectable entertainment for a long time, and it had come at last. The role of women had increased significantly over the past twelve years. Always active in the church and WCTU, they now had physical culture classes and reading and language clubs—something to appeal to almost every joiner. To spruce up the appearance of town, the Ladies' Improvement Society was trying to grow trees in the park down the center of the Boulevard. The council supported the endeavor by passing an ordinance forbidding damaging the trees.

The council also entreated the Ladies' Improvement Society to suggest names for the streets, to replace the unimaginative A, B, C that the community had been burdened with since the original survey. The ladies did their best and came up with such imaginative gems as Alamo, Dolores, Alameda, Hermosa, Indio, Alta, Fremont, and Cumbres. Regrettably, the councilmen ignored these suggestions and settled for the mundane First, Second, and so on. Even the Boulevard lost out in the shuffle, to become just plain Third Avenue, and one street named Smith became Twentieth. Such lack of ingenuity ill suited Durango.

The same "foggy bottom" thinking also forced Durango and La Plata County to be one of the few Colorado precincts to vote against women's suffrage in November 1893, by nearly two to one. Before the state vote was tabulated, the *Herald* chortled that suffrage had "undoubtedly received" a final death blow; then, with egg all over its editorial face, it had to concede that Colorado had approved women's suffrage. Ladies no doubt had something to say to their husbands after that vote. Apparently, town suffrage meetings, advocating "recognize your wife as your equal," swayed few males. No logical explanation was apparent for the local conservative attitude.

This negativism carried over into the area of race relations. Hard times evoked feelings of animosity, especially when one's job or living standard was threatened. Minorities easily became convenient scapegoats for a host of ills. The press gave occasional glimpses of these prejudices. For example, there were disparaging comments about a "colony of Japs" temporarily infesting the city. Although only twenty-seven Chinese were found to be living here, anger flared in 1894 when another opium den was discovered. A police raid netted six pipes, lamps, "dope," and four "hop fiends." Much to the "super" Americans' dismay, the three women and a man nabbed were all white. The Hispanos and blacks, surprisingly, did not come in for much discussion, except for unusual instances, like the fight between two "colored inmates" of one of the houses on Railroad Street. Blacks were too few to represent any possible threat, and Hispanos "knew their place."

As 1894 drew to a close, Durangoans were shocked to find that Ed Steans, their accommodating postmaster, came up $1,800 short after a government audit of his accounts. He had been his own worst enemy, the *Herald* concluded, and then dropped the matter. Christmas, 1894, glistened brighter than the previous year, when there seemed little cause for levity. To top off the day, the Commercial Hotel's freshly painted and papered dining room advertised Christmas dinner of consommé royale, French peas, chocolate éclairs, roast prime rib, mashed potatoes, mince pie, and coffee, tea, or milk, all for 35¢. Or if one preferred, turkey, veal, or ham and other entrées were available in "one of the best dining rooms in the city."

The years 1893 and 1894 encompassed an end and a beginning. Some of the enthusiasm and optimism of the early years wore out. An unidentified resident commented in the late fall of 1893, "Of course we have suffered severely, but not so extensively as in other portions of the state. . . ." Durango, as the *Herald* summarized it in 1893, was "neither dead nor booming." Because the smelter was able to keep going that year (1893) without suspension, the depression's impact had been blunted somewhat. Though there were problems, the financial crush was less perhaps than in Silverton or Denver.

That "indomitable spirit of hope and confidence," the community's badge of honor, was revived in 1894. A shutdown at the smelter proved to be only temporary, and by the end of the year both it and the coal mines were running and reportedly doing a "good" business. The three banks, Smelter, Colorado State, and First National, remained solvent throughout, as did the new Durango Savings Bank; these institutions kept Durango afloat when other cities faced bank failures. This blessing should not be underestimated. As Durango bounced back, so did La Plata County. Reminiscent of 1880, the Denver and Rio Grande "boys" organized another town. In March 1894, the Hesperus Town and Improvement Company, under the guidance of Albert C. Hunt, former governor Alexander Hunt's son, surveyed and platted Hesperus near the coal mines and along the tracks of the Rio Grande Southern. The company ran excursion trains to the site for prospective investors in real estate. Hunt and the others were not so distressed by the hard times and the uncertain future that they were prevented from starting such a venture. Nor was the Durango Land and Coal Company, which, staring at a dead real estate market, cheerfully notified its stockholders that the "worst was over" and Durango was doing very well.

The worst was over but not its aftermath. Well into 1898 Durango suffered from the depression, and the turn of the century came before good times returned. A. P. Camp summarized well in November 1897, when he said:

Business has increased materially over last year. Money matters grow easier all the time. There is greater activity in business circles. I consider the prospects are very bright from now on for continued improvement. We have doubtless seen the worst and the rebound is here.

Conservative banker Camp viewed the situation more realistically than the optimists of 1894.

Durango always oozed more than its share of optimism. The shock of the depression, with its lingering aftermath, forced a reconsideration of the present and future. The easy expectations of 1881 or 1892 no longer sufficed. The gregarious city boosters choked on their verbiage and fell silent until a new group came forward. Thus passed a time of trial.

6. King of the San Juan Basin

Depression still gripped Durango when 1895 arrived, though it appeared that the worst was over. A throng of optimistic statements proclaimed the depression's end, the dawn of a better day. Serious-minded residents wondered. Was this the dawning of a new era? The hellfire of the depression certainly purged the glow of 1892. The answer proved slow in coming; two decades would pass before it could be measured.

The town recovered slowly, and not until 1898 did it shake off the aftermath. The turn of the century came before the local economy fully recovered. Druggist Jack Parsons called 1900 the very best year since 1892, and old-timer Robert Sloan concurred, feeling that the outlook was "exceedingly flattering."

Seven years later Durango received another severe setback. A national financial panic caused by speculation and a weak banking system spread from the East throughout the country. Before it ran its short course, both the Colorado State and Smelter City banks closed, a disaster that had been avoided in the longer and harder 1890s depression. Poor banking practices, weak leadership, and lack of regulation pulled them down. Officially, the panic ran into 1908, then better times resumed. There was, however, nothing to console those who lost money in the bank failures in this day before federal deposit insurance. Burns Bank opened in May 1910, partly in response to the 1907 failures, to join the older First National.

By 1910 a comfortable routine had returned, one that would continue until America's entry into World War I in 1917. Durango's business district stretched from the depot down Main to Eleventh. Second Avenue offered only weak competition, despite its earlier promise. The real heart of Main ran from Seventh through Tenth. A quick survey of the businesses revealed the usual grocery, paint, clothing, hardware, and drug stores, hotels, blacksmiths, real estate offices, restaurants, bakeries, and saloons (twenty-two of the last—by far the most numerous individual business). Evidence of the changing times, "automobile concerns" and moving picture theaters, made their appearance. It was a solid business community for a town Durango's size (4,686 by the 1910 census), one which served a farming, ranching, mining, and urban clientele.

The founders would have been proud of their "baby." Through their Durango Land and Coal Company, the survivors still maintained an interest. Over the years those dividends kept rolling in, though slowing noticeably during hard times. By 1908 over $400,000 had been paid to investors, not a bad return on the original investment. Such familiar names as William Bell, William Palmer, and John Porter continued to hold office or serve as directors. Their dominance and that of their company, however, were drawing to a close. Most of the original townsite lots were gone; their interest in the Porter Fuel Company had been sold in 1906, and their other La Plata County coal lands were sold or useless. Their only remaining local assets were a few lots and their one-fifth interest in Durango Railway and Realty Company, a company that by 1908 had not made a dime in profits.

President Bell accurately forewarned stockholders in his 1908 report: "The Company has reached a stage in its life when its future earnings will of necessity be on a very reduced scale. . . ." In dollars and cents the venture had been an outstanding success and contributed far more to Durango than it took out. Few people, then or since, have fully appreciated what these men and their company achieved.

Their one continuing hope for profit rested with the aforementioned Durango Railway and Realty Company, a firm that grew out of an 1891 experiment with a horse-drawn streetcar line down Main Avenue. If ever an idea came along at the wrong time, this was it. People objected to the "obstructing" of Main, and the crews complicated matters by being abusive, insulting, and "invariably" pulling away from the depot before all passengers got aboard. Within a short time, lack of business killed the experiment. At this point, 1892, the Realty Company stepped in, purchased the right-of-way, and changed over to electric power. The company owned extensive tracts of land between Animas City and Durango and anticipated that the streetcar line would improve property values and offer the convenience of transportation needed to lure buyers.

Overcoming objections to the earlier line, enthusiasts proudly hailed their "metropolitan streetcar line." Amazingly, it survived in a year (1893) that proved fatal to many other business ventures. Overcoming ice in the winter and breakdowns, the two cars clanged up and down Main from the depot to Animas City, passing each other on double tracks just beyond the river bridge, a bargain ride for the nickel fare. Unfortunately, neither land sales nor streetcar business turned a profit.

People also pointed with pride to their electric lights and power, the mark of a truly progressive community. Since 1887 several small companies had taken turns providing electricity. In 1913, following the national trend, they were incorporated into the larger Western Colorado Power Company, which served much of the region from Delta through Durango.

The alliance between Durango and the power companies had its rocky moments. In 1905, for example, high rates prompted a call for municipal ownership, a call that went unanswered. That same year Durangoans watched with more interest the building of the Rockwood Plant, which they read would be the second largest power plant in the world; it slipped to third before its completion and then joined the also-rans. Even without world ranking, Rockwood became a favorite picnic spot, and it was always fun to watch the "wheels go round." The too-high-rates squabble broke out again in 1907, and the city council fussed about it for a while before the company reduced them.

The company voiced its own complaints. Their poles were being defaced by bills, cards, and other paraphernalia tacked to them, and they wanted it stopped. One of the councilmen countered that the poles were such an eyesore that they should be completely covered with paper. The council responded by passing an ordinance, which included having all the poles painted green. This problem never was resolved to everyone's satisfaction. Poles and wires criss-crossed the skyline, framing the view; progress had come to stay.

The company, meanwhile, did its best to lure more customers into using electric appliances. A July 6, 1909, advertisement in the *Durango Evening Herald* promoted things every home needed: an electric desk fan for keeping cool; an electric toaster to solve the burnt toast problem; an electric washing machine to do the family wash more quickly and better; the god-send of hot days, an electric iron; the electric curling iron which would not singe hair but keep an even temperature while keeping a girl's even temper; and finally, what all babies recommended, an electric heater to solve the problem of cold milk. Electricity definitely improved all aspects of Durango life. What home could be without it?

Durango's power plants, especially its main one located next to the river just beyond Thirteenth Street, purchased tons of local coal. Coal mining flourished as never before or since in the years 1895–1916. La Plata County mined an all-time record in 1907, 189,357 tons. As much as that seemed to be, it represented less than 2 percent of that year's Colorado total. Enthusiastic newspaper reporters, however, seldom let facts stand in the way of their story. In 1897, without batting an eye, they reported that the local mines produced 200,000 tons, when actual production proved to be 74,000. La Plata County never became one of Colorado's great coal fields, yet it did employ a sizable work force, 164 miners in 1900 and 311 miners in 1908. Except for the Hesperus mines, all the coal was found within an hour's ride of Durango.

The Porter Mine held onto its place as the largest, largely due to its contract with the smelter and the opening of the railroad to Telluride, where Porter operated mines. The same company also owned the second largest operation, the Hesperus Mine, making it the dominant coal concern. After the smelter, the Porter mines, according to the *Herald,* January 8, 1898, "turned more money loose each month than any other agency." Small amounts of coal still were coked, mostly for smelter use.

This period of peak production was also the time of greatest labor unrest and deaths in the mines. Notoriously dangerous because of gas, dust, and cave-ins, coal mines claimed a steady toll of victims. At least six Durango miners were killed before 1900, all because of falling rock; a spot-check of later years found one death in 1900, two in 1905 and 1909, and none in 1911. A state report on ventilation in Durango mines rated them from "not very good" to "fairly good." How many miners contracted black lung because of this and generally unfavorable working conditions will never be known.

Deaths, always tragic, never evoked the same reaction as strikes, which closed operations and endangered the local economy. These were tumultuous years in Colorado coal and hardrock mining, a pattern Durango imitated. In 1894 the coal miners marched out, demanding safety legislation, regular payment of wages, and an end to the scrip system (company money). In 1897 a local wildcat strike over increase in wages slowed production, and the great smelter strike of 1899 shut down all the mines. In May 1902, the miners struck again, demanding an eight-hour day and a wage increase; the wage scale was said to be lower than that of other Colorado districts. A citizens' committee was organized to investigate the complaints of both sides. The miners' resources soon neared exhaustion, while the companies bided their time. It ended in June with the miners being granted the choice of either three dollars per day or pay based upon tonnage mined.

The threat of a strike next year elicited this comment from the *Herald* on November 5: "The Durango miners already have an eight-hour day, with good wages and are not compelled to take their pay in scrip or trade at a company store." Apparently the miners concurred and peace returned to the La Plata coal mines, if not to the rest of the state. During the tragic 1913–14 days that led to the Ludlow "massacre" near Trinidad, the Durango mines operated steadily, in a small way undermining their co-workers' efforts. Union organizers achieved little success among these men.

Other changes were also taking place on the local scene. The Porter Company was sold to the Union Pacific Coal Company, a subsidiary of that railroad, in January 1906, for $850,000; coking coal was needed for the Arizona smelters. The vein at Porter declined rapidly and the mine was abandoned in July 1908; the camp around it, with its one general merchandise store and seldom over a hundred people, soon disappeared, too. Union Pacific interests declined as well; the introduction of electricity changed refining methods and cut the need for coke. The new owners had more luck at Hesperus, where operations continued into the 1920s. The coal behind Perin's Peak was finally tapped (1901), thanks in no small measure to the construction of a railroad spur to the site from Franklin's Junction on the Rio Grande Southern. The Boston Coal and Fuel Company, superseded by the Calumet Fuel Company in 1906, controlled that operation. It built the company town of Perins, a hamlet with a population in the hundreds, a company store, and a boarding house. Fortunately it avoided the evils usually associated with this type of endeavor, probably because of Perins' small size, nearness to Durango, and more progressive company attitude. The Perins' mine became the area's greatest producer before mining ended in 1926.

Other coal mines produced in a small way, supplementing the total county tonnage. Only occasionally now were new discoveries reported. Durango coal mines never overcame their competition, isolation, and small minable deposits to emerge as more than locally significant. The high hopes of the early eighties went unrealized. Production certainly satisfied local demands, however, and shipments warmed homes and businesses and generated power throughout the San Juans.

Closely related to coal mining and to railroad development were the smelters or, as it came to be, the smelter. Under Amy's direction, the San Juan Smelter never recovered from the mining crash of 1893–94, although its potential stayed high and interested parties circled the floundering firm. In 1895 Denver's Omaha and Grant Smelting Company leased it and before the end of the year purchased the plant. Amy sold his fine Third Avenue home and returned east because, according to local gossip, his wife did not like Durango.

The new company brought more capital, skilled management, and stronger backing than the smelter had enjoyed for years. Experienced metallurgist Franklin Guiterman was sent as plant manager in a wise move. Guiterman began to modernize and improve, only to suffer a damaging setback in late September when fire destroyed several buildings. Down but not out, he rebuilt and established the smelter within a year as one of the major ones in Colorado, and *the* major one for the San Juans, making Durango a true regional smelting center. Guiterman's management was the best the plant had had since Porter, and he held an advantage over Porter in having strong financial backing, excellent transportation, and prospering mining.

Just when Durango's future seemed secure, a new turn of fortune blighted the outlook. The era was closing for the independent smelting company; the advantages of a large, monopolistic corporation proved too enticing. As a result, the major smelting corporations hammered out an agreement and a firm emerged that eventually became the gigantic, monopolistic American Smelting and Refining Company. Omaha and Grant was absorbed, and with that Durango found itself a small fish in a large pond.

Instinctively mistrusting conglomerates, Durangoans became wary. Before long the smelter trust was accused of being secretive, impersonal, and interfering in local politics. Dave Day and his *Democrat* took repeated swipes at the "combine." Spits and hisses aside, the community could do nothing. Like it or not, twentieth-century industrial organization and attitudes had bridged the isolation gap.

Relations with the AS&R soured when a bitter smelter strike hit Durango in 1899 and then spread throughout Colorado. A strike that started in Durango and eventually paralyzed the entire state's smelting industry seems inconceivable, but it happened just that way.

Demands for an eight-hour day incited the rebellion. The men wanted the same pay for eight hours that they had received for ten or twelve hours. Guiterman countered by offering hourly wages, shrewdly manipulating them so that one had to work the same longer hours to earn the previous scale. The background for this deviousness was obvious. The Colorado legislature had passed an eight-hour bill, one of labor's pet projects, over management's heated objections. Immediately a court case challenged the bill's constitutionality, but AS&R preferred not to wait for a protracted judicial decision. Guiterman posted his notice on June 1, to go into effect June 15; this forced the issue. With unabashed guile, the company declared that no one would be required to work more than eight hours. Here lay the blame for the strike. Guiterman went so far as to post the notice when he was leaving town; no one else had authority to deal with the workers.

Unlike the coal miners, the smeltermen unionized—Durango Mine and Smelter-men's Union No. 58 of the Western Federation of Miners. They had already appointed a negotiating committee, which accomplished little since neither side would give an inch. Guiterman did later make one fascinating proposal: in any settlement reached with Pueblo or Denver workers on the issue, Durango should receive a differential, because it was a "more costly place to live" than the other two communities. Negotiations failed and the men walked out, closing the smelter and triggering a strike throughout the state.

Though it started here, it was not settled here. The focus of attention shifted to the larger smelters, particularly in Denver. Within days, side effects became evident—Silverton mines closed, Porter shut down, and the coke ovens cooled. Durango businesses soon felt the pinch. As the strike dragged on, men crowded onto trains leaving the area. Then, as railroad revenues dropped with decreased shipments, crews were laid off. Weeks turned into months with no settlement in sight. What had started peacefully with only a few bad feelings degenerated into acrimony. The "be of good cheer" slogan turned sour. The blame was laid on outside agitators, a darkly mysterious group.

The first break came when the Colorado Supreme Court, working in exceeding haste, declared the eight-hour law unconstitutional. This signaled enough for some smelter workers, who began returning to work in late July; Denver, Pueblo, and Durango stubbornly held out. In early August a committee of Durango merchants, headed by Harry Jackson and John Parsons, tried to resolve the impasse. No success met their efforts. By now Durangoans were running scared; a summer's prosperity was contingent upon the immediate termination of the strike.

Fortunately, the end was near. The men gradually returned to work at the Durango plant, at first without any violence. The strike officially ended on August 15, when the beaten local union conceded; Denver gave in the same day. But it had lasted one day too long. Louis Kaneck, an Austrian who worked at the smelter, was shot and killed by a party of masked men. Although the coroner's jury decided parties unknown committed the deed, the union received the blame, probably justly. Kaneck had been a "scab," and scabs were despised for eroding the strikers' solidarity. A few days before, two other scabs had been escorted out of town. "Let us hope that Durango and La Plata County [have] experienced the last labor trouble for many years to come," prayed the *Herald*, August 18.

Durango suffered from this strike, more so than from the coal strikes. Even in such gloom, however, a silver lining was apparent, at least to the Pollyannas. "Durango has reached the low ebb. Now is the time to invest. Never again will values in real estate and farm lands be so low." Even the five-month-old union survived the ordeal and local opprobrium.

Four years later management and the union went at it again. This time the Western Federation called its members out in Denver in July 1903 for an eight-hour day. At the end of August, Local 58, too, marched out. Guiterman, now in charge of the AS&R's Colorado department working out of Denver, felt the whole weight of the strike on his shoulders. He handled it firmly, as he had earlier.

The Durango strike appeared to be an afterthought. The workers were never unified, and they faced the combined opposition of AS&R and an aroused Citizens' Alliance, which remembered too clearly the long days of 1899. The Citizens' Alliance promised men who desired to work the right to do so. This technique had been used successfully elsewhere to break strikes. This group also set out to get "agitators," which, spelled out, meant Western Federation of Miners officials and organizers. WFM leader Frank Smelcer, after winning a case for calling a worker a "damn dirty scab," was promptly arrested for carrying a concealed weapon. Seeing the handwriting on the wall, he pleaded guilty, paid his fine, and shook the dust of Durango from his feet, returning to more hospitable, strongly unionized Silverton.

Such harassment, combined with the fact that many of the smelter force did not quit work, doomed the local strike. Within two weeks the plant was again running smoothly and the crisis had passed. With a sigh of relief, residents turned to news of the general mining strike that had paralyzed the state. The years 1903–04 were bad ones for Colorado. Durango was lucky to have had as little trouble as it did. The local union, its spirit and membership broken, limped along for a few more years, finally collapsing in December 1909. With the AS&R firmly in control, no more threats arose. The town could continue to glory in its title of "smelter city," even if a few doom-sayers, shaken by recent events, believed it should have more than one major industry.

Local mines never developed sufficiently to become the smelter's major customers; those came from the outside. Mining engineer Thomas Rickard could applaud Colorado mining in 1898 for having long since passed through the "kindergarten stage," but Durango mining never even reached it. He pointed out that mining required money, and he might have gone on to say that rich ore veins helped, too. Durango mines possessed or acquired neither. Durangoans invested in mining all right, continuing their earlier practice of sending their money to better-known, outside properties. They were much more likely to invest in a property such as Silverton's Little Giant Mining Company than one in La Plata Canyon; familiarity bred contempt, one might surmise.

Mining continued throughout these years in Junction Creek (Oro Fino District) and La Plata Canyon, with the Neglected Mine in the former and the May Day in the latter arousing the most interest. Lightner Creek generated a few rumbles, rarely any profits. La Plata "City," which had its own newspaper for a while, was the only mining camp with even a remote claim to the name. A small settlement grew near the May Day Mine at the mouth of the canyon, taking the mine's name but consolidating it to Mayday. A branch of the Rio Grande Southern ran to that village. Short of capital, cursed with pockety veins, handicapped by poor transportation, nearby mines failed to produce as expected. But faith never foundered, and in 1914–16 eyes turned toward Cave Basin, beyond the site where Vallecito Reservoir would one day charm tourists. Although Durango liked to think of itself as the launching point for that prospect, Bayfield had a better claim. It was of no consequence, however, because Cave Basin never hit pay dirt. Meanwhile, the old reliable, La Plata Canyon, was rumored to have a bright future with "strikes of good luck falling thick and fast." Such is the lure of mining.

More intriguing was the possibility of gas and oil in the area. George Franklin, who helped develop the Perins coal, was one of the most active prospectors in the gas and oil exploration. One well reached 800 feet. It all proved to no avail at the moment; technology, capital, market, and steady producers were all lacking.

As hardrock mining sputtered and gas and oil prospects failed to materialize, railroad building drew to a close. One unfulfilled hope for it lingered on, that of a southern outlet to break the Denver and Rio Grande's stranglehold. While several "paper" railroads planned such a project, none got beyond the survey point. Finally, in 1905, to forestall competition, the D&RG built the locally famed "red apple" line to Farmington. Initially a broad gauge, it was wisely converted to narrow gauge. The years 1900–1905 were full of rumors involving railroads and local coal deposits, but the only tangible result was the red apple line, so-called because of its chief freight. Small Aztec and Farmington provided little traffic volume. The only other construction involved the Rio Grande Southern spurs to Perins and to the mouth of La Plata Canyon.

Disappointed, though not deterred by this turn of events, Durangoans continued to push for a southern outlet in occasional newspaper articles. Just as often, they delighted in kicking the D&RG around for not having enough cars, too high rates, "beastly" service, and generally "rotten" methods. Dave Day waxed eloquent about D&RG sins. One year, 1907, he complained about the dilapidated condition of the depot, nominating it for membership in the Pioneer Association or for a "pension" from the Cliff Dwellers' League. His hyperbole included tales of cockroaches and bed bugs that played baseball on the depot's ground floor. Others scored the depot's environment, which included saloons, low-class boarding houses, and a budding red-light district. That was not the fault of the beleaguered D&RG, however.

The Denver and Rio Grande tried to counter such adverse images, with little success. The new president of the company, Henry Mudge, visited town in 1915 and spoke glowingly of bringing in broad gauge connections and expansion. It would never happen.

The days of the railroad as king of Durango's transportation were numbered. Shortly after the turn of the century, the automobile huffed and puffed through the streets, and at the 1913 Colorado–New Mexico fair the community probably saw its first "aeroplane." It arrived and departed by train, carefully boxed; in between it took off and landed at the fairgrounds, the pilot claiming to be the first licensed aviator to make an ascension from Durango's altitude or higher. This new wonder of the age circled the city, ending one of its flights unexpectedly in a pasture with an out-of-commission engine. For sheer contrast, it should be mentioned that in the decade just past, the stagecoach had lumbered in and out of town on the Farmington route until the red apple ended its career.

Still watching over Durango with conservative, business-oriented eyes were the city fathers. As the years rolled by, government gradually became larger and more costly; the 1897 city budget of $33,700 jumped to $71,200 by 1914. Wishes to the contrary notwithstanding, there seemed to be no way to prevent this trend. A taxpayers' federation in 1896 scrutinized city and county expenses to "increase receipts, reduce expenditures and lessen taxation." Among others, Thomas Graden, Charles Newman, Frank Guiterman, and A. P. Camp organized themselves into committees for those purposes, with good intentions but little staying power.

There was no way these plans could succeed—citizens were continually demanding more and better services. The sewer system was just one example; another was a paid fire department, with all of its three members, in 1897, down from seven three years earlier. Salaries rebounded, along with other expenses that had been sliced during the depression's dark days. The regular wage scale for labor was two dollars per day in 1898, and by 1901 the city was granting a fifteen-day vacation to all regular members of the fire, water, and police departments. This progressive measure drew the ire of taxpayers, who on other occasions had petitioned to reduce the police force now that the town was orderly (1895) and to reduce city officials' salaries (tabled indefinitely, 1897).

Conversely, petitions also asked for more services, like those Third Avenue residents who wanted to keep cattle off their lawns and restrict one of their neighbors from keeping so many cows. Others sought enforcement of quarantine laws during a diphtheria scare and an ordinance to prevent children from crossing lawns on their way to and from school. Pity the poor council, besieged from all sides.

Throughout these years nothing proved more troublesome than the continuing sidewalk imbroglio. Injured pedestrians, victims of defective wooden sidewalks or their own carelessness, did not hesitate to sue. Petitions repeatedly referred to some aspect of the trouble. Finally, the council responded and called for bids on concrete sidewalks. An opportunity to join with Animas City to build a sidewalk between the two was rejected, as was annexation, a practical plan that was still a generation away from realization. High costs, real or feared, guided deliberations. No one was sure that Animas City was really worth the expense.

On other occasions the council posted a reward for the apprehension of anyone bathing in the Animas within five miles of town (keep that drinking water pure!). A no-smoking edict for council sessions was passed in 1899 and blithely ignored. A running battle with prairie dogs was fought in the cemetery, with the winsome creatures triumphant as late as 1912. Sending delegates to the Colorado Good Roads Association was an idea the city officials concurred with. They also authorized installation of a drinking fountain on the corner of Ninth and Main and were pleased when the WCTU donated one; it was no coincidence that the saloon block began within a stone's throw of that fountain. The council joined in celebrating July 4 by allowing the fire "apparatus" to be used in the parade and showed a practical bent by granting someone named Mitchell the right to sell pencils on the street in order for him to "raise funds enough to get out of the city." Occasional sessions were disrupted by passionate outbursts, as in 1909 when an emotional alderman charged his fellow council members with being "dishonest, corrupt and unlawful." A meeting later, he retracted what he had said. These men energetically supported a Durango "clean up day" and financially helped a citizens' group purchase the land for the site of the future post office (Main and Eleventh). On several occasions they instructed the marshal to crack down on gambling.

There was rarely anything unusual in their deliberations, and they generally handled the issues in a competent, if not always farsighted, manner. "Routine" would describe most council meetings. Nor did their constituents seem very different in their attitudes and demands from earlier or later Durangoans. In the matter of ordinances, the council was still reacting to specific situations, rather than planning for potential ones. In 1901 the ordinances were revised and published, a vital achievement.

The horseless carriage presented a new problem that required action by the council in 1910. A local license fee was established and, with an eye toward economics, owners were told to make their own license plates and attach them to the rear end of the vehicle. Anyone driving over ten miles per hour in the business district or eighteen in the rest of the city risked arrest; five violations resulted in the loss of one's license. Each car had to have a "gong, bell or horn" and lamps; no machine could be operated "without full use of both hands and arms and one foot and leg." None of this cruising down Main with your arm around your best girl!

Enforcement of the speed limits fell to the police, who had their hands full. In 1912 the council authorized the rental of a stopwatch for thirty days or longer to time the speeders. It did little good—the police were left standing on the corner in a cloud of dust. Durango loved its fast new toy. Next year the marshal was instructed to enforce the ordinance strictly, and the officers of the Durango Motor Club were urged to request members to observe the limits.

This was, however, the Progressive era, a time when Americans urgently sought to reform themselves and their country. Reformers attacked many problems, including corruption and inefficiency in city government. Durangoans joined the cause enthusiastically. This issue came naturally to local progressives, who argued that a city manager-council government (one of the progressive reforms) would be economical and efficient. What taxpayer could resist? In 1911 a citizen-initiated election approved charter government and after a slight delay of one year, delegates were elected for a convention. Although voter apathy made the mandate less overwhelming than the newspapers predicted, the charter convention went ahead with its work in May 1912, charged with completing its task in sixty days. Two old-timers, Harry Jackson as president and Alfred Camp as vice-president, chaired the meetings; the rest of the twenty-one-member group were relative newcomers. Submitted to the voters in September, the charter passed better than two-to-one, although national, state, and local election campaigns nearly crowded it off the newspaper page.

The city charter was a forward-looking one for its day and time. It provided for an appointed city manager to oversee the day-to-day functions of government. It also allowed those three progressive ideals—initiative, referendum, and recall—and the granting of municipal franchises only by vote of the taxpayers. To ensure no smoke-filled-room decisions, the council was charged to "sit with open doors at all sessions" and to keep a journal. Durango also became a home-rule city with this charter. A 1915 attempt by some malcontents to amend the charter was handily defeated, the *Weekly Democrat,* July 2, 1915, crowing over "a victory for the People."

Residents could well be proud of their new city government. Proud of their government, proud of their town, they unabashedly promoted them. No greater honor could be bestowed than to be called a booster. It was said of Charles Newman at the time of his death in 1906 that he was a valuable friend of Durango, one who "ever and always boosted" the city and its future. The Durango Board of Trade carried on as the chief spokesman, although it was getting a little hoary with age. Finally, in 1914, it joined with the Durango Club, a social organization, eventually to become the Chamber of Commerce. Regardless of name, the goals remained the same, to promote the town and southwest Colorado. They pushed for that bewitching southern railroad outlet, a sugar beet factory, and better roads. They maintained a reading room and were desirous of cooperating with anyone in the "great San Juan Basin," including Fort Lewis, which had evolved from a military post through an Indian school to a high school by 1916. Regional rivalry diminished; mining towns like Silverton no longer posed any consequential threat, and ones like Rico collapsed, pitiful shadows of their former selves. A few brickbats were hurled Cortez's way and Denver received a few jabs now and then, as in 1912 when the *Democrat* called for its readers not to trade with Denver's "commission pirates."

Durangoans pushed the San Juan Basin concept, intending to make their community its hub. This trimming of sails from earlier bombast, which advocated Durango as practically the center of the universe—certainly of the whole southwest—demonstrated new awareness. The 1890s depression and the 2-percent growth rate per year in the decade, and 4-percent the next, ended grandiose dreams.

As conceived by Durangoans, the San Juan Basin stretched from Pagosa Springs on the east to Cortez on the west. North to south, it ran from Silverton to the Farmington area. More correctly it should have been called the Animas Basin, but the name San Juan translated into bigger things. This area encompasses 10,000 square miles—those boosters still thought big. This vast domain crossed political, economic, cultural, and state lines, and Durango never completely succeeded in its exaggerated aspirations. The basin was simply too big and diverse and its potential conqueror too small.

The city worked hard on the basin idea, paying particular attention to building goodwill between town and country. With the stabilization of mining and the slowed community growth, farming became more important to the overall economy. It grew steadily, particularly after the opening of the Ute Strip, the last outpost of the old frontier.

Agitation to move the Utes for their crime of simply being in the way finally succeeded in 1895, when Congress passed a bill that gave the Utes the right to choose individual allotments or move to a new reservation at what became Towaoc. Those who chose allotments formed the nucleus of Ignacio and the Southern Ute community. The rest of the reservation was thrown open to settlement by presidential proclamation; the magic day was May 4, 1899, at high noon.

Another Oklahoma land rush in the making? Durango gleaned state and national coverage; not since the 1889 fire had it provided such a hot item. The D&RG published a glowing pamphlet on the inviting opportunities, arable land, and irrigation water available on the Ute Strip. The company and town sat back to await the rush. Dave Day voiced Durangoans' attitude when he called the opening one of the most important movements ever known in southern Colorado.

Durango was only one of the starting points, but it naturally considered itself *the* spot. Horse rentals reached unheard of heights, people crowded into town, and townspeople fussed about lawlessness. "Boomers" stampeded toward the promised land, to the sound of blowing whistles and bells. William Mason, owner of a fast horse, galloped to the land he chose, staked it, looked around, and "noticed that there was no one else in the race." The event proved disappointing to Durango, since the crowds never reached expectations and, once they fanned out, became thin indeed. Some violence came in the aftermath—one of the claimants for land that James Frazier staked shot him. He survived, however, to homestead his parcel. The Utes had already taken much of the good agricultural land, so many of the rushers met only disappointment. Undesirables moved in along with the rest, and it took a while to weed them out. One J. M. Simons and wife stole a team of horses in June to go east, but the sheriff waylaid their excursion and canceled their plans.

For those who stayed, life on the homestead was harsh indeed. Frazier wrote, "Many a time we all wished we had never seen the Animas Valley or left sunny Kansas."

Another old-timer, who grew up on a Sunnyside homestead, would not talk to the author about it seventy years later, so grim were his memories. For years irrigation was nonexistent, grubbing the land backbreaking, rainfall unpredictable, isolation stupefying, transportation poor, and the comforts of life few and far between. Days in a tarpaper shack created dismal memories. Homesteading pictured by that D&RG pamphlet contrasted sharply with homesteading reality.

Durango worked diligently to tie the area south of town into its economic orbit, working particularly to improve the roads. La Plata County found so little money to spare for roads that farmers built or maintained their own in lieu of paying the poll tax; convict labor was promoted as another cheap alternative. These efforts notwithstanding, the roads remained generally poor—spring weather ruined the best efforts. Disgusted travelers agreed with the *Weekly Democrat*, May 19, 1911, when the editor commented, "We can never profit by our scenery unless there is some way of getting to it. Good roads will make the San Juan the Switzerland of America."

These were the two waves of the future, farming and tourism. Local agricultural production grew and diversified during these years—sheep and cattle, wheat and barley (staple of the local beer), dairy products, and a budding fruit industry. The change to an agricultural economy would shape the coming generation. Thanks to the farsightedness of its leaders, Durango stood ready to serve as banker, broker, merchant, and cultural center—and to make the economic decisions for its hinterlands. What impact agriculture would have on its urban character remained to be seen.

Over these twenty years Durango endured its trials and cheered its successes. The fact that it took them all in stride was a mark of its maturity. The old order gave way to the new, not through revolution, but evolution. Ahead lay the promise of additional change, forecast by the developments in the years from 1895 to 1917.

7. Days of Heartache and Ragtime

From the melancholy "gay nineties," past toe-tapping ragtime melodies, to the dawn of the jazz age in less than a generation, life in Durango increased in tempo. Or to put it another way, from the horse-and-buggy days and the friendly saloon, to the airplane, car, and prohibition, Durangoans had not beheld such change since 1880–81.

For a moment just imagine the change that came with more general use of the telephone and electricity, the coming of the automobile and motion picture theaters, and the potential of the airplane. Electric lights transformed home and business, arc lights illuminated the streets, and by 1909 one could telephone long distance within a radius of seventeen hundred miles. Young Robert McConnell, whose parents purchased the Amy house on Third Avenue, remembered, "We had electric lights but nothing else electric; we also had bicycles, horses, dust, and mud." The dust and mud would stay, the rest would change.

The community took the movies to its heart. Before 1909 three theaters opened. Sensing profit potential, a group of locals organized the Durango Film Producing Company and were busy in 1914 photographing the "scenery, ruins and points of interest" at Mesa Verde. The real impact of movies actually came a decade later. Not so the automobile; its impact was immediate. By 1911 Durango had three agencies and an automobile club, and the town posted speed limits and required licensing. The grand total of automobiles was thirty-two.

The car eased farmers' isolation and changed recreational, social, and community patterns before long. As early as 1910, for instance, cars transported the baseball team to Cortez for a game. Almost instantly, drivers tried to set records, claiming the fastest time to Hesperus (23 minutes), La Plata (70 minutes), and Animas City to Trimble Springs (10 minutes). Remember, these were set in 1911 over unpaved roads! Many a pleasant afternoon ride in the country was punctured by a flat tire or two; and a long trip, such as one to Phoenix, received detailed newspaper coverage. That type of travel reeked of adventure, as these auto pioneers made repairs, slept in garages, barns, and rooms, and often cooked their own meals. Such trips were seasonal. In winter, their cars on blocks, the owners walked or returned to the faithful all-weather horse. The early automobile could not buck snow and cold weather.

Already the Durango Motor Club endorsed better county roads and a highway system connecting with outside points to encourage tourism. This scheme fit perfectly into the goals of the Board of Trade and newspaper boosterism. Durango must be on the "highway map," trumpeted the *Herald*, October 2, 1913. "Again we say, let all unite on pushing good roads and the Spanish Trail-Grand Canyon highway." For the next fifty years the Spanish (later Navajo) Trails theme buttressed promotion.

Durangoans were well aware of the tourism potential even before the automobile made its appearance. Indian ruins in the Mancos Canyon had attracted attention as early as the 1870s when John Moss and party established Parrott City in 1874. The famed western photographer William Henry Jackson photographed some of them that same year. Durango's early role was ambiguous. Locals enjoyed visiting nearby ruins, but their reception of visitors was mixed. Before the Rio Grande Southern reached Mancos, Durango served as the gateway to the cliff dwellings, over roads locally called good; one jarred visitor commented, however, that "this must be understood in the Colorado sense." Another 1889 tourist considered Durango a difficult place to obtain much information. While the completion of the Southern ended the city's first role in the saga of Mesa Verde, interest continued to run high.

By then the ruins in and on Mesa Verde had been discovered and a new dimension added. The race for relics started instantly. In March 1889, more than 1,000 relics, skulls, skeletons, sandals, pots, and the like were displayed in Durango before being shipped elsewhere. The indiscriminate looting and collecting aroused concern; in fact, as far back as 1886 the idea of a park to preserve the ruins had been considered. In 1891 Swedish archaeologist Gustav Nordenskiold, the first to make a careful collection at Mesa Verde, was chagrined to find himself arrested in Durango for devastating the ruins. Regrettably, his indignation did not prevent his release, or his taking the collection out of the country.

Two of the newly formed archaeological society's expressed purposes were to save the ruins located on Ute land and to stop vandalism. It took more than just a local effort, however. After the exhibition of relics and photographs at the Chicago World's Fair, visitation increased along with vandalism. Durangoans themselves were not above reproach, either. Their collections grew year by year, and a mummy was actually featured in one of the county fair parades.

Although feeble attempts to preserve the ruins had led to naught, there were people with concern enough to refuse to give up. Out of the Colorado Federation of Women's clubs marched determined Virginia McClurg to spearhead the battle. She and similarly concerned women saw the national park finally established after nearly a decade of fighting for it. They became the Colorado Cliff Dwellings Association, and in this troupe was a dedicated nucleus of Durango women, including Jeanette Scoville, Estelle Camp, and Anna Boyle. The Reading Club, one of the town's first organizations (dating from 1882), strongly backed their efforts.

The Durango ladies did all they could in the fight, serving as hostesses for Mrs. McClurg when she brought groups to see the ruins, coordinating local support, and perhaps undertaking their most daring venture when three of them went to Navajo Springs in 1904 to try to convince the Ute leader Ignacio to sign a lease for the cliff dwellings. They failed in their overall plan, returning home with only some exciting stories to tell. Victorian ladies were not used to a night in an Indian camp. They did not fail in their campaign, however. In June 1906, President Theodore Roosevelt signed the bill creating Mesa Verde National Park.

The struggle for the park showed Durango women at their energetic best. Jeanette Scoville, for instance, was a charter member of the Reading Club, the Village Improvement Society, and the Ladies Library Association, besides her activity on behalf of Mesa Verde. These women were determined to clean up the last remnants of the frontier past and stood foursquare behind the WCTU. The arrival of the first woman dentist in 1907 pleased them. Women were taking a more active role in business and the professions, breaking out from the teacher-housewife mold of earlier years.

Durango's role vis-à-vis Mesa Verde was changing. Mancos gained early supremacy, securing park headquarters and trade, an advantage Durango was determined to overcome. The advent of the car and better roads served Durango well, since it could offer much more in the way of accommodations and attractions than Mancos. Within a decade, it would surpass Mancos. By 1916, the visitor total topped 1,000 for the first time. Two years had passed since the first cars struggled into the park, the drivers, like thousands to come, not failing to stop for photographs. Just demonstrating that they could safely negotiate the curves, grade, and "knife edge" cliff-hanging road was the important thing.

Multiple tourist blessings were bestowed on Durango. Even before Mesa Verde, the San Juan National Forest, once known as the Durango and San Juan Forest, had been established (in 1905) with Durango as headquarters. Approval for it was not unanimous. Some local citizens joined with vociferous Western Slopers to oppose acrimoniously this infringement upon their sacred rights to exploit natural resources. In the long run they lost, although the issue stayed alive for years over such questions as grazing leases.

Eventually these developments altered the local economy, making it one strongly based on tourism and recreation. At the time, however, only a few farsighted individuals could conceive of what might transpire. From those thirty-two pioneering Durango cars, Mesa Verde, and the San Juan National Forest, came formidable changes.

The women did not stop their efforts, either. Undaunted, they moved into the men's world of politics, behind the scenes at first. Several ran for delegates to the 1912 Charter Convention, but lost. Durango's involvement in the Progressive era was not limited to its new charter. Those probers of American life, the Muckrakers, were uncovering gruesome details about America's food, enough to turn their readers' stomachs. The resulting alarm swept the country, and Durango women and men joined with compatriots elsewhere to curb the adulterated food evil. Between 1902 and 1916 they crusaded against adulterated oleo, butter, and meat, and deceptive advertising. State food inspectors, secretly visiting town in April 1912, found meat markets and bakeries violating federal and state laws. Over all, Durango's food conditions were found to be in need of a "thorough cleaning." One's appetite evaporated when he read that a meat shop featured 150 pounds of spoiled meat on sale, another contaminated its hamburger, and a bakery employee coated unprotected cakes and cookies with a dust frosting as he swept the floor.

These same reformers also worked for a better water system, completion of the sewer system, and modern schools. In the end, all were achieved, including a new high school building, the pride of the community. "Each of them stands as a monument over a battle fought for their possession," noted the editor of the *Herald*, February 26, 1917, who went on to say: "When new improvements come upon the future, let us remember that no argument will possibly be brought against them, that was not brought against every one of the above works. . . ."

Unfortunately in many ways, the reform drive of the Progressive era increasingly focused on one question, prohibition. Americans are known to prefer taking the simple path to the national elixir, hence the drive to end slavery before the Civil War and now the one to end the liquor problem. For Durango this meant "drying up" the saloon row and depot pocket, which, as promised, would also bring an end to the red-light district, drunkenness, wife beating, poverty, and crime. Bring on the promised panacea!

The red-light district seriously disturbed growing numbers of virtuous citizens. The natural zoning of this social evil was reinforced in the ordinance revision of 1900–1901, which continued the limits for dance halls, prostitutes, and gambling, and retained conditions under which liquor might be sold. "Lewd women" or, worse, "decoying females" and their male counterparts, "habitués of low resorts, gamblers and pimps," were carefully defined and regulated, for all the good it did.

Hardly missing a trick, Durango's red-light district prospered. Sharp jabs from reformers and newspapers began to take their toll, however, after the turn of the century. An exposé of the morphine habit and its "fiends" (a crisis occurred back in 1892, when the local morphine supply neared exhaustion) did little to enhance the district. Nor did stories of miners being rolled, attempts to lure "innocent" young girls into a life of shame, "crime breeding saloons," unlicensed prostitution, and Sunday drinking and gambling in violation of the city law help the district. As a result, open gambling was shut down on July 1, 1905, and saloons were forced to close at midnight. After more bitter struggle between "wets" and "drys," the city voted dry in 1914 by a narrow margin. On January 1, 1916, an era ended when the saloons were shuttered here and throughout Colorado, as prohibition became the law of the state. For George Olbert it was more than the end of an era. He had to close his Bismarck Saloon and sell the property. The saloonkeeper was the victim of this purge, and Olbert, for one example, drifted through several other business ventures before his health failed and he retired.

The red-light district left behind its own legend. Few old-timers who saw the 250-pound lady faro dealer dressed in a "voluminous white mother hubbard" pedaling her bicycle ever forgot it. "When she rode that bicycle down the street, she looked like a miniature circus tent in motion." By far the most remembered madam was the legendary Bessie Rivers, who came to town in the 1880s and resided here for the rest of her life. She was described by those who knew her as a pretty, "high type," wonderful woman. Bessie became a fixture in the community and overcame, as much as anyone ever could, her profession's stigma. The reformers did not end established prostitution, however. It continued into the 1950s, when the amateur trade, roving professionals, and the back seat of the car terminated the need for a fixed district. Nor did they solve the liquor problem, as the 1920s were to show. That wonderful male institution, the saloon, was *hors de combat*, only to be resurrected later, for the tourist trade, in a form nearly unrecognizable to the old-time devotee.

The newspapers did a lot to effect reform, and these years saw perhaps the greatest period of personal journalism the town ever experienced. Fearless, outspoken, egotistical Dave Day, of Ouray's *Solid Muldoon* fame, stands head and shoulders above his contemporaries and linotype descendants. Brought to town to strengthen the Democratic party, Day was controversy looking for a cause. One of the men who helped bring him to Durango reportedly exploded one time about the $800 it cost him. "Damn if I wouldn't give twice that amount to send him back." For a while Dave served as agent to the Southern Utes, until accusations, brought primarily by local Republicans, dragged him into court, charged with dishonest dealings, nepotism, and vote peddling. The commissioner of Indian Affairs found him innocent. Such was Dave Day. He returned to his paper, now called the *Democrat,* and battled on with his notorious rapier pen and quick quips. No rival could match him.

The *Herald,* in Day's terms the "Bladder," seldom escaped his wrath; the fact that it championed Republicanism had a lot to do with his attitude. The *Herald* turned on "Durango's blight" in kind, and the feud enlivened slow days in the newspaper business. If that had been all, Dave Day would not be significant, but he also cajoled, badgered, and promoted his adopted home. His style made Durango famous and quotable. He supported causes, at least ones that he approved. For example, he suggested coal miners unionize for better wages (but he became highly incensed when his printers struck in September 1910), and he committed the political heresy of backing Teddy Roosevelt, mainly because he advanced the creed of Day's great hero William Jennings Bryan. He is best remembered for his writing:

Sunday baseball is preferable to the average Sunday sermon.

The Lord loveth a cheerful giver—but the expanse of divine affection does not extend to bribery.

Muck-rakers seem to have the beef trust canned.

When hams go down we chew; when soap takes a tumble we wash; when whiskey—well, it goes down daily.

The shower last night was abundant while it lasted and purely local. No rain at Trimble or below there. Just rained on the just.

Col. Day, as he was called, wrote until his death on June 20, 1914. Durango, all of Colorado, has not seen his like again.

His great love was politics, and years later the story is still told how on election night, 1896, he sat on the corner of Ninth and Main with a big box of "good sized" firecrackers. Every time a report came in of a state's voting for Bryan he lit one, threw it just as high in the air as he could, and yelled "Bryan," followed by a loud bang that echoed down the block. The overriding issue in the 1890s was free silver, and the 1896 election between Bryan and McKinley, the battle of the standards, evoked as much feeling as politics probably ever have in the community. Even the *Herald* and Day agreed on the issue and candidates. Bryan ran and lost nationally in 1896, 1900, and 1908, but not in Durango or La Plata County. Bryan in 1896 gathered 2,796 votes, McKinley 88. Look at the *Herald* in 1900, headlining "Our Savior Crucified Upon the Cross of Gold." Dave Day never lost the faith, but the *Herald* eventually returned to the Republican fold. Politics, partly serious but generally sprinkled with a large dash of frivolity, became deadly serious on the silver issue. When Henry Teller, Colorado's silver champion and senator, came to town in 1898, an enthusiastic crowd gathered to hear the "leader of the great cause" make a "telling speech." Beyond that, local issues predominated, each party trying to maintain its hold and "turn the rascals out." One time in 1906, that all-American Socialist Eugene V. Debs arrived on the scene. Politely received, he found a few converts. Running on the Socialist ticket, Debs received over 300 countywide votes for president in 1908 and 1912. The Socialist tide ebbed soon after, having been a reflection of the labor unrest and general dissatisfaction with the times. Apathy rewarded dull campaigns; few could compare for excitement to 1896 or 1912, when Theodore Roosevelt, Woodrow Wilson, and William Howard Taft battled over progressive issues and the presidency.

Local partisans fought vehemently over politics, fortunately with little lasting bitterness. One reason, certainly, was that the rival groups for power proclaimed similar interests, came from a common background, and had no real fear of each other. The earlier pattern of a common cultural and ethnic heritage continued largely undisturbed. In the 1900 census only 17 blacks and no Orientals or Indians were reported in Durango (this return is somewhat suspect on the grounds that there were obviously some Chinese). And the county, except for an increase in Utes, followed the same trend. Immigration had declined since the 1880s; only 437 foreign born were living in Durango in 1900. The number rose by 1910, but the percentage of the total population remained in the 11–12 percent bracket.

The power elite found this mixture easy to work with. They shared aspirations and backgrounds. The old guard was giving way, however, in this period of transition. Gradually it yielded the reins of power, many, like Porter, going west to California and returning only seasonally for a visit. Only a few, such as A. P. Camp, would be around by the 1920s. In their places emerged men like Jack Clay, who came in 1902 with the power company. There was no break in the leadership tradition, just a changing of the guard.

Not everyone, of course, fit into this predominantly Anglo-Saxon mold. For them another Durango existed. As naturally zoned as if by ordinance, the Mexican Americans found themselves isolated south of Sixth Street, "south of the border," as it was called, in Webb Town and beyond in Mexican Flats. To the west across the Animas in "Chihuahua" others huddled in shacks. For these people, born on the wrong side of the racial tracks, opportunity remained limited, despite the fact that most Anglo Durangoans were blind to racism.

Joining with them across from the smelter were the recent Eastern European immigrants who worked the long hard shifts there. The Fantos, Girardis, Anesis, and others were able to bridge the gap, blending into the melting pot and achieving middle-class respectability. Blacks grew enough in numbers after 1900 to start their own African Methodist Church, in itself a subtle form of segregation. A few black girls crashed the color line and worked on the "line" across the tracks. Generally the blacks were left alone unless they became involved in some escapade or were needed for an election victory; the *Herald*, on November 7, 1904, stated it was doubtful any other western community possessed in its "colored population people of higher order of intelligence and integrity" (who undoubtedly all voted Republican). Even though the census taker seemed to be unable to interview them, the Chinese contingent held steady. They secured their own little business section on Tenth Street, just around the corner from the saloon block. Here in 1910 were found laundries and a restaurant. For a while, one of the saloons even employed a Chinese monte dealer.

Indians wandered in and out of town for trade but found no permanent welcome. Navajos from the reservation occasionally were hired to dig ditches or do farm work and other hard labor for low wages. This practice triggered at least one flare-up when "Mexicans" attacked a Navajo crew for working for cheaper wages and demanded that white men be employed instead. Rather an interesting reaction, considering their own predicament.

Partly out of pity, partly out of Christianity and the Progressive era, Durangoans were continually exhorted to remember the poor. This task was left mostly to the churches and the Salvation Army. The latter, particularly, provided sustenance, doling out grub and garments. Tramps, on the other hand, came up empty-handed in Durango—city marshals saw to that.

Life was harder for non–Anglo Saxons. They held the low skilled, physical jobs, the proverbial last hired, first fired. Usually living in substandard dwellings, they discovered that the amenities of life, which the middle class took for granted, only slowly filtered down to them. They found themselves facing an unexpressed, but no less real, segregation. Certainly not to be condoned, Durango's attitudes only mirrored those of America during these years.

For other residents, the quality of life improved steadily after the crisis of the 1890s. Their life-styles epitomized the last years of the Victorian era and the change that came to prewar America. Their lives revolved around the Main Avenue business heart and the Third Avenue social center. The evenly paced life provided the cultural, social, and business contacts they preferred.

They could spend a Sunday afternoon driving out to the "Spa of the Rockies," Trimble Hot Springs. A rumor once had it that the electric streetcar line would extend out there. It never did. After pedaling their bikes to the spa, numerous choices awaited the athletically inclined: croquet, tennis, golf, and archery for "invigorating out-of-door" amusements, or bowling, billiards, and swimming indoors. In 1909 and 1910 a group of Durango's and Silverton's finest organized the Electra Lake Sporting Club, leased a reservoir from the power company above Tacoma, and set about to create their own private resort. The upper class was starting to acquire affectations.

Fishing and other outdoor activities gained devotees, as more leisure time became available to the middle class. Bicycling went through a big craze in the nineties and maintained its popularity for years. The YMCA, however, boomed and faded during the depression, though it had its own rooms, library, gym equipment, and offered an alternative to the "saloon" life. Ironically, it was located upstairs over a saloon, with all those temptations. High school sports became a bigger part of the scene. Generally the students backed them, but not always, as evidenced by one distraught reformer's diatribe in the December 1910 *Toltec*, the student newspaper. He mourned the fact that the high school had no debating or literary societies: "Athletics should not claim all our attention. Let us wake up and get busy." Townwide, the baseball team continued to uphold local athletic honors, the smelter being a consistent sponsor.

Durango provided a number of parks within the city limits and paid a "park keeper" thirty cents per hour to maintain them. The intelligentsia were not ignored either. With the help of money from steel millionaire Andrew Carnegie a public library was built (1907) on Second Avenue. It took three years of dickering before the money and enthusiasm coincided. The Ladies Library Association donated over 2,000 books, which were housed in rooms in the Red Men's hall until the library opened. With an "opera house," library, movie theaters, an excellent school system, and a variety of clubs, the community had emerged as the cultural center local leaders had intended it to be.

A few blades of crabgrass contaminated this otherwise idyllic setting. The "city of homes" underwent one of its periodic housing shortages in 1905. Newcomers found few houses and high prices. Real estate, always considered a prime money-making scheme, was a royal road to wealth for many Durangoans. The Animas River remained polluted, despite fines and surveillance, and smelter smoke, intensified by coal and wood smoke, sullied Durango's deep blue sky and sharpened its distinctive aroma. Sanitary conditions, until people became more concerned and the sewers were finished, spawned health and aesthetic sores. Big and small animals loped at large in spite of the efforts of police and the local Humane Society. It would be years before conditions improved— never resolved, just improved.

Against these "evils" stood the legions of the middle class, particularly the Ladies Civic Club, which aggressively sought "making the city beautiful" projects. It backed "clean up" days, pure food inspection, tree planting, control of juvenile delinquents— just about everything.

Neither the ladies nor anyone else could do much about the weather, which dealt several hard blows. The drought of 1901 was a record breaker. The Animas had only pools of water left in it before snows and rains broke its grip. Droughts seemed to come in 33-year cycles; the next serious one would be 1934, then 1977. Remembered longer was the 1911 flood, one of those once-in-100-years phenomena. High water roiled down the Animas and most nearby rivers and streams, leaving destruction in its wake. The D&RG lost its Animas Canyon tracks, water flowed four feet deep through some of Durango's streets, and homes in Mexican Flats found themselves islands. Bridges throughout the Basin disappeared, washed away; hundreds of thousands of dollars' worth of damage was done.

Another blight that would not go away was the high cost of living. Blamed on isolation, transportation costs, whatever—it elicited lively discussion but no solutions. The problem was pushed under the community rug in hopes it might disappear. Like kids and dogs, it persisted.

Kids were changing, and not for the better, according to the older generation. Crusty senior citizen Dave Day wrote in August 1907 that when he was growing up no good-looking maiden had to sit around holding her own hand. "Now days" Durango youths appeared more susceptible to cigarettes and pool than to interesting and instructive conversation.

What was it like, growing up in Durango? Louis Smith recalled when he was a youngster in the late 1890s and early twentieth century:

> It was the nice, friendly agreeable town. Now that was before cars, of course, and in the evening the streets belonged to the kids. They had what they called arc lights at intersections. But after 6:00 the streets belonged to the kids. Gosh, under the arc-lights they was out there playing hide and seek or kick-the-can or shinny, and the only ones in the street would be some old coal hauler or someone with a broken down wagon. And at a quarter of nine, they used to ring the fire bell down there; that was the curfew.

Richard Macomb had a *Denver Post* route through the saloon block, an experience he never forgot:

> We sold quite a few papers at the bars. I was instructed by Taylor Maddox. He took me around the first night I went out on the route. He took me along and he told these bartenders that I would be bringing the papers in and I was not supposed to know anything about what went on in there. I wasn't supposed to say a word to anyone about who was in there or anything like that, which was all right too. I used to go down to the red-light district, which at that time was run by Bessie Rivers. She was a very generous person and she did a lot for charity.

Delivering newspapers in that environment might be frowned upon by today's parents; for Macomb it was a start toward eventually becoming a highly respected banker.

Marguerite Cantrell, daughter of Harry Jackson, clerked in her father's hardware store, and she also remembered Bessie. "She would come into the store to buy something, and the girl that was waiting on customers, and even some of the young men, didn't want to wait on her, so one day my father told me to be as nice to her as I can." Marguerite was, and her father later told her about Bessie Rivers. "A lot of people don't like to have her come in the store or bring her girls in, or do they like to wait on her. Don't you ever be that way. Her money is part of our bread and butter." Young Miss Jackson could be high-spirited in her own way. One time she defied Durango tradition.

> In the old days no lady walked in what they called the saloon block. If a lady was seen in that block you knew what kind of a lady she was and you definitely didn't walk there, and one day I decided I would do it. I was about eighteen and I decided I would just show them you could do that, so I did.

But by the time I got to the store, my father found it out, and so I didn't ever do that again.

Every generation feels the need to challenge parental authority.

Considering the booster attitudes, it was surprising to find Durango described as "small and insignificant," "quaint little town," and just "ordinary little railroad, coal-mining town." Comparisons of the present to the past probably influenced the remembrances to an extent; undoubtedly the boosters erred in the other direction. Not everyone, after all, wanted to live in Durango. Victoria Day, moving here from a ranch outside Ouray, regretted every step in this direction. Looking at her new home, she said to Dave, "I wish this house would burn down or the river would come up and wash it away." She eventually came to like the town.

Life was hard work for homemakers and breadwinners. Remember spring house cleaning?

Beating the rugs, taking the tacks out of the rugs and hanging them up on the clothesline and whopping them with a sort of a giant egg whip, until the dust got knocked out of them, then cleaning the floors and tacking the rug back. Everything got scrubbed and put back in the room to go with that clean rug. Dusting was a chore. All kinds of knick-knacks sat around, fragile and had to be carefully dusted. Cushions got recovered and curtains cleaned or new lace ones put in.

These were spring memories for Helen Sloan Daniels, granddaughter of Robert E. Sloan; even life on Third Avenue included its share of hard work. Across Sixth Street spring cleaning was just as laborious, and for the husband, the job at the smelter was harder physically than his Third Avenue counterpart's. Alva Short tapped a furnace there while waiting to take up a homestead and settle on the lower Florida Mesa south of town in 1905.

Working at the smelter they paid $2 a day, but you had to board and room yourself. There was some awful hard work there moving that ore around at the bottom, but the work I had wasn't too bad. . . . I didn't like the fumes over there very much. Fumes from the furnaces, everything that came out there was hot, boiling hot. I didn't like the fumes too well.

He also labored in the coal mines on a part-time basis to make additional money. Farmers often worked in the mines both here and in Silverton during the winter to bring in extra money and to help with the expenses of opening a homestead.

Others remembered the Colorado–New Mexico fair, a fall feature with games, races, and exhibits, as an exciting break from the usual routine. Halloween pranks, including the ever-popular soaped windows and tipped-over outhouses, rankled elders and occasionally brought grief to perpetrators. Memorial Day, however, faded when the ranks of the old veterans thinned and a new generation found other interests. Christmas and New Year's celebrations changed only gradually over the years. The biggest change came with the emergence of the jolly fat Santa Claus. After the depression more money was available for presents to fill those Christmas stockings. No child's or adult's eyes could have failed to light up when beholding the variety of gifts and "goodies" available in 1897—toys, homemade candies, perfumes, mixed nuts, books, suits, fruit cakes, sterling silver, and on and on. Today's shopper would find the prices inconceivable. New Year was a time of reflection and anticipation. The *Herald*, December 31, 1914, said, "Wherein we have failed in 1914, let us strive to succeed in 1915. Life to a large extent is what we make it." The Gem Theater presented six reels of movies for ten cents that evening, the Hermosa WCTU a twenty-five-cent chicken dinner on the first, and the Graden Mercantile Company entreated: "Kindly accept our thanks for your friendship and our best wishes for a prosperous and happy Nineteen Fifteen."

There was tragedy in Durango, too. Mrs. Vernon Helton vividly remembered her father, Sheriff William Thompson, being mortally wounded on Main Avenue in January 1906, while trying to stop some illegal gambling. This still unclear, deplorable affair involved a feud between city and county law officers over gambling enforcement. The town was not as violent on gambling and drinking as this outburst might indicate.

The "Denver of Southwestern Colorado, the Gateway of the San Juan Country, the Gem of the State," had weathered an era of change since 1894. It had emerged as a modern city by 1916, one that possessed all the "essential requirements." Its newspaper coverage now included national and international news, baseball and football scores —and the latest gossip.

Twice during these years, Durangoans braced for war. The first time they would just as soon forget. In March 1898, as war tensions were building and patriots were chanting "Remember the *Maine*, to hell with Spain," a national wire service reported Durango to have burned President William McKinley in effigy. How unpatriotic! No red-blooded American would oppose his policies toward "barbaric" Spain and add fuel to the fire with provocative speeches (quoted by the wire service) condemning the president and offering to reimburse Spain for the explosives used to sink the ill-fated *Maine*. Durango was mortified. And it all turned out to have been a hoax. Apologies and a full disclosure did little to assuage local embarrassment. When war was declared in April, volunteers flocked to the colors, and at a rally the evening the news was received, folks turned out in large numbers to cheer lustily the patriotic speeches.

The "splendid little war" ended so quickly that it hardly affected the community, which, after the initial outbreak of war fever, returned to the more profitable activity of recovering from the depression. Now again, in 1916, its residents readied for another conflict. They read in their newspapers in August 1914 that war had broken out in Europe, and subsequent coverage adequately followed events. More and more newspaper columns were crowded with national and international issues: the United States' problems with Mexico, the intervention to try to capture Pancho Villa, the German submarine campaign, the sinking of the *Lusitania*, German war atrocities, the election of 1916, and a preparedness campaign to enable Americans to save the world from the Huns. By the winter of 1916–17, Durango appeared to be ready to march to war. Where she headed she knew not. But it was evident that she would never return to the prewar days, so recently cheery and mellow.

PART THREE

Be of Good Courage
1917-1941

Have not I commanded thee? Be strong and of a good courage; be not afraid, neither be thou dismayed . . . .

Joshua 1:9

8. Over There and Back Here

Remember the Saint Mihiel salient, Belleau Wood, the Argonne Forest, and the 1918–19 flu epidemic? How about four-minute men, wheatless days, the Hun, and the Bolsheviks? A dwindling number of Durangoans remember all these things from the days of their youth, now a part of yesterday.

Years of trial, days of fear—1917–1919. Conformity was expected. Americanism propounded. President Woodrow Wilson said on the eve of American entry into the war, "Once lead this people into war and they'll forget there ever was such a thing as tolerance." Seldom has America been so regimented. The federal government, through its war boards, poked and pried into American life, for instance, operating the railroads and curtailing free speech, which always before had been sacred to the corporation and the individual. Had it not been for wartime exigencies, Americans would never have tolerated such infringements on their liberties. Even in far off, isolated Durango, World War I changed lives, surprising for a war that lasted only nineteen months for the United States.

To the accompaniment of train and smelter whistles, the community swung into the war spirit with cheers, patriotic words, and ringing band music. Residents stood ready; since 1914 they had been inundated by increasingly pro-British, anti-German propaganda. In late months it had become virulent. War passions boiled even before the April 6 declaration. The *Durango Democrat*, April 13, set the tone for the homefront:

> A WARNING—If there are any pro-German, pro-vandal, anti-president or anti-Americans in this neck of the woods who have an insult up their sleeve for the STARS AND STRIPES they had better get it out of their systems, for they will find the sledding damned awfully rough from now on.

After lauding three "patriotic" members of the Elks for climbing Smelter Mountain to plant an American flag, the article concluded, "Our flag floats high above our heads, sending a message that Durango and its environs are Americans all, Americans all and forever!"

"Americans all and forever!" Pity anyone foolish enough to be out of step. Marguerite Cantrell remembered her German grandparents: "They would say, they're

German and you don't want to have anything to do with them. Well, it was kind of hard to take when you were so German yourself. Yes, there was quite a bit of feeling." Durangoans, and other Americans, had fallen prey to subtle, and not so subtle, indoctrination. The Germans, the "Huns," threatened democracy, Christianity, and peace. Anything German-tainted was automatically bad. Out at Hesperus, the manager of the Hesperus and Porter Fuel Companies, William I. Gifford, received a coded message on April 6 instructing him to hire a day and night watchman. The company could not be too wary of sabotage.

Emotions overcame reason after this tempestuous start. On just the rumor that a "German sympathizer" had said Americans don't understand the Kaiser, the *Herald* barked on May 13, "We think Durango needs an organized band of 200 night riders from which to detail a squad to handle such things as that." A year later the *Democrat* called anyone who demeaned the purchase of liberty bonds a "damn dirty liar" and hinted that there were gallons of yellow paint lying idle in town. In January 1918, A. L. Wright of Perins was arrested for uttering threats against President Wilson; and because of his pro-German sympathies, he spent the rest of the war in prison. His cause was not helped when he was found to be a member of that radical labor union, the Industrial Workers of the World. Six months later at a "German Barbecue" all German school textbooks and literature that could be found were burned, along with an effigy of the Kaiser. The school board hopped on the bandwagon of bigotry and banned the teaching of German.

The Animas City council appealed to residents to plant gardens, a sign of the general commitment and a challenge that people in both communities accepted. Fearing shortages, a few people went on an early buying binge to store up flour and sugar, but such tactics were quickly labeled "unpatriotic."

No matter where one looked, there was the war, presided over by Uncle Sam. At the movies the four-minute men delivered patriotic exhortations during the changing of reels (this was the era of one-projector theaters); workers were urged to purchase bonds to achieve Durango's designated goal (the city topped $139,200 in the second liberty bond drive); women organized a Council of Defense and joined the Red Cross; and everyone was touched by meatless and wheatless days. Most even collected things from cherry pits to tinfoil for war needs. Macaroni, fish, eggs, and cheese were substituted for meat; corn and rye bread and "graham gems" for wheat. On the first anniversary of America's entry into the war, the *Toltec* told its high school readers, "Let us, now one and all, show our 'Uncle Sammy' what we can do this summer and work, work, work." Durangoans could honestly boast that they helped produce a united home-front effort.

Eager boys volunteered, hoping to fight the Hun, and others were drafted (346). Some got over there; a few never came back. For all of them and their families, World War I acquired a special meaning. New father Ed McDaniel recalled the war and the draft for another reason. "I just missed the first World War by the skin of my teeth, you might say. They called me in and rated me 4-A. My health was perfect, but the doctor who did the examining was the one we had for our oldest son when he was born and he knew the situation. . . . They were getting right close to my number when the armistice was signed."

Although most townspeople remained a long way from "over there," they had an excellent idea of what was going on, thanks to the newspapers. By mid-1918, with the thwarting of the last German offensive, victory was sensed. In late July, news that the Allied armies were launching their own great drive turned excited celebrants out in a spontaneous parade, headed by the Salvation Army band and its captain hammering the big bass drum, abetted by the clamoring whistles of all the engines in the railroad yards. Now everyone could finally relax a little and mumble about the suggestion that men wear kneepants to conserve cloth and cheer when the food ban was lifted on ice cream cones. The end came on November 11, the "Greatest Day in History," trumpeted the *Democrat*. Hesperus coal manager Gifford put a somber tone on the celebration, noting in his journal that no demonstration occurred, and thankfully no new influenza cases did either.

Americans moved from the war to a far greater personal peril, the flu epidemic. Bessie Finegan, a nurse, pictured it vividly. One of the fortunate ones, she came down with the flu but recovered.

> There was nobody on the streets that didn't have to go. Everything was shut down. Everybody on the street wore white surgical masks. I don't think it helped much, because everybody seemed to get the flu anyhow. All the nurses got it. The whole town was in mourning. [There was a family that caught it one evening.] Well, by morning the mother, the baby, and the daughter-in-law were dead. Two things happened to you. Suddenly you couldn't breathe, your lungs seemed to collapse, or else you hemorrhaged, and you hemorrhaged. They didn't have nurses, even in the hospital; the nurses were sick. So people, good people, just volunteered.

The epidemic hit urban and rural alike, although the latter appeared to fare better. Louis Smith, working on a ranch outside town, was afraid to come in until "long about March" 1919, when it started to slack off. It terrified people, and fear may have contributed to their death if they contracted the flu. John Bryce, farming at Sunnyside while ill, recovered and commented, "I think a great many people were in a state of mind to be terrified about it and were in poor condition to resist it." Some Durangoans moved to the country and some farmers journeyed as far away as California, but there was no escaping it. If the situation was bad here, it was worse in Silverton. The flu proved even deadlier at higher elevations.

Businesses shut down, schools closed, and people tried to avoid contact with each other during the height of the epidemic in October-November 1918; then the wave seemed to recede, only to advance again in January and again, especially among school children, in March 1919. Newspapers printed possible cures. The local Red Cross chapter established temporary hospitals, prepared masks, warm broth, and cotton pads, and generally assisted where needed. All the time, the flu rampaged while medical personnel watched helplessly. Whiskey seemed to be the only effective "medicine."

The city council reacted quickly as best it could. It recommended placing placards on houses where the "Spanish influenza" was discovered and instructed the health officer to see that all rooms in which victims died were fumigated. A ban was placed on dances, lodge meetings, and public meetings; churches were permitted to hold one Sunday service, but Sunday schools were restricted. Pool rooms, movie theaters, and the like were closed, and the council even went so far as to quarantine people arriving from other towns on the railroad. This happened in January 1919, when Durango, still suffering, saw Telluride, Rico, and Montrose caught in a raging epidemic. The railroads protested, but the council would not yield, even extending the ban to the Farmington branch of the Denver and Rio Grande. Within the knowledge of the day, the city fathers tried to do the best they knew how.

The war and the flu frame memories of these years. Christmas 1918 was symbolic of the disruption. The quarantine regulations canceled the Christmas eve dance and lists of quarantined patients replaced seasonal good wishes. The *Democrat* warned its readers to watch out for Hun toys; buy nothing made in Germany. Only then could one be sure he was not fattening the pockets of "baby butchers." So much for the real Christmas spirit—benevolence, love, and goodwill. Durango and America never have seen another epidemic such as this one.

For the younger children, whose families escaped unscathed, the era retained a magical appeal. "We made our own entertainment. You didn't have things to do, you didn't seem to have a whole lot of athletic events, no such thing as little league," recollected Leonard Glazer. "You went down to the river and fished and those that liked to swim would go up to what was called the sandbar, which is an area just west of the Riverview subdivision." All you saw in the winter were sleighs and sleds; adults "just didn't go anywhere." For nine-year-old Leonard, his hometown was a playground.

One visitor to the town has never forgotten the wooden sidewalks and the unpaved streets with knee-deep mud. For Nurse Finegan and other women this presented problems. "Most everyone walked," she recalled, but the women found the stylish long dresses and hats a problem. "When you stepped, it [the dress] dragged. You had a big hat pinned on with hat pins and you had to hold it with one hand and your skirt with the other. Any bundles you had, you had to tuck under your arms the best you could. The good old days, you can have them!"

The city government continued the costly struggle to replace board sidewalks with cement but took no action on paving the streets, probably indicating the tightened municipal finances, which, in 1917, caused the consolidation of the police and fire departments. The days of great growth and expanding business were now well behind. Already in bonded debt for previous improvements, the city tightened its belt.

Austerity did not shield the council from criticism. Complaints kept coming. The streets were so rough, "monuments to city neglect," that they jolted the fillings out of his teeth, complained one jarred traveler; another waxed angry about the stray dog problem. Stock occasionally ran at large, once ruining the lawn of James McHolland, who came before the city administrators to protest irately. Nor did the new fifteen-miles-per-hour speed limit on Main endear the council to some citizens. The council voiced its own complaints: Animas City used more than its share of local water; kids continued to ride bicycles on sidewalks; and jokers kept removing the "iron policemen" stationed at intersections.

Nor had folks stopped sinning. In spite of Prohibition, "booze" could be found, the fabled "white mule" already a daring attraction at some parties. State agents tried to stem the tide, serving only as thumbs in the dike of the flood to come. Gamblers and "chippies" flaunted their brazen ways as well, agitating reformers who thought the law should have put a stop to such nonsense long ago.

More positively, the Salvation Army remained active to help the unfortunates, assisted by the churches. Over the past twenty years church influence had ebbed because of the altered needs and attitudes of a different age. The church's day as a communitywide force withered. Chautauquas partially replaced them, though not until the summer of 1919 did the first Chautauqua tent go up in the city. Its promoters promised a program that would appeal to young and old, one that offered "culture" and respectable entertainment. By 1919, this popular American institution had declined from its national peak; Durango languished behind the times, but no matter, better late than never.

There was no reluctance to promote the city and the region. Convinced Durango was slated to be a "most popular" tourist center, the Durango Exchange advertised vigorously. It pushed for better highways, arguing patriotically that shifting the transportation burden from trains to trucks would allow the former to be better used for "busting the hell out of the Kaiser." Although little appreciated at the time, a salient point had been reached. There would be no more unchallenged years for the railroads—truck transportation had come to stay. In the same flag-waving vein, patriots wanted the government to build a railroad from the south to tap the coal fields, thereby contributing to the war effort. Uncle Sam did not buy the idea, and the southern outlet died again. Durango wholeheartedly supported the Spanish Trails concept; that highway running from Pueblo to Mesa Verde was in fairly good shape.

Hand-in-hand with the drive for promotion went the drive for improvement. Homeowners were chided for failing to cut weeds in August 1918. "A disgrace," moaned the *Democrat*. "Durango, we are sorry to state, looks ragged in many spots." How could they turn the "prettiest little city" in the Rocky Mountain region into a trashy "wayside station"? A bit of racial slander crept into the article: anyone who failed to cut weeds ought to be forced to "move down in Mexican Flats, where weeds are not supposed to be quite so much of a disgrace." Boosters also agreed with Dana Bartlett, who had written about Los Angeles a few years before: the "climate has a cash value" and "ugliness has no commercial or ethical value." Unfortunately, the desire for wealth and jobs superseded complications of increased population. Bessie Finegan reiterated many others' sentiments when she observed that, "the smelter was the one industry. Noticed it for a while, then didn't know it was there. Missed something if [I did not] get up in the morning and find sulphur. Thought something was wrong and it would have been." Farmer Bryce commented, "Nobody paid any attention to it. They just thought that was one of the things that had to be lived with."

The worth of one old-time booster attraction, the Colorado–New Mexico fair, was being questioned. In the fall of 1917 the press openly discussed its fate. It seemed that farmers and ranchers had lost interest in bringing exhibits, and some people favored turning it into a carnival or simply abandoning it altogether. Another smaller group wanted to push the fair "as never before" and make it a success. In its place eventually came the La Plata County Fair and the Spanish Trails Fiesta.

These years, thanks to war-related needs, saw a final rally in local coal mining. The years 1917 and 1918 were the last good ones, averaging nearly 140,000 tons, 70 percent of which came from the Perins and Hesperus operations. One hundred and thirty-seven people lived at Perins, the camp, according to the 1920 census returns, probably down some from earlier peak days. The miners were mostly Mexicans, Italians, Greeks, and Germans. The little company town, nestled below the mine tipple with all its houses drably alike, had been "dry" from the start. The nearest saloon sat just outside company jurisdiction, a mile south. Young teachers came from Durango for the school term, teaching all eight grades in one room. "Lovely people," remembered one of those young ladies, Minnie Rowe, who received fifty dollars a month to teach the children of the thirty or so families living there. Night school for some of the single miners turned out to be a fiasco, because Minnie could speak no Greek and the miners no English. Nor did it help when one of her students decided to write love notes to her.

Table 1

COAL PRODUCTION MAJOR MINES, 1887–1925

Porter Mine		*Perins Peak Mine*	
1887	2,800 tons	1901	7,463 tons
1890	6,030	1904	15,000
1894	37,128 (estimated)	1908	65,999
1896	39,646 (estimated)	1910	71,103
1899	49,280	1914	63,297
1901	45,116	1918	60,527
1905	59,547	1920	67,971
1907	47,459	1923	53,770
1908	11,553 (closed in July)	1925	42,499

These were by far Durango's largest coal mines. Durango newspapers of the 1880s listed anywhere from eight to twelve coal "mines," while the state coal inspector found only seven in 1890. During the peak years of 1900–1910 a high of six and a low of two operating mines were reported. This trend toward fewer companies, each with larger production, reflected the adoption of machine mining methods and corporation control. Smaller mines with less capital and hand methods simply could not compete.

The City and Black Diamond mines in the Horse Gulch area, the San Juan and Champion mines south of Durango, and the Lightner Creek Mines west of town trailed the big two. Their production was much lower, although the City Mine topped 30,000 tons in 1909.

A post office, boarding house, and occasional store made up the "business" district of Perins. Isolated culturally and geographically from its larger neighbor, Perins was rarely a newsworthy item in the local press. The killing of saloon owner John Jakino on August 14, 1915, proved an exception. And when the confessed murderers tunneled out of the La Plata County jail, Perins jumped in and out of the headlines for weeks.

Although it made no profits from local coal mining, the Durango Land and Coal Company declared a last big dividend in December 1917, when it sold its Crested Butte coal interests to the Colorado Fuel and Iron Company for $105,000. Those two senior citizens William Bell and John Porter continued as president and vice-president. Their only Durango investment, the railway and realty company, still yielded nothing, and they candidly told stockholders that a broad gauge railroad connection to the south would be the only thing to make the town and their holdings prosper. They, too, had caught the southern outlet fever and would die land-poor waiting for its arrival.

Shades of the old (the Durango Land and Coal), heralds of the new (trucks)—the times they were a'changing. Males were more than mildly disturbed when the Barber's Union advanced the price of a shave to the unheard of level of 25¢ and a haircut to 50¢. "It's hell we can't lay in a supply before the advance goes into effect," grumbled one man on the street. Inflation certainly seemed worrisome, but something even more insidious lurked on the horizon. The "Bolsheviks" were on the march, under the bed, a threat to Durango! In 1919 the *Democrat*, on that most patriotic of all days, July 4, comforted the concerned, "After all, only one kind of man can be a bolshevik—a fool." Others were not so sure that Bolsheviks alone threatened America. Having made the world safe for democracy only months before, they believed that maybe now the time had come to look into other evils. The intolerance, the hatred generated by the wartime hysterics, would not be turned off so simply by the war's conclusion.

9. Durango, We Love You!

Nineteen-twenty—the first year of the new decade, the first year of a new America. The effects of World War I receded quickly, the Progressive reform movement waned, the business ethic returned in full vigor; and Victorian morality, which had shaped society for so many years, seemed quaintly out of date. This was 1920, with women given the right to vote, jazz and new dances sweeping the land, and Prohibition the law, if not the will, of the land. Durangoans were preoccupied in 1920 with the "Black Sox" scandal, involving gambling in the 1919 World Series, and whether the queen of Hollywood, Mary Pickford, would marry the swashbuckling Douglas Fairbanks. Nor were the Bolsheviks out of mind for long, in this the year of the "red scare" and numerous arrests of those radicals. Such concerns in themselves indicated a changed community, one more caught up in the world around it than isolated in one of its own.

The automobile made great inroads in the twenties and thirties. It was no longer the exception to own one. Durango's attachment to the motor vehicle began in the 1920s. Even though the price of gasoline reached the unheard of price of 31¢ per gallon in 1924, drivers took to the road. Almost all aspects of life, from churchgoing to business methods, were affected. Even taxis made their appearance; the Cannon Ball Stage Company motto promised "Promptness, Courtesy and Safety." As roads improved, more tourists arrived and trucks eventually took the freighting business away from the railroads. Again in the early twenties the southern railroad outlet scheme was revived, only to die once more. There the matter rested, but not in peace.

Even more enthralling was the airplane. World War I had shown how useful it could be, and in the next decade pilots and planes barnstormed America giving exhibitions. No special insight was needed to recognize that this was the fastest way yet to overcome isolation. Great agitation arose for building an airport.

Private sources seemed unable to do more than talk, and finally in 1929 they turned to the City Council. The council proved agreeable and underwrote a study, which recommended Reservoir Hill as the most suitable site. After some haggling over price and acreage, Durango purchased a site from, among others, the Durango Land and Coal Company, which had long ago filed on land there. The municipal airport officially opened on Saturday, October 12, 1929, with an airshow. Observers that day saw all sides of flying when one of the Douglas bombers, here for the opening, crash landed, demolishing the plane. Fortunately no one was injured. One of the stunned onlookers, city manager William Wigglesworth, had seen the complete transportation cycle—the first stagecoach, train, automobile, and now plane arrive in town. After the speeches and other ceremonies, the field commenced operation, but the promised daily air service to Denver remained far in the future. The Pikes Peak Air Commerce Company, for instance, pledged to fly monoplanes to Denver via Alamosa, Pueblo, and Colorado Springs in 1930. The depression delayed those promises.

Nevertheless, Durango had caught a vision of itself as the air hub of the San Juan Basin, and with commendable spunk kept the dream alive throughout the hard times. The airport was improved with the addition of such things as a radio beacon, until it became not only one of the earliest on the Western Slope but also one of the most modern. The use of the field, however, remained limited to small planes, which upon take-off found themselves instantly gaining 400 feet of elevation as they sailed over the rim of the mesa. They had no margin for error. When that famous pilot Wiley Post and his more famous passenger Will Rogers landed here in July 1935, the event created front-page news. They stayed overnight at the Strater, where Rogers was besieged by a crowd of admirers, and the town gained a measure of fame from its mention in his syndicated newspaper column. Within a few weeks, on August 15, both men died in a plane crash near Point Barrow, Alaska.

Rogers and Post were only a temporary attraction; no matter, air enthusiasts envisioned an unlimited future for the long run. Tourism would multiply, the transportation problem would disappear, and growth would come. Growth, after all, was still the motto.

More meaningful to individuals was the inaugural broadcast in December 1936 of Durango's own radio station, KIUP, only the second on the Western Slope. Radios had come a decade earlier, and many a night was spent fussing over a crackling, hissing little box, trying to bring in an outside station. Now there was no need to work the dial so hard, and radios were found in most homes by the time of America's entry into World War II. In this day of instant news, it is hard to imagine the impact that the radio had: politics, sports, entertainment, education, the list goes on—all were affected. And what the radio could not provide, visual presentation, the movies did. The 1920s and 1930s were Hollywood's great days locally and throughout the United States. Feature films, cartoons, newsreels—within weeks moviegoers could see headline events, and ladies might easily keep abreast of the latest fashions. Although it seems mundane now, the telephone company continued to improve its local and long distance connections, further tying Durango to the rest of the country. Speed, ease, comfort, convenience, and availability came with improvements in transportation and communication between the wars.

Community leaders approved of these developments and worked avidly for them. The changing of the guard, noted earlier, was now complete. Sixty-eight-year-old Ike Kruschke retired in 1920 after nearly forty years of Durango merchandising, and Thomas Graden, Alfred Camp, and John Porter all died during the decade. Of Porter it was said, and equally true for them all, "In the passing of John A. Porter a great link with the past has been obliterated. The world has lost a builder, a developer. The San Juan has lost a loyal friend and supporter." In their places came some of their sons, Robert H. Sloan at Graden Mercantile Company and A. M. Camp at the First National. Mostly, however, new leaders materialized, though they were just as Durango-oriented and conservative in outlook as their predecessors.

They emerged at an opportune time. Business and businessmen were being rehabilitated after the heyday of the progressives. Pride in the self-made businessman had been resurrected. Business rode triumphantly tall nationally in the 1920s, although it should be kept in mind that Main Avenue businessmen had not suffered much loss of influence at any time. The new leadership took up where the old left off. Take Jack Clay, for example. He served on the Chamber of Commerce, school board, city council, as mayor, on a state planning commission; and it was said of him when he left in 1937 that he was a "civic minded, pusher, booster, big hearted," substantial citizen. As local manager of the Western Colorado Company, Clay perhaps had more free time than some of his contemporaries, although they all pitched in for the betterment of their community. J. P. Channell (owner of Channell Motor Company since 1923), during his four years as president of the Chamber (starting in 1928), pushed for lower railroad rates, money to improve Wolf Creek Pass and highways, strengthening of rural La Plata County, and "merchant institutes" to improve business techniques.

Clay and Channell indicated what needed to be accomplished and how to do it by their involvement. Others joined them wholeheartedly, including Judge William Searcy, who came down from declining Silverton; John Turner, founder of the Turner Investment Company back in 1906; and Frederick W. Kroeger, who purchased and then reorganized what became the Farmers Supply Company. They lacked the interlocking enterprise power of a Porter, a concept which disappeared as business and the economy diversified. These men focused almost all their attention on one principal occupation or business, perhaps dabbling in others on a smaller scale. As a power elite they held less individual control; as a group, however, they continued to guide Durango's destiny. In election after election, they backed their own for city council and retained a tight little power structure.

Without question this was the last period when a small group of men could run the show. Dentist Schuyler Parker, who practiced throughout these years, felt the merchants and Chamber of Commerce were the strongest influences. He went on to point out one change from the earlier days of Camp, Porter, et al.: "You know that is strange, you go into lots of towns and you know right away who's running them. As I look back on it, there's been nobody running this town, no individual. I guess Main Street runs the town." Lester Gardenswartz, who opened a sporting goods store before the crash of 1929, felt, "The town was run by a group of men that was running the Chamber of Commerce. It was a clique, we had a hard time breaking into it." That no individual or family came to dominate was understandable. No business or industry assumed that role, nor had any of the pioneering families. Leadership in such a situation naturally came by consensus or by committee.

Those on the outside saw something sinister about this. The focal point of discontent, the so-called Parsons Coffee Club, convened in that drug store every morning. Depending upon one's point of view, it either did or did not chart Durango's fate over a cup of coffee. One person thought the group was just a focal point for rumors; another called them forward-looking businessmen, a force in the community.

Although their impact on Durango cannot be measured in hard facts and figures, without question they were masters of their own businesses, which they tried to keep as tightly knit as possible. They did this by establishing prices, adhering to them, and freezing out any newcomers who dared to challenge them. For a long while local merchants shrewdly gained profits based upon their isolation, lack of competition, and monopolistic practices. Two examples were the dry cleaning establishments, which allied themselves in an old-fashioned, nineteenth-century business pool to set charges and allot business, and the stores that sold sporting goods. The latter agreed to keep the prices above the nationally advertised level and succeeded because of their isolation and local agreements. Both were eventually challenged and forced to back off. With the coming of national chain stores, such as Piggly Wiggly in 1924, the days of these business methods were numbered.

Coming into its own economically at this time was agriculture. It had grown steadily in the first forty years of the twentieth century, shown clearly by the increase in farm acreage from 151,000 in 1910 to 371,000 in 1940, and by the development of the "dry side" and the brief boom of the little settlement of Marvel (Marvel even went through a frenzy of oil excitement in 1924, which quickly fizzled). Everything went along smoothly until the interstate water compacts apportioned the water, and the dry side found itself dry once more. Development languished, Marvel's boom collapsed, and the more speculative dry land farming replaced the irrigation.

Leaders of early Durango had planned that it would dominate the region, and its successors built upon that foundation. Throughout these years their creation was the agricultural center of the San Juan Basin, the chief shipping point for farm and ranch. In truth, farmers had nowhere else to turn. "We were dependent on town for everything we had to buy," John Bryce commented. "Of course, there were a few little country stores where people didn't buy more than the day-to-day necessities." Farming was a hard life, electricity did not come until nearly World War II, when the presence of the REA finally forced Western Colorado Power to string lines into rural areas they previously claimed did not have enough population to make it profitable. For Bryce, electricity was wonderful, but the tractor brought the biggest innovation. "The biggest change in my mind was when we could go from horses to tractors. Farming is pretty hard on some of this soil, pretty hard on horses."

As Kroeger, who had been a farmer and stockgrower, demonstrated, more of Durango's businesses catered to the agricultural market. And both Channell and Kroeger were active in the Grange, strengthening its usefulness. Why? Agriculture overall had suffered from economic doldrums during almost this entire period. Building it up again meant building Durango, something the merchants and Chamber of Commerce could afford to overlook only at their peril. The farmers themselves tried, but the individualism inherent within the occupation proved insurmountable. Despite pleas from businessmen and local newspapers, they could not bring themselves to take a more collective step and they suffered as a result. There was a real question, however, of where they could turn for help. The Republican-controlled federal government offered sympathy, not panacea, and state and local agencies possessed no wherewithal.

Nevertheless, the town took on a more agricultural mien during these years than it had had before or has had since. Visitors to the community alluded to it as a small, rural town, which indeed it was, regardless of its boosters' efforts to the contrary. Saturday was the big business day; on that day the farmers came to shop, eased along by the Model T, then the Model A, as Ford's creations zoomed to the top of the popularity chart. The banks stayed open a half day to accommodate rural business. Where once the smelter pay-day dominated the business cycle, now the farmer reigned supreme.

During this time the Durango Exchange, which became the Chamber of Commerce in 1930, was working at two levels, nearly at cross purposes with each other. It encouraged farming, the farm trade, and goodwill between town and country, while at the same time trying to convince tourists of Durango's urban image.

Its efforts on behalf of the farmers centered on securing a sugar beet factory, which would have been economically, but not odoriferously, good for both town and hinterlands. The attempt failed, through no lack of effort; geographic, climatic, and economic barriers scuttled the plans. The basic philosophy of the organization was to promote whatever seemed auspicious for business and for Durango. Its members continued to be what they had always been, advocates of community interests, such as its potential as an industrial center. They joined with the Western Slope in areas of mutual interest, encourged people to "buy Durango," and pressured the D&RGW not to suspend or cripple service, an especial threat once the depression started. They tried to sell Durango as a convention center and proved surprisingly successful in 1931 when the town served as host to at least three state meetings.

An increasingly substantial portion of their effort was directed toward selling the area as the "complete vacationland." Tourism was seen as the means to another end: as one pamphlet encouraged, "Come to PLAY and you'll want to STAY." The magnitude of the effort was evident in the Exchange report of 1925, which showed that in the three-month period starting in April, nearly 2,000 letters had been received inquiring about Durango; well over half dealt with vacation and road information. Besides answering letters and publishing pamphlets, the Exchange furnished an exhibit for the Overland Park in Denver, the largest tourist camp in the capital; put up highway signs; and tried to publish articles in national magazines and newspapers.

All these efforts rankled neighboring communities, which also sought to corral their share of the tourist trade and disdained Durango's attempts to grab more than its due. In 1934 several New Mexico cities warned tourists against coming to Durango because there was not enough water to drink. Although this happened during a bad drought, Durangoans waxed indignant that a rival would stoop to such tactics. Durango had never had a water shortage and never would, thundered back the *News*. Also, there seemed to have been some defections within the "troops" of boosters, forces working for "deterioration and decay," charged the Exchange. Regrettably, the report did not elaborate further.

The Chamber did not miss a beat when it replaced the Exchange. The president of the Chamber, Charles Beise, wrote to Jack Clay in March 1936:

> It is our hope to serve you [Western Colorado Power] and Durango, to attract more tourists to our basin, to obtain better roads, to encourage more friendly relations between the cities of the San Juan and to make Durango a better place in which to live.

In the mid-1930s it published the "Spokesman," proclaiming with its masthead, "Boast the Colorful San Juan—Enchanting Vacationland." "If you don't like Durango you can set to work to correct the problem," the editor remonstrated, "or move on!" Malcontents apparently muttered about the "guys who run the town" (perhaps the Parsons Coffee Club), to which the "Spokesman" replied that the ones who howl the most "are the ones who won't take any responsibility or serve."

Overcoming latent opposition or just plain jealousy, the Exchange and the Chamber attained their goals within the limitations imposed by contemporary attitudes. They kept tabs on highway programs and money, advanced Durango's interests and tried to block projects inimical to those interests, promoted intercommunity understanding, fostered community studies, and encouraged tourism. They encouraged growth and in so doing laid the groundwork for the years that followed. They planned better than they could have imagined.

Those groups and all boosters of that time should have taken a measure of satisfaction from what they saw around them. Even with the trials of the depression, the town continued to be the hub of the San Juan Basin. Growth might have slowed, but that was far better than decline. Nor were there any serious challenges to the crown of supremacy. Cortez had not developed as expected; Mancos, Bayfield, and Marvel gave no competition; Farmington stayed smaller and economically weaker; and the remaining mining towns were pale shadows of their former selves. For these reasons it is obvious why Durango vigorously pushed the San Juan Basin concept—it reigned economically, socially, and culturally as the unchallenged monarch. Tourist-oriented maps gleefully pointed out this fact by having all roads radiate from Durango.

One example of Durango's success will suffice. It became the unchallenged gateway to Mesa Verde, the region's chief tourist attraction. With the transfer of the park headquarters from Mancos to Mesa Verde, that village lost its last claim, and its rival found clear sailing. As visitor totals steadily climbed, profits rolled in. A 1939 government pamphlet about the park pictured roads and railroads going first to Durango, then to the ruins. Rio Grande Motor Way offered a round trip to Mesa Verde for $7.50. Even KIUP got into the swing in 1937 by featuring the park on its "Intercommunity Day" program. Since no other nearby community commanded a radio station, Durango was alone in that field of promotion. No one could stand against her. Everything seemed to accrue to her advantage.

Enthusiasm soared to new heights. Wade Folsom, son of the pioneer dentist, wrote a song about his hometown. After praising sunshine, sparkling streams, and quaking aspen, he reached the chorus, the chef d'oeuvre:

Durango! Durango! In the empire of the West,
You're the sweetest and the best.
Durango! We love you, queen of the great southwest.

Perhaps the song might better have been left unresurrected from its long dusty, sleep; yet the words express so well the era and its attitudes.

Even here, "where the sunshine ever gleams," clouds came. The 1929 crash, trailed by an ever downward spiraling depression, gripped the United States. Durango could not hope to escape it. For a while the community appeared to lead a charmed life. While city officials debated a municipal airport and approved a record 1930 budget of $101,000, up from the $90,000 average of the twenties, the country sank into the morass. Regardless of the fact that the Rio Grande Southern went into receivership in December 1929, and the Rio Grande suffered sharp freight reductions, local confidence was unshaken.

By mid-1930 doubts began to surface; the *Herald-Democrat* warned readers on October 31 that "extravagance may be partly responsible for the depression, but frugality has greatly aggravated it." Frugality! Readers had little to spend and, with farm income long depressed, Main Avenue began to feel the pinch. Encouraging words inspired a temporary rally; the new manager of the Kiva Theater, Mark E. Berkhimer, announced he was surprised to find Durango "a picture of thrift rather than one of business depression." That picture faded in November when the American Smelting and Refining Company closed the smelter. Long a declining proposition that reflected mining's plight, the company saw no other recourse. It shut down with a promise to reopen as soon as possible. Over 200 men were suddenly out of work, and the "smelter city" learned what hard times were. As doubt became fear, Durango plunged over the brink.

Now the council was confronted by citizen groups seeking to relieve unemployment. What had been discussed only in whispers, in hopes that it might go away, was now brought into the open, where it should have been when the first symptoms appeared months before. In January 1931, the city donated funds to the community welfare council and set aside money for land clearing jobs to give the "very needy a chance to earn a few dollars."

The aforementioned agricultural woes and the precipitous decline in local coal mining, down to the 20,000-to-30,000-ton-per-year range, magnified the troubles. The Calumet Company at Perins weathered a brief 1921 strike, only to come to an end in 1926 when faced with a depleted coal vein and declining market. The village turned off the lights for the last time then, and local coal mining ceased to be of significance. Remaining production came from outlying county mines. The arrival of natural gas as a heating and industrial fuel in 1929 doomed coal. This cleaner fuel, along with the closing of the smelter, eventually resolved the pollution problem. Schuyler Parker vividly described the coal days: "You know, this town was a dirty town; the smoke from the smelter was everywhere and the coal dust would settle on the snow and be black snow a couple of days after it had fallen and we didn't think anything about it. That was what was to be expected of every town that burned coal." For every action there is a reaction, and even in the darkest of situations (closing the smelter), something good may come (cleaner air).

Durango's coal mining never grew beyond a local, sometimes regional enterprise. Shielded by isolation, the mines monopolized this market and occasionally took advantage of problems in other parts of the state to ship to a larger market. Such occasions were few and far between; one classic example was the Colorado strike of 1913–14. Prohibitive freight charges to and from remote Durango can be blamed for preventing a fuller exploitation of local possibilities, while also being credited with preventing ruinous outside competition. In the end, the smelter and railroads, with a strong assist from San Juan mining, kept the coal mines profitable. By the 1920s little remained of this once flourishing market. Durango's black diamond had reached the end of the first period of its history.

Local hardrock mining, never healthy, limped along at a slower and slower pace, in such bad shape that the depression hardly affected it. With times so bad, one phase of mining was rekindled. Panning was tried in hopes of turning up some color, enough gold at least to help buy food. Not since the 1870s had the La Platas seen such activity, and it all paid off with the discovery of the Red Arrow Mine on the La Platas' west slope. The Gold King Mine in the canyon snagged a few headlines from the twenties up to the mid-thirties, but mined investors' pockets more successfully than it produced ore from its spotty vein. The Neglected Mine flourished briefly again in the late 1930s, much to the delight of such old-timer families as the Jacksons and Sloans, who still retained interests there. None of these efforts could begin to perk up the industry or provide enough jobs to make a dent in the depression.

Durango was going to have to rely on its own resources to weather the depression. It was the 1890s all over again, only worse. Leonard Glazer remembered belt tightening and learning to get by on less. Then came the closing of the smelter. A relief store opened downtown, where it dispensed free food and provided stopgap aid. Rich Macomb and others who had jobs volunteered to contribute fifty cents a week to a fund to help those out of work. "Anything we could do to try to help the rest of the crowd. It was tough going." Tough going, indeed, and help remained a day late and a dollar short.

Sporting goods store owner Lester Gardenswartz reminisced about trading a box of shotgun shells for a turkey. He went on to say, "We had tough times in Durango, but still we never had any bread lines in town. Everybody seemed to be helping one another to get by." Jackson Hardware and other stores were forced to extend credit when debts became overwhelming; they could not turn away old customers. Thomas Mason "tried to feed the town" with credit in his grocery store and went broke, about $200,000 in debt. Twenty years later some former customers were still paying on their debts, although a greater number would, or could, never come up with the money. This was not the only store that went bankrupt. Others recalled houses being boarded up simply because their occupants could not afford to live in them. Some families moved in together to share expenses. A mother remembered the little boy from across the street who ate ravenously when he came over for lunch one day. Her young son asked him why he ate that way. "Well, if you hadn't had anything but squash to eat all winter you'd eat fast too."

Helen Murray lost her job at Graden's, and her husband cleaned chicken coops to bring in some money. Near Animas City a shanty town sprang up, nicknamed Hooverville, for the much maligned president. "They'd build it out of anything they could get, boxes, corrugated tin, or anything they could get," Bessie Finegan said. "Just to put a roof over their heads. Anything you could crawl under and keep dry. It was a shabby town." People rambled in and out of town, thinking that some place, any place, would be better than where they had been. Durango might have appeared to be less affected than other places, but no jobs existed here and pitifully little relief for transients.

In the mind of a now middle-aged woman, one experience stands out. She lived on a farm and eagerly looked forward to the weekly trip to town with her mother, because Mom always bought her that supreme treat, an ice cream cone. This particular Saturday, they finished shopping and started home without that treat. "Mommy, my ice cream cone." "I'm sorry, honey, but we can't afford it." A long, hard cry produced no magic and the ride home was devoid of joy. Forty years later, that lost ice cream "was the depression" for this woman. That was it—a feeling, an image. It cannot be fully understood by those who have only read about it. John Parker summarized it well when talking about the 1930s and the good old days: "They may be great to read about in history books, but I wouldn't go back."

It must be noted, however, that if one had money during the depression, he could quite likely make money. An interviewee agreed times were hard; however, he "stretched his nickels" and invested in real estate. It was easy enough to buy up foreclosures. He turned a 250-percent profit on one ranch when he finally sold it. So the old Durango propensity for making money on land went on, even in the depression's depths.

Help, when it finally came, emanated from Washington. Durango and La Plata County voted overwhelmingly (60 percent) for Democrat Franklin Roosevelt and his vaguely stated New Deal in the 1932 election. This completely reversed the 1928 results, which gave Herbert Hoover a similar winning percentage. The New Deal met with voters' approval, since they backed Roosevelt again in 1936, before starting a string of majority votes for Republican presidential nominees that lasted until 1964. The situation had deteriorated so far by 1932–33 that Durango was willing to try almost anything.

Fortunately, the banks weathered the depression-inspired banking crisis and emerged from Roosevelt's "banking holiday" in solid condition, except for the Durango Trust, which teetered on its last legs and eventually closed, only partly because of the hard times. Durango's banking houses again stood firm against the pressures of an economic whirlwind. Everyone could be thankful. This ameliorated the depression's local impact and saved depositors further grief.

Its proponents hoped and prayed that the New Deal would do something, and it responded with a near miracle. In the now famous 100 days, an assortment of federal agencies and relief measures were scattered over America. Money and aid from Washington came to the rescue. One of the first things the New Deal did was to amend the Volstead Act to permit the sale of 3.2 beer and wine. While the WCTU never forgave Roosevelt this transgression, the measure was an attempt to create jobs, raise revenue, and probably bolster sagging spirits. Before April was gone, the city council approved ten beer licenses and happy days were here again for the drinking crowd. By the end of 1933 the "noble experiment" had been repealed nationally, and Durango's drinking establishments resurfaced legally.

The council quickly petitioned Washington for a Civilian Conservation Corps camp. One of Roosevelt's pet projects, the CCC provided jobs, room, and board to unemployed young men. Durango got its CCC camp and a lot more from the New Deal. The CCC camp stayed open through 1940, weathering several rumored closings. Democrats and businessmen always rode to the rescue in the nick of time. Several other camps were in the immediate area, so Durango was especially blessed.

A branch office of the Homeowners Loan Corporation provided relief for hard-pressed owners by refinancing mortgages. No depression image is etched so clearly, even today, as having to leave a home or farm because the family had no funds to pay the mortgage or taxes. Farmers and ranchers were helped by the Agricultural Adjustment Act. Some $36,000 was given to county farmers in 1933–35 for reducing crop acreage and livestock production before the United States Supreme Court ruled the measure unconstitutional. The sweeping Works Progress Administration funded numerous Durango and La Plata County projects, including road repair and building. Jim Sartoris, who came to town with the WPA, pointed out that constructing horse barns, caretaker house, and grandstands at the fairgrounds was one of its major efforts. The crew also put in sewers, curbs, and gutters, oiled streets, and performed a variety of other jobs. Critics voiced objections about federal work projects being boondoggles. Not so, replied Sartoris, "They [employees] worked very hard. There was a lot of criticism. I know they used to ridicule people about the WPA this, and the WPA that, but believe me, it had its good points. Because they worked for what they got."

Merchants agreed voluntarily to the codes of the National Recovery Administration, adhering to fair competition, minimum wages, maximum hours, and forbidding child labor. Shoppers were admonished to trade only with stores that displayed the NRA symbol, the blue eagle. Compliance would provide jobs and fairer prices. Who could object to tampering with the free enterprise system for such worthy goals? The system worked fine for a while here, as elsewhere, before enthusiasm waned and the NRA became an albatross. By January 1935, a vigorous drive had to be launched to enforce stricter compliance; mercifully, the Court declared the NRA unconstitutional later that year. By then many thought the NRA had gone too far down the road toward socialism and a planned economy. The codes had attempted too much and proved to be ill-conceived, but so great had been the depression's gravity that they seemed necessary. Now with times slowly improving, their implications were reconsidered, and the NRA came in for a barrage of criticism.

The National Youth Administration financed the expense of local archaeological excavations, as did a WPA project. The State Historical Society, under Civil Works

Administration sponsorship, employed persons to interview old-timers, and the Public Works Administration underwrote a series of lectures on southwestern archaeology. WPA funds ($86,000) went into construction of Smiley Junior High School in 1936–37, providing jobs, income, and a needed educational facility. Before it was all over, hardly a person in Durango had not been touched and in some way benefited from the New Deal.

The major project, far overshadowing all others for money invested and long-range impact, was the building of the Pine River or, as it is known today, Vallecito Dam. Planning began in 1936, construction in 1938, and the dam was dedicated on September 1, 1941, at a cost of $3,300,000. The man who shepherded this windfall was fourth congressional district Congressman Edward Taylor, a long-time champion of Western Slope water interests. Durango papers could not say enough nice things about him. The project epitomized the New Deal at its best and was its greatest achievement in Durango and La Plata County.

In the end the New Deal gave the region a tremendous boost and heralded much future government activity. As indicated, this did not occur without dissent. The editor of the *Weekly Herald* wrote on December 26, 1940: "When any people succumb to the lure of political coddling and give up their right of private action, even in a small degree, they have taken the first step toward state socialism. . . ." The price, not fully realized at the time, was that the community was hooked to the federal money trough. The day has not yet come that it has backed off.

The economy still looked bleak when 1941 arrived, a situation that worried local leaders. It looked bleak for an entirely different reason from 1932, however; government aid was drying up. A Chamber committee studying current conditions finally telegraphed Representative Taylor and Colorado's senators:

> Durango is facing an economic situation that is frankly appalling. Completion of the Pine River dam coincident with removal of three CCC Camps and coupled with the dismantling of the Smelter . . . is resulting already in the actual migration of many of our people who are attracted to industrial centers where defense operations are in progress. Unless Durango is definitely brought into sharing a portion of the defense program we are facing worse conditions than in '32.

They really wanted to stop the dismantling of the smelter and have it put back into operation, having given up a previous idea of converting it to an ammunition factory. Promises and rumors to the contrary, the smelter never reopened, and now AS&R was pulling out completely. How far had we come in twenty years; what had happened to the laissez-faire initiative, the doctrine of self-help that former President Hoover had espoused? The Chamber of Commerce, representing local business interests, had become so addicted to federal help that there seemed to be nowhere else to turn in 1941. What would the merchants of 1881 have thought? Durango's leadership had undergone an amazing metamorphosis during the depression. Rightly or wrongly, this transformation would guide the destiny of the town. The very group that has often in the days since decried federal dependence was clamoring to get on the federal gravy train.

In a way different from what the committee and the Chamber imagined, they would be granted their wish about the smelter. Extraordinary things were going to happen across the river.

10. The Only Bonded Whorehouse in America

The roaring twenties and the depression thirties evoke visions of the Charleston, bootlegging, the stock market crash, and "Buddy, can you spare a dime?" Durango saw much of this, certainly; yet a great deal from the earlier years survived. These were days of less growth, of transition, of concern about morals and old virtues and, at the same time, of more relaxation and stability.

The intolerance of the First World War characterized the twenties. The Ku Klux Klan marched in Durango as it did throughout Colorado, this being the strongest Klan state in the Rocky Mountains. Blacks were not the intended victims; the town did not harbor enough of them to warrant getting the sheets out. Catholics and Mexican Americans posed the threat to the Klan's brand of Americanism. Conveniently, the two "enemies" were often combined into one. Thus Durango's latent racial prejudice exploded, fueled by the turmoil of the times.

The Klan came in the early 1920s and became by 1924 a strong, insidious force. The usual secret mumbo-jumbo ritual and hooded trappings came with it, along with cross burnings on Smelter Mountain and occasionally over by Greenmount Cemetery. Both spots were handily located near Spanish communities. These were racist activities, without doubt, but they were obviously laced with political implications as well—1924 was an election year and the Klan primarily backed Republican candidates at the state and local levels. The two newspapers chose opposite sides; the *Democrat* and Rod Day strongly opposed, but the *Herald* certainly leaned toward the Klan and its "all-American" goals. Several of the *Herald* staff were Klansmen or strong sympathizers. This stirred a hotly contested newspaper fight, at least on the *Democrat's* part, in the second half of 1924 over politics and related matters.

That year saw the Klan's high tide both in Durango and the state; the candidates they backed did well. In 1925 they roamed, holding meetings. A basinwide rally at the fairgrounds in August was followed by a "silent parade" of cars loaded with members. They burned crosses and interrupted one startled minister to give a Klan eulogy at a member's funeral. Then they gradually disappeared, their venom spent. Those who lived through these days did not forget how membership or nonmembership sundered old friendships.

The Klan caused "quite a lot of trouble, friction," created enemies, hurt business, "didn't do the town a damn bit of good," were typical comments. One Florida Mesa farmer remarked that it was popular out there but, curiously, showed no antipathy toward Indians. The Klan stayed single-mindedly anti-Catholic and anti-Mexican, a fact Ethel Nelson well rememberd as a member of St. Columba Church. At first she and her friends laughed about it, thought it was a sort of nonsense, then it became serious.

They threatened to burn down the convent and little Sacred Heart Church and things like that, and at that time we had a priest by the name of Father [Wm.] Kipp . . . [who got] so excited—he wouldn't speak about it on the altar because that was immoral, but he would get down on the aisle and get so excited he would walk back and forth. . . . We got to the place where we didn't feel free to walk downtown, or be as casual as we always had been.

The Klan sent out word that they were going to drive the nuns out of the convent. So Father Kipp bought a double-barrel shotgun and he called the Chief of Police to put a notice in the paper that he had a shotgun and that if he needed to, he would use it.

She believed that the Klan picked on the other Catholic Church, Sacred Heart, predominantly a Mexican-American congregation, more than it did on her church.

Anna Gomez, a young girl at the time, thought the hooded hooligans looked like "spooks." "We were scared of them," she said. Her husband Max, on the other hand, recalled the Klan members as somewhat cowardly. "They got brave enough that sometimes they would burn a cross right by the depot, but mostly you would see them up on the top of Smelter Mountain."

The Klan failed in its goals, choking on its own reputation for violence and its involvement in national and state scandals that hurt local efforts. It failed because of spirited Catholic opposition and strong objections by other citizens. Wetter Grocery charged Klan members a dollar more per gallon for kerosene they apparently intended to use in a cross burning (extra profit was donated to the church offering). More directly, a group of Catholic young men pitched into one Klan parade, routing the hooded marchers. And it failed because, for all its high-sounding principles, it was a prejudiced, bigoted group, which appealed to others of the same ilk. It promised so much more than such a dogmatic organization could deliver. Of all the people interviewed, none admitted to being a Klan member and only a few even admitted knowing anyone who was. It is not something one brags about today.

Who joined the Klan then? Well, as one woman pointed out, the way to tell was to check clotheslines on Monday morning after a big Klan weekend. Those whose lines had extra sheets became prime suspects. The Klan is thought to have found its true believers among the borderline middle class, people who had not risen high enough in the social or economic order to avoid feeling threatened. This was partly true locally; however, the Klan seems to have drawn membership from all classes, as a Durangoan said, "just ordinary guys and a few professional people."

The fears and prejudices that hatched the Klan did not die, unfortunately. Several years later several of the "most vicious Klan" ladies tried to get Nelson fired from her beauty parlor job because she was Catholic. One person thought Durango's racial prejudice dated from that organization's debut, but it really predated the Klan by decades. The community had long tacitly segregated its largest minority and continued to do so. Such segregation was racial, certainly, and also economic: "If you only made $2 for ten hours a day, that's about all you could afford. They could live on land with some of those shacks down there that didn't cost very much. . . ."

Max Gomez still remembers years later the discrimination of the 1920s. The Mexican, he observed, had two strikes against him and was sure to be the last hired and the first fired. The image he projected in many Durangoans' minds, according to Gomez, was that of being either lazy or a thief. Like many of his contemporaries, Gomez worked at the smelter, as a carpenter, and was saved during the depression by a New Deal job. The Mexican Americans still inherited primarily the lowest paying, unskilled jobs, and they knew their place from decades past.

So did the Indians who came to town to trade, fewer now that the little settlement at Ignacio had been founded. The big problem with the Indians was whiskey. They could not legally purchase it, because of the best of federal government intentions to prevent a growing problem on the reservations. But Indians secured it clandestinely through others, a profitable business, and then drank it as fast as possible before they were arrested. This only led to worse problems and did not resolve the basic issue.

Drinking, of course, was a taboo in the twenties for everyone, white or red. In spite of pious Klan disclaimers, Durango became a center of bootlegging, as did Silverton, where empty mines easily concealed stills. The Klan supported Prohibition but could do nothing to enforce it, perhaps demonstrating the group's fundamental weakness.

Newspapers detailed numerous arrests and trials for violations of prohibition until they were hardly newsworthy. The council, meanwhile, was granting a suspicious number of soft drink licenses, finally rejecting Nick Sena's application after his arrest and conviction of bootlegging. Both interviewees and newspapers pointed to the south end of town and to the nearby hills as prime spots where the stills bubbled away. An October 1931 raid netted one large still, thirteen men, and eight women, all of whom gave addresses south of Sixth. Eastern European immigrants were blamed, fairly or not, for causing much of the trouble. If it had not been for customers north of Sixth, however, bootleggers would never have been so active, so the guilt was widespread. Business was transacted fairly openly. One bootlegger distributed moonshine to his customers on his coal route, and another painted milk bottles white and peddled his wares around town. Recent immigrant Angelo Dallabetta was surprised to find drinks being sold at a Second Avenue hotel when he arrived in Durango.

Almost everybody has a favorite Prohibition story. One lady recalled that when her brother spilled a little bootleg on the floor, it ate away the paint. She asked how he could drink such "pure poison"; he replied that he drank it because he liked the taste. For everyone who lamented the fact that when he wanted a drink with his friends he had to break the law, there was another who enjoyed the thrill of lawbreaking: "Kind of fun to go to those speakeasies, because you had to give a knock at the door and then they would see who you were and then let you in." Several felt that Prohibition completely changed the social picture, considerably undermining the old society.

One reason that law enforcement suffered a loss of face was made clear by Ethel Nelson. She worked at the Elite Beauty Shop at the time, which just happened to be next door to the Chamber of Commerce. One night as she was leaving work, she saw a party featuring moonshine going on inside the Chamber. Among those attending were the president of the Chamber, the city manager, and a federal agent! Medical reasons for enforcement certainly existed—a drink could be deadly. As Nelson mentioned, a lot of people suffered a great deal because they were stupid enough "to drink that stuff."

When Durangoans were given the chance to vote on Prohibition again, they spoke strongly for repeal, better than two-to-one in 1933. Thus ended the noble experiment, which caused more trouble and expense than it was worth. The WCTU lost the war but won a battle; the saloons never reemerged in their old form. Taverns replaced them and Durango soon acquired a reputation as a drinking town.

Eastern European immigrants, who earned Klan disapproval for their religion and "un-American" influences, again received more blame for flouting Prohibition than was fair. They had come to work in the smelter and the mines, and many settled south of Sixth, with its cheaper housing and convenience to their work. A subculture developed, subsisting with and replacing to a degree the previously dominant Mexican-Spanish one. In the 1920 census Durango reported 437 foreign-born whites, 10 percent of the population. The leading immigrant groups were Austrians and Italians, a decided change from previous years. They, too, had followed the immigrants' rainbow to America's pot of gold. For this town, perhaps the best known success story of the group was that of the Fantos. Rose Fanto became a living legend in her day for her generous support of charities, her helping hand, and "beautiful red wine." She and her miner husband scrimped and saved until they had enough money to open a tavern, which became a social center for the south end of town. Her career and reputation did not put her above reproach. In 1941 the city council threatened to take away her liquor license for keeping "girls and women, commonly known as 'Come on Girls.'" They threatened—and then renewed the license.

Thanks to the opportunities created by World War I and finally being given the right to vote nationally, women in the 1920s found themselves moving into the American mainstream. Although still found in their traditional roles—housewife, clerk, teacher, and so forth—women were advancing into new areas such as archaeology. Helen Sloan Daniels studied, photographed, and reported on petroglyphs found northwest of town in Falls Creek. She also directed the National Youth Administration museum project that excavated eight Anasazi sites.

Interest in the Anasazi reached all-time heights in the 1930s, a "virulent epidemic," archaeologist Robert Lister described it. Times were hard and selling Indian relics was one way to bring in money. People like Zeke Flora, who found nineteen mummified human remains in Falls Creek, had time on their hands and an interest in amateur archaeology. Unlike Flora's efforts, much of what passed for archaeology was simply pothunting, looking for souvenirs, and severely damaging sites for further study. The famous southwestern archaeologist Earl Morris spent three seasons digging local sites, the last fieldwork he would do. He also enjoyed many a relaxing Sunday "digging" trout out of Electra Lake, which had become a fisherman's Valhalla. What he and others had uncovered were Basket Maker II sites dating back to 300 B.C., earlier than any previously known. For a brief while Durango nearly rivaled Mesa Verde in archaeological interest.

Durangoans became so enthusiastic that they formed the San Juan Archaeological Society, whose members were active in excavation projects. They published "Sherds and Points," covering a wide range of topics, before World War II ended both the society and its publication.

All this pleased those who wanted to see Durango publicized and promoted. The city fathers certainly desired it, and they did their best to present the best possible civic image. Their meetings were now generally routine; conditions did not force issues as they had earlier, and the need for haste had disappeared. The council handled more "quality of life" matters now. For example, complaints about loud phonographs blaring from Main Avenue business establishments moved the council to ask the offenders to desist. The Farmers Supply Company was taken to task and its stockyard declared a nuisance, when it was used as a feeding lot instead of its intended purpose as a shipping point. On another occasion, complaints about dumping garbage outside the authorized dump ground spurred a movement to establish city regulations for garbage cans and to contract one company for collection. The concept of government protection for public health did not wane with the demise of the Progressive period. Sam Herons found his license revoked when, in the consensus of the council, his ice cream wagon became "very unsanitary."

On a happier note, a municipal golf course was established on the mesa, charging ten dollars per year per family or a fifty-cent greens fee per day in 1933. Before yearning for the good old days, golfers should remember the nature of the times. Hillcrest, according to a 1936 Durangoan, tested the "skill of the most accomplished golfer." In the last summer of prosperity, 1929, the council helped underwrite band concerts and maintained a public campground for tourists.

Another attempt to merge with Animas City came to naught. Old rivalries and lack of pressing reasons for that action doomed the idea to continual inaction. Animas City nearly tripled its population between 1920 and 1940, but at 712 people it still posed no threat to its competitor.

Not conceiving the tempest that would be unleashed in the future, the council approved its first zoning ordinance in April 1941. The idea was simple enough, to protect residential sections, prevent congestion, conserve property values, and direct city growth in accordance with a "well considered" plan. Few could argue with any of these reasons, so the ordinance went into effect. A generation later, a discussion of city and county zoning guaranteed an explosive situation.

No one could zone sin, however, and sinners went about their business unrepentant. Betty Hickey replaced Bessie Rivers as the leading madam, indeed Durango's last "official" one. Betty joked about operating the "only bonded whorehouse in America," which resulted when three merchants guaranteed her bond during a dispute over rent and land. Like Bessie, she maintained a surprisingly positive profile within the community. When Betty joined the WACs during the war, reportedly as a recreational director, an era ended. The price for a visit had risen to $5, except during Fiesta when, "due to wear and tear" on the girls, it shot up to $7.50.

The south end of Main down near the depot festered. It was a source of trouble with beer parlors, gambling, dance halls, and white slavery—almost all of the vices, according to reformers who endeavored to close it. Not until several shootings and a 1939 murder was action finally, but slowly, taken.

The most infamous murder between the world wars was the one involving the editors of the *Democrat* and the *Herald;* it took place on Main in broad daylight, when Rod Day killed William Wood in April 1922. The feud had grown out of newspaper bickerings and personal conflicts. Both men were sons of famous San Juan pioneers, and the killing created a scandal. Even though Day eventually was acquitted of murder, he sold his interest in the paper, ending the Durango career of this famous newspaper family.

More typical of the kinds of troubles confronting the police force were "wet nosed kids with smart alec complexes," fast driving, drunkenness, and the repeated round-up of those still elusive stray dogs. The breaking up of a youthful burglary gang provoked this February 19, 1932, comment in the *Herald:* "The duty of the community to its rising generation must be assumed fearlessly if parents shirk their responsibilities."

These problems could not be blamed on the school system. Seldom had it been held in such high esteem and worked so successfully, thanks primarily to Superintendent Emory Smiley. Both students and teachers interviewed had only good things to say about this shy, retiring man, who was small only in physical stature. Coming to Durango in 1903 as high school principal, he later served thirty-seven years as superintendent, determined that every child should receive the best education possible. Possessed of a remarkable memory and the gift of remembering names, it was said of him that he knew every child by his or her first name; he frequently visited classes in the five-school system. Under his strong, efficient administration, the system blossomed to include a new high school and Smiley Junior High, named after him over his sincere protests. He had his struggles with students, school board, parents, teachers, and townspeople, but Smiley worked hard, and everyone knew where he stood on educational matters. No educator has ever had a similar impact on the community. His wife summarized his career clearly when she affirmed, "He just devoted his entire life to the schools of Durango. His whole life was wrapped up in the schools."

Some people liked to blame the movies for the juvenile problems. After all, such films as *Gambling with Souls,* the most "daring picture ever made, real life in the raw," were shown at the Kiva Theater. Fortunately Hollywood redeemed itself with features like *Mutiny on the Bounty* and those ever popular westerns. Matinees were the youngsters' Saturday treat, if money could be spared.

Something new for both young and old appeared in the late 1930s, ski runs. One was referred to optimistically as "Durango's Sun Valley." None of them quite reached that standard. The most accessible was Chapman Hill, built partly with WPA help. The other, twenty-two miles north on Highway 550, foreshadowing Purgatory, was promoted by the local ski club and featured a tow, all for the price of twenty-five cents per day for adults, a dime for children. From these beginnings grew this important segment of the town's economy. Cheaper in those days, skiing was also less encumbered with traffic and lift lines.

Though it would seem in many ways to have been a simpler, less pressure-filled time, it was not, by any stretch of the imagination. More liberal in some ways than previous ones, these years still caused their share of uneasiness. The *Democrat* in August of 1920, for instance, carried an article about "social diseases," without once mentioning them by name. That they were discussed at all offended some people. Women could smoke and wear rouge without comment, but "respectable" people broke the law by drinking bootleg whiskey and visiting speakeasies, something which would not have happened on such a scale in Victorian America. There were new problems to worry about, along with the old ones. Everyone was aware of state, national, and international crises almost while they developed, thanks to radio. Then there were the plagues of childhood illnesses, old age, and those social disgraces the ads forever mentioned—"bad breath and B.O." Combined with the depression troubles, these things made the thirties an ulcer-producing decade if one ever existed.

Durangoans joined secret societies as readily as ever. In fact, the uneasiness and changes of the twenties pushed them into lodges in record numbers. Here with their "brothers" and "sisters" they could find a sense of belonging as they acted out their ritual offices. People joined lodges with more enthusiasm than they joined churches, further diminishing the significance of the latter. A 1921 survey found twenty-two different lodges, including Elks, Masons, Red Men, and Woodmen of the World. The G.A.R. marched no more, however, as the Civil War became only pages in a history book. In its place trooped the American Legion. The pioneers of the San Juan rode on, their ranks noticeably thinning by the 1930s. They and later arrivals in general ignored a historical moment in 1930 when no celebration marked the golden anniversary of Durango's founding. Even the Daughters of the American Revolution, steeped as they were in the town's history, missed the September date. Perhaps the depression thirties provided little incentive for remembering better days.

Even with new forms of transportation, economic woes kept many people close to home. Trimble Springs fell upon hard times after the Victorian 1890s; it survived several fires and a general decline in popularity of such resorts to become more a road station than a resort. Anyway, few people considered riding a bicycle out there any more, not with the car available. Pinkerton Springs, with music, dancing, and swimming, seemed more in tune with the era. But its place in the sun proved short-lived.

The automobile precipitated the greatest social change. Its impact on dating, church attendance, school functions, recreation and morals, and on crime, bootlegging, and business patterns was unprecedented. It changed the whole life-style. Durango motorists took to their cars with uninhibited zest. One of the first victims of the transition was the streetcar line, which, in the last year of its existence, showed a rumored profit of twenty-five cents.

A Durango Athletic Club thrived briefly. In 1924 it urged physical fitness: "Throw away your medicines and keep away from doctor bills. [Were they high then, too?] After the lethargy of the winter months, the best spring tonic is proper exercise." The 1930s brought a great upswing in interest in softball, maybe because Durango opened the first lighted softball field in the Western Colorado system in 1933. Town teams battled one another each season, joined occasionally by a CCC team. The high school football team played the first night game in the basin in 1934. The local boys were ready but not the Norwood eleven, which must have been slightly in awe. They lost 73–6. "Something of a sorry affair," bemoaned the sports reporter. Sports fans could easily keep up with the national scene as well. During the World Series, the newspapers carried an inning-by-inning report, and sports broadcasts on radio became much more common.

The old guard social leadership ceased to be in the teens and twenties, never to be replaced. No families came to dominate, as those on Third Avenue once had done. The times militated against that, and the community structure already was becoming too fragmented to encourage it. The upper crust continued its whirl, with parties and summers at Electra Lake and its own social season; however, it did not have the impact of previous decades. Victorian sociability fell victim to the roaring twenties.

What was Durango like? Everyone has slightly different memories of it. Sporting goods merchant Gardenswartz cherished it.

> It was a rural town. We had a little summer business. It wasn't what you'd call a tourist town. Durango was the hub of the San Juan Basin, just like the hub of a wheel. You'd see a customer maybe once or twice a year. . . . I remember when twenty fish was what you were allowed, and it was nothing to go out on the Pine River, which was 99 percent open water, 'cause every farmer would let you fish on his place. The water was open and you used to catch some of the most beautiful fish you ever saw in your life. . . .
>
> There was never a lot of money, but you could always make a beautiful living in Durango, if you were willing to work at it.

Leonard Glazer humorously described his attempt to collect a donation from Betty Hickey for the Spanish Trails Fiesta. Two to three thousand dollars were needed every year to put on the show, and the Fiesta committee appointed citizens to solicit merchants. About four o'clock one afternoon Glazer visited Betty and found her vexed.

> About that time she laid me low; she said, "You can take your Spanish Trails Fiesta and b-e-e-p it!" I said, "What's wrong?" "A fellow came down here the other morning at 7:00 A.M. to collect for the Fiesta and anybody ought to know better than to come at 7:00 to a house like this to make a collection! We're not in business at 7 o'clock in the morning."

After calming her, he convinced Betty to donate some money. "We were always real good friends. In fact, she never let anyone else collect for the Fiesta Committee."

Will Rogers left behind this insight. Even during his short stay, he gained a perceptive glimpse.

> Towns are like people, they are proud of what they have. Trinidad, Colorado, with enough coal to melt the North Pole down till it runs, then Wiley hit a

beeline over the tops of the mountains to Durango, a beautiful little city, out of the way and glad of it, gold, silver and Mesa Verde Cliff Dwelling Ruins, where civilization flourished before it started to go backwards. . . .

The era came to an end in December 1941. Suddenly prohibition, the depression, softball games, and the Klan seemed unimportant. The community had been cheerfully planning for Christmas. The annual light display blinked on, on Friday, December 5; all merchants kept their lights off until 7:30, then with one glorious flash the season was ushered in. The Kiva's double feature starred William Powell and Myrna Loy in *The Shadow of the Thin Man,* and "America's beautiful blond sweetheart of swing," Carole Landis, in *Cadet Girl.* The Elks Club sponsored a Colorado featherweight championship fight Saturday evening.

On Sunday the Japanese attacked Pearl Harbor. The "day which will live in infamy" lives still in the minds of those who sat shocked by the news from their radios that afternoon.

Within the next three days the Western Colorado Power Company began issuing "War Bulletins." Saboteurs were plotting vandalism and employees could not be too careful: "Especially, *visitors* to power plants, dams, substations, etc. should be *scrutinized carefully. Give out no information,* unless properly authorized. *Be Alert. Analyze. Scrutinize."* Durango raced equally as fast to check the "desperado of the Far East," who desecrated the "calmness and sacredness of a beautiful Sabbath Day." A defense committee was organized, patriotism pledged, and full support to the national defense effort promised. The city council unanimously passed a resolution calling for residents to give wholehearted aid to the war effort and promising the city's cooperation. For better than a year, the country's first peacetime draft had given young men a number and a potential appointment with Uncle Sam. Now they volunteered. As one of the power company bulletins emphasized, "We are at war. Conditions are not normal." They would not be for Durango for four years, if ever.

DURANGO IN THE TWENTIETH CENTURY
A PICTORIAL REVIEW

The twentieth century has never had the same fascination for Americans as the nineteenth. This seems to hold true for the photography; although more photos exist, there is less choice among them. Tomorrow, the cynics say, does not exist, and yesterday was but a dream, so live for today. For whatever reasons, starting with the second half of Durango's first century, photographs that show the town and its activities prove harder and harder to come by. Many individual and promotional pictures can be found but few of the community shots that were so typical of the earlier century.

Here they are, however—twentieth-century Durangoans captured in all walks of life. Some were heroes, a few villains, and most just ordinary people trying to make a living in a community beset with continuing problems.

By the turn of the century Third Avenue was beginning to resemble the quiet, tree-shaded residential neighborhood its founders envisioned in 1880. These two spic and span children must have just come out of their home — no self-respecting youngster could be that clean for long. *Western Colorado Power Company Archives*

Durango's black community was never large. This woman, identified only as a well-known charwoman of the early days, held one of the positions open to minority individuals. *Amon Carter Museum*

130

An interesting group of Durangoans posed before the Palace Grocery & Meat Market. In 1900–01 oranges sold for 35¢ per dozen, men's suits, $12–$20, and a full set of false teeth for $5. A five-room house on Third Avenue was $600, one with six rooms and two lots, $2,000. *Durango Herald*

The Boston Coal & Fuel Company's engine, Perins Peak, on a siding next to Graden's Wholesale Grocery warehouse. It ran from Durango to Franklin Junction, via the Rio Grande Southern tracks, then labored up a spur line to the mine. Occasionally the extra thrill of a derailment highlighted the downward journey. *Duane A. Smith*

"You load sixteen tons and what do you get, another day older and deeper in debt," lamented a folksong from the coal fields. The crew of the City Coal Mine about 1910. Most of these men lived south of Sixth Street, which left them only a short walk to work. Obviously, the crew was getting ready to start its shift. A careful study of this photograph reveals much about coal miners and their equipment. *Duane A. Smith*

The Porter Mine in Wildcat Canyon. Durango lies beyond the hill to the northeast. Several Rio Grande Southern cars are visible, and one is being loaded with coal at the mine tipple. The small settlement was behind the photographer. *U.S. Geological Survey*

132

The longest lasting and most significant of Durango's satellite coal camps was Perins, shown about 1910. Although a company town, it did not acquire the bad reputation many of these communities did. The mine tipple can barely be seen at the right. The drab houses look much alike; the school stands in the center. *Duane A. Smith*

Sans the typical saloon nude, the boys lift their glasses to toast an unknown photographer. Located near the depot, this was one of seven saloons in the area in 1910. The cluster south of Sixth Street, with its accompanying girls, served the railroad clientele and that end of town. The bar has since come uptown to reside in splendor in the Strater. *Strater Hotel*

Durango has witnessed many "races" in its day, from the opening of the Ute strip to today's jogger's. Since the 1880s one of the most popular has been horse racing, starting with the first track on the mesa where the Riverview subdivision now sits. This race took place at the fairgrounds, probably at the turn of the century. *Goodman's, Inc.*

The boys at the Bismarck Saloon, with George Olbert, the owner, standing in his white apron; some of the boys look pretty young. Apparently a pool game was in progress. Were they drinking Coors? Perhaps they sang a chorus of "Beer, beer, glorious beer!" but their days of such fun were numbered. *Linda Mannas*

A group of "eager" young scholars at Park School in 1910. Located south of Sixth Street, Park had the most multi-cultural student body of any Durango school. Some of these youngsters don't seem too enthusiastic about posing for this picture. *Center of Southwest Studies*

Horses would not hold still for a parade shot in 1912, nor would the young bicycle rider on the right. The Utes traveled from Ignacio to participate, having become something of a relic and a "must" for such events. *Linda Mannas*

Getting to Durango in the old days by car was an adventure, as proven here by members of the visiting Los Angeles Chamber of Commerce in 1911. Fortunately for civic pride, this fording took place south beyond Fruitland, New Mexico. *Western Colorado Power Company Archives*

Other Indians also played a role in Durango's present and future, though having departed long since. Their heritage, the cliff dwellings of Mesa Verde National Park, held out tourist potential, even if, for the moment, upstart Mancos rivaled Durango as the "jumping off" point. Until this wagon reached the park in 1912 or 1913, only horses and mules could navigate the trails. These long-forgotten people celebrate their achievement. *Mesa Verde National Park*

136

The 1911 flood was one of those that Durangoans remembered for a long time. The water eventually got as high as the top of the arches on the Main Avenue bridge; in this picture it is already flooding some of the nearby homes. *Center of Southwest Studies*

Perhaps Durango's first "aeroplane" about ready to take off from the fairgrounds. Fragile in appearance and here only for an exhibition, the plane foretold great changes. *Jackson Clark*

The Yanks are coming — they had a long way to go from Durango's depot in 1917. A goodly crowd gathered to see them off, complete with flags and fair ladies. Notice the number of cars parked around the area; most of them were probably Fords. They doomed the streetcar, which can be seen about a block away on Main. *Goodman's, Inc.*

Down came the poles in 1924, to be replaced by new modern ones. Parsons Drug Store, a Durango fixture, is just to the left; here met the "club." Most of this block on the right was destroyed by the 1974 fire, as was Graden's store on the next corner in an earlier blaze. Graden's was an outgrowth of the lumber and flour mills started by Thomas Graden and Robert Sloan in the early 1880s. *Western Colorado Power Company Archives*

138

By 1923 the housewife found a greater selection when she went to the market, and the friendly clerks and owners Thomas Mason (second from right) and Walt Ambold (left) of the Mason & Ambold grocery were ready for her. According to their advertisement, they were exclusive agents for Chase & Sanborn coffee and teas, besides offering staple and fancy groceries, meats, and bakery products. *Center of Southwest Studies*

Durango, like many American cities, served as an immigrants' "melting pot." With coal mines and the smelter operating in the 1920s, foreigners found jobs and a home south of Sixth Street. The Daughters of the American Revolution sponsored an Americanization school, with some success, as this group of proud graduates and teachers testifies. *Center of Southwest Studies*

The Rev. John Everington and a group of stern-faced Methodist men in the early twenties. Organized in 1881, the Methodist Church remained one of the strongest Protestant denominations in a community that has always been "well-churched." *First United Methodist Church*

"Brother, can you spare a dime?" The 1930s depression was no fun. These fellows are sprucing up the CCC camp on Reservoir Hill about 1933–34. The camp was good for Durango and for the men who found work and room and board there. They also entered some very good softball teams in the Durango league. *Center of Southwest Studies*

Will Rogers acquired a liking for Durango during his brief stay here in 1935. Durango was, he quipped, "out of the way and glad of it." Will drew a crowd wherever he went on his overnight stay. Within three weeks he and his pilot Wiley Post (Mrs. Post is climbing aboard) were dead in a plane crash. *Strater Hotel*

The Spanish Trails Fiesta, now Navajo, has always been a popular Durango attraction. This is a mid- or late 1930s photograph of an "old-time" car. It was from the Elite Beauty Shoppe that some members of the next door Chamber of Commerce were discovered drinking during Prohibition. *Ken Periman*

Railroading brought excitement regardless of the era. Incredible as it seems, this washout southeast of town about 1934 did not derail the train. By the thirties, cars and trucks were making serious inroads into railroad traffic, and the D&RGW was feeling the pinch. *Duane A. Smith*

Durangoans did not know exactly what was going on at the rebuilt smelter during the war. They found out later that part of the operations dealt with uranium. The old smelter was pretty well gone by this 1942 photograph. A few old and a few new buildings were being utilized as a roasting and leaching plant. *Western Colorado Power Company Archives*

World War II needs called for 4-H'ers and others to raise as many cattle and sheep as possible. A September afternoon in 1942 saw the boys and girls exhibiting their efforts at the fairgrounds, where, only a few years before, the New Deal had underwritten the construction of the stands. *Western Colorado Power Company Archives*

World War II is over and it is a time to celebrate at the 1946 Fiesta. Already Durango is profiting from its western image, as a "stagecoach" rebuilt in 1888 by Harry Jackson, lumbers down Main. The crowd does not seem all that interested. *Jackson Clark*

143

Monarch Airlines initiated daily service at the La Plata airport in November, 1946, a year before this landing. A one-way ticket to Denver cost $18.35. That same November, parking meters were installed in Durango, so the community was really coming of age. *Amon Carter Museum*

Seldom photographed Mexican Flats stretched beyond Durango's southern limits. On this July, 1949 afternoon no train is seen on the once busy D&RGW tracks and the smelter is smokeless. *Amon Carter Museum*

The family unit has always been an important adhesive for Durango society, especially south of Sixth Street, where it helped ameliorate the problems of minority groups. Everything seemed rosy for smiling Ruth Montoya, her two sisters, Sophie and Esther, and a young friend on this summer day in 1949. *Ruth Martinez*

Children's styles change along with the times. Compare this photograph with the turn-of-the-century Third Avenue pose. By the late 1950s the out-of-doors was becoming a major tourist attraction. *Durango Herald*

145

"Around the World in 80 Days" paused momentarily to film near Durango, while Mike Todd, according to a local story, flew to New York to obtain further financing to complete the movie. Stars Shirley MacLaine, David Niven, Cantinflas, and Buster Keaton, with a D&RG locomotive, appear bemused by it all. *Mike Todd Productions*

"Camelot" comes to Durango. On June 18, 1960, John Kennedy, seeking Colorado's Democratic votes, visited Durango, which hosted the state assembly. He talked about water problems, promised a better natural resources program, lashed the Republicans, and observed that "the West has been made by easterners who moved West." Shown with him at the La Plata airport are his brother Ted and future Supreme Court Justice Byron White. *Durango Herald*

Skiing gained enormous popularity in the 1960s and 1970s. Dolph Kuss is instructing this class on some fine points in the mid-sixties. Durangoans by then had three nearby places to go — Hesperus, Purgatory, and Chapman Hill. *Durango Herald*

". . . For it's one, two, three strikes you're out . . ." Baseball has always been popular, from town teams to barnstorming major leaguers. Basically, however, it has involved kids like these "Old-Timers" warming up at fairgrounds field. *Dolph Kuss*

147

Ft. Lewis changed Durango in many ways, not the least of which for some Durangoans, the introduction of college athletics. When this photograph was taken in the 1961–62 season, the school was still an agricultural and mechanical junior college, country cousin of what was then Colorado A&M. The cheerleaders face some long afternoons in the sixties, when Fort Lewis was usually the conference doormat. *Center of Southwest Studies*

A lot of footballs have been fumbled since the first high school game in 1893. Durango High has had its ups and downs, including, according to Coach Vern Fuller, having to blast rocks to level the playing field in the late 1930s, and provide at least a few inches of dirt for the players to land on. Seldom have the troubles equaled the 1–19 seasons of 1977–78 pictured here. *Durango Herald*

148

This is the morning of August 25, 1974, when Durango's worst fire was slowly being brought under control. All the buildings from Gardenswartz Sporting Goods to Levine's had to be torn down because of damage. The Main Mall is now on the site. *Durango Herald*

The depot is one of Durango's oldest remaining buildings (1882) and has come a long way since Dave Day recommended it be declared a relic. Once in a decaying crime pocket, the depot and surrounding area have been refurbished into a tourist mecca. More people take the train from Durango now in a year than used to in a decade or better. *Richard Gilbert*

"There is music in her jingle, there is music in her roar, like a will-o'-wisp she travels. . . ." The train intrigues young and old, and over 120,000 ride it to Silverton in a summer. Durango benefits heavily from these tourist dollars. Changes are coming, however, as the Denver and Rio Grande prepares to sell the line. For the first time in nearly a century it will have no connection with the town to which it gave birth. *Richard Gilbert*

"Bound to Boom" it was said of Durango in 1880, and 99 years later Main is busy as ever. Traffic, tourists, a multitude of businesses, a touch of the outdoors — Durango has it all. Look carefully, for some of the glory has departed by the very success of the dream. *Richard Gilbert*

PART FOUR

Rise up, the Winter Is Past
1942-1969

*For, lo, the winter is past, the rain is over and gone;
The flowers appear on the earth; the time of the
singing of birds is come . . . .*

Solomon 2:11–12

11. Catalyst of a New Durango

The days of World War II are not so long ago, a mere generation removed. But it might as well have been the Civil War for most Durangoans, who either did not reside here then or were born later. Such has been the transformation since those epic days of the forties.

Bessie Finegan, already an old-timer of thirty-five years' residence when the war broke out, recalled the war years this way:

> During the war just loads of people went out to California to work in the defense factories. Lots of people went out there, so Durango was kind of bare for a while. Lots of young men went into the army. They wanted to get in the army in those days.
>
> During the war, that's when the women started to work. They were supposed to stay home in the kitchen. When the war came on there wasn't any men around, the women found out they could do things. When the men came home, the women found out they could do those things and they were not very anxious to go back to the kitchen. And a lot of them never did. . . . And they found out they're just as good as men and can do almost anything.

Here was one of the great American social changes in microcosm; neither the town nor the country has been quite the same since.

Just as the worried city leaders had foreseen, and Mrs. Finegan observed, the attraction of higher paying wartime industries lured workers. Durango was never able to match the challenge. How could the city compete when advertisements from the likes of Boeing Aircraft appeared in the *Herald?* The company offered free transportation to the West Coast, on-the-job training with pay, varied types of factory work, and far better wages than unindustrial Durango could match. As if these were not enough, Boeing ended with this pièce de résistance: "No other job will give more evidence of patriotic duty." The appeals of patriotism, job variety, higher wages, and positions for men and women could not be resisted.

The same was true of military enlistment. Young Ken Periman, just finishing high school, described it: "War was glory then. I hated my father because he wouldn't let me go in at sixteen. I tried to lie about my age and that didn't work either. He wouldn't let me join the reserves until I was seventeen." As the boys—and girls—marched off to war, the community saw to it that they received a proper send-off, at least in the beginning. A "breakfast-lunch" served by the American Legion Auxiliary left no one hungry, a speech by a local celebrity promoted the proper patriotic fervor, and the high school band escorted the group to the railroad station. As the war dragged on, such celebrations became less frequent, much to the disgust of the superpatriots. "Dare we get blasé about seeing men off to fight?" questioned the *Herald* as early as April 16, 1942. Understandably, such high-pitched war fever could not be sustained. This was not 1917; much of our national naiveté had worn off.

As 1942 slipped into 1943, then 1944, and finally 1945, the county casualty list lengthened (fifty-one killed and missing), and places like Midway, Bizerte, Normandy, and Iwo Jima became household words to those who had never been 100 miles from home. Notices of missing in action, wounded, POW, or, the most dreaded, "killed in action," rarely missed a week in the newspaper. News of and letters from servicemen and women received more and more space. "Home on furlough" always warranted a few lines, and a local whose name appeared in a column by the famous war correspondent Ernie Pyle gained instant acclaim. Yet mere words cannot describe the heartache and anxiety that such items generated for the readers who watched loved ones go into a war larger than any that had come before it in Durango's memory.

Life went on back home, though with some differences. The Parsons Coffee Club continued to meet. "Every morning we'd meet and we'd fight the war, we'd talk about everything that was happening in the world," remembered one unreconstructed member. They read and talked, as did all Durango. One could not escape the war—it called attention to itself from the magazine, the radio, the newspaper, and the movie theater.

Newspapers gave good photographic coverage of it. One wonders why so many pin-up poses of leggy Hollywood starlets in scanty (for that day) attire were included; perhaps it was to build up homefront morale as much as battlefront. Speakers also came to town to stimulate bond drives and promote other patriotic endeavors. The *Herald*, which had been anticommunist for so long, began in 1942 to paint "our Russian Allies" as "good guys" and Joseph Stalin as a pipe smoking, friendly near neighbor. Such were wartime exigencies.

Unlike 1917–18, nationalist hysteria did not run rampant, probably because the Japanese never settled permanently in Durango, and Americans did not suffer another German phobia. The only outgrowth of national anti-Japanese feeling was an attempt to secure a relocation camp to house Japanese deported from the West Coast. Few humanitarian motives were involved—it was simply an effort to give the beleaguered local economy a boost. The Chamber sought help from anywhere, without much success. As its president wrote in 1942, "Sometime ago we saw the necessity here in Durango of doing something that would maintain our present town's population. . . ."

What they finally secured was a reopening of the smelter to process war-needed vanadium, a key ingredient for producing a rust resistant, stronger grade of steel. Vanadium mining boomed to the north and west, primarily near the Utah line. Under government regulation and guidance, prospecting and mining for strategic metals flourished. Never before had the industry been so regulated, even to closing down the "nonessential" gold and silver mines and establishing metal prices. All this proved to be too much for an old-time Silverton miner, Charles Chase, who exploded in a Durango meeting, "I have the horror of organization. We are over-organized." Many others concurred; the "monster" of the New Deal seemed to have gone raving mad.

The United States Vanadium Corporation ran the mill with about fifty employees, a far cry from the AS&R days. The ore came from the Dove Creek area, with just a bit from local discoveries. There were actually two plants across the river; the second, built in 1943, operated under an army contract. The nature of the work there, confessed the *Herald* in September 1945, was a "military secret." Presumably, the writer continued, it was connected with the production of uranium. His presumption was correct, although not until well into the postwar years would this be confirmed. Actually both uranium and vanadium are found in a common mineral source, carnotite.

What uranium meant to the military, Durangoans, and the rest of the world was revealed in August 1945, when atomic bombs were dropped on Japanese cities. Durango was blasted into the atomic age; it had helped to usher it in by producing uranium for government use.

Wartime demands also revived lagging coal mining. La Plata County's production doubled to 72,000 tons by 1945, paralleling a nationwide pattern. Local production was still only a drop in the bucket in the Colorado picture, however, and as soon as the war ended it slumped once more. Neither of the big districts—Perins or Porter—revived, and it was obvious to all that the spurt would be only temporary.

The homefront was more regimented than during peacetime, though less than it had been during World War I. What war meant was, first to last, registration and rationing. No one escaped the long arm of the government. Ration books were required for food and other essentials, such as gasoline and tires. "Will your wife tell her age?" asked the *Herald* on April 30, 1942. "She will if she wants a sugar card," the writer retorted. In the matter of tires, those in need found passenger and truck tires and tubes available only after military demands had been satisfied, and then only on a prorated system with leisure driving needs at the bottom of the list.

Food, too, was in short supply, as the country strained to feed its own troops and help its allies. Farmers found the market much to their liking; they and the housewives became familiar with the ration point system. Each item carried a certain point value; in 1944, to illustrate, cheese had a value of ten points to the pound, chuck steak five points, and pineapple juice four per can. Out of the ration book came the little coupons. The OPA (Office of Price Administration) changed these values to match supplies and would put some items on a free list, though the shopper was lucky if she could find them at the local store. Periodic scarcities of such items as coffee, cigarettes, and women's stockings frustrated many a shopping trip.

As they had in 1917–18 Durangoans bought bonds, struggling on occasion to meet quotas. In 1942 John Fankhauser, county chairman, was moved to remind locals, "Now let us all pitch in and help raise this $18,000 May quota." Early in the war, when the drive went "over the top," a ceremony celebrated the milestone. Later on, enthusiasm waned. All types of gimmicks, from free motion picture tickets to a queen and attendants, were used to encourage purchases. The town also cooperated in the war efforts, from saving kitchen fat to collecting scrap paper. Groups like the Boy Scouts were particularly helpful, "covering every inch of the city" to pick up materials. War demands mounted and each drive prompted a slogan. In 1944 it was "Help get those supplies [scrap paper] over to the invasion forces in time."

Few refused to pitch in and help. Planting a victory garden, practicing civilian defense drills, buying bonds, and saving tin—all counted toward the war effort. Durango and Animas City school children did a multitude of things, from collecting needed items to purchasing savings bond stamps, and Fort Lewis Junior College students helped harvest crops. Women who had never thought of it before canned food, and the Red Cross had people of all ages involved in such activities as preparing surgical dressings. By 1945 clothing for war-torn nations was being gathered under the banner of the United Nations.

In some ways Durango hardly seemed touched by the global struggle going on around it. High school athletics continued unabated with marked success. When the Demons, as they were known, managed to defeat Cortez twice in football in 1942, after several seasons of bitter defeat, local pride knew no bounds. In basketball they were even better, winning the state "B" consolation tourney in 1943. These achievements in the San Juan Basin League were more a reflection of size than superiority. It was Goliath facing David, with the outcome being the more logical, if not the biblical, one. After a galling defeat, the *Silverton Standard*, February 9, 1945, observed, "Silverton had little hope of defeating Durango when they went to that place Friday, fighting the elements to get there. Just why Durango gloats over beating Silverton is more than we can figure out." To win seemed to reinforce civic pride and confirm that Durango ranked best in the Basin; Silverton could go ahead and fume if it wanted to. For those less enamored with athletics, the high school band received "superlatives" as one of the best in the state during these same years.

The racial attitudes noted earlier lingered unchecked, the most obvious manifestation being fights between groups of boys, one side Anglo, the other Mexican-American from south of Sixth Street. One might have been able to attribute these feuds to youthful feeling of oats, if the pattern had not already been established. Gilbert Lujan, who grew up during these years, remembered the gang fights but was never bothered by them personally. The city fathers finally called the "ringleaders" in to try to put a stop to the combat, but this temporary bondage did not reach the root of the problem. As Lujan recalled, each group "didn't go out of your territory too much." The war would bring change even in this arena.

The Denver and Rio Grande Western suffered through the "Perils of Pauline," while managing to continue operating. Narrow-gauge locomotives were needed more in Alaska to help in the war effort than they were in southwestern Colorado, where most of them ran. Requisitions for those engines kept coming from Washington. Only by the narrowest of margins in 1942 and 1943 did protests and pressure from the community and county keep the local trains running. Abandonment of the distressed Rio Grande Southern appeared only to be deferred for the moment. With the steady improvement of air connections, the trains did not seem to be so important any more, at least in the eyes of Washington planners. Speed, safety, and rapid wartime expansion of air transportation convinced Americans that airlines were here to stay. Western Air Lines proposed to include Durango on its "feeder" route from Albuquerque to Salt Lake City as soon as wartime restrictions were lifted.

Having fended off the threat to that hallowed institution, the narrow-gauge railroad, the Chamber moved on to promoting as usual. It cheered the Denver and Rio Grande in 1944 for producing a promotional film on southwestern Colorado. Wartime travel restrictions kept tourism at a minimum, regardless of promotion efforts. The town and chamber reached a level of maturity by not feeling threatened by the rise of a new neighbor, Gem Village. They welcomed it and wished success to "Rock Hound" city. In the end they measured it well; Gem Village never posed the remotest menace to Durango's prestige and power.

War, of course, generates its own particular concerns and rumors. No community was immune. Obviously many of these related directly to the war and activities of men and women in service. Others of a more peripheral nature caused moments of anxiety, too. Wartime marriages and an increase in divorce troubled the homefronters. Was lack of a "proper courtship" the reason? As early as 1942, decaying marriages were looked upon as "one of the most impressive war problems." A December 8, 1944, *Herald* news item touched upon a much less momentous worry, American "doughboys" teaching young French girls the Boogie-Woogie, the new dance craze. "American dance music packs as much dynamite as American bombs." Chaperones at dances concurred!

The major concern of those with relatives or friends in the military was their safety. Letters from those overseas gave the stay-at-homes a flavor of the war and encouragement for greater homefront efforts. And for the first time militarily, women claimed some attention. Lt. Elizabeth Dill was typical. A public school nurse before the war, she joined the service in February 1942, becoming supervisor of a hospital operating room in England. When she was sent to the Normandy front in 1944, a letter published in the paper concluded by saying that in her two-year absence from home, she had never met anyone from Durango. A certain parochialism crept in among the patriotism, yet Durangoans were becoming more worldly-wise, and the cultural isolation that had hindered the community was breaking up in the wake of "unintended" travel, movies, and the radio.

The war brought change, both expected and unexpected. Dentist Schuyler Parker, who served in both world wars, felt Americans and dentistry gained from the experience. People learned the advantage of having their teeth worked on and maintaining proper dental hygiene. "Naturally, a man when he got out of the service and married that beautiful girl—he told her she had beautiful teeth and he was sure she was going to keep them. So he sent his wife to a dentist."

Leonard Glazer deftly summarized a major change: "Well, the young people, naturally, especially the males, left Durango, which made quite some difference in the population because they were taken into the service. It did create a different atmosphere in the area." He went on to call attention to another trend which argued auspiciously for the future. Because of crowded living conditions elsewhere, "a lot of families moved here to live during the war while their husbands were in the service, and it made quite a difference in the general population." The same chemistry that had attracted so many others years ago generated its magic once again and many stayed at war's end.

The potential for change and the desire for continuity stirred cross-currents for the future. Alton Dorsett, who, as he expressed it, "found Durango" and became owner of the newspaper, remembered his first impression: "This was really a closed community. They didn't want any strangers, they didn't want anybody new coming in. . . ." Although they (whoever "they" might be) resisted it, change was coming as surely as the war was drawing to a close in 1945.

Signals waved from all directions. The visitor total climbed at Mesa Verde to nearly 1,500 in June, double what it had been a year ago and equal to a year's total a generation before. Durango faced a critical housing shortage; construction, which had dipped drastically during the depression, had not regained its momentum. The Chamber of Commerce's housing committee, created to "probe the possibility" of building new homes, deliberated while people kept coming and the problem worsened. Inquiries poured into the Chamber about jobs, homes, and vacations, and were dutifully answered and noted in the press as proof of Durango's popularity. Before the year was three-fourths gone, an estimated 100 newcomers had come to work or purchased farms or ranches nearby. The town's population, which had grown by only 25 percent between 1910 and 1940, jumped 27 percent in the forties, mostly after the war.

The very busy Chamber also set up a committee to provide employment for returning veterans and war workers. As the economy stood at that moment, it would have a difficult time absorbing many of them, a matter that worried community leaders. The need for community planning for the years ahead also surfaced, to be foolishly swept under a rug, whence it reemerged at a later date to plague city officials.

The years ahead held more promise than Durango had known in well over a generation. The town Dorsett saw would soon be no more; even the predictions of the Parsons Coffee Club did not foresee what was about to take place. Old Durango, with its charms and vices, metamorphosed. The depression, New Deal, and war catalyzed a reaction that has not stopped yet. As one housewife commented, "I was born and raised here and things aren't like they used to be at all." She hit the nail on the head, while also believing that the formation of Lake Mead and the dropping of atomic bombs had changed the weather!

12. This Is the Place

. . . I wanted to come back to Durango. This is where I wanted to stay. I
didn't want to go anywhere else. This was it. Once I got in here I didn't want
to leave. [Offered a position as postman for eighty-one cents an hour], I said,
"That'll do it. Count me in. I want to live in Durango. I don't wanta leave
this place."

Jim Sartoris, former WPA worker and more recently an army engineer, came home in
1946. He came to stay and he was not alone. In the next two decades Durango grew, as
growth once more became a dominant theme.

The town he returned to was like, yet somehow different from, the one he had left
to join the military. He noticed the change; so did others. This change, just starting,
would become another dominant theme. Reveille sounded for Durango.

Like the rest of the United States, this town did not escape the war's aftereffects.
The Russians reverted to the role of threatening Communists, shedding their wartime
"white hat." The cold war's icy chill gripped America, reaching into every nook and
cranny, including Durango. Communism was on the march and America had better be
prepared.

The major impact of world conditions on the local scene was the reactivation in
1948–49 of the mill across the river, which had closed in 1945 at the war's conclusion.
The Vanadium Corporation of America, a worldwide company, leased the uranium and
vanadium plant and soon had it running around the clock. The work force soared to over
200, putting it back to the AS&R levels. Once more a milling operation became the
largest employer. The operation was obviously a large one, though not until the Atomic
Energy Commission relaxed security measures in 1956 did facts supplant estimations.

Durango's mill, one of several in Colorado (the VCA operated another at Naturita,
for instance), was a major uranium concentrate producer. The VCA also owned mines
and drew ore from them, as well as from other mines in all the four-corner states. The
amount of money pumped into the local economy proved substantial and was one of the
major factors in bringing about the postwar boom.

The impact of the VCA touched every town in the area. Colorado's far Western Slope underwent a mining resurgence, generated this time by uranium. Some Durangoans joined the rush with gusto, finding to their dismay that the best prospects were several hard hours' travel distant rather than at their front door. Better roads were needed immediately to transport ore from mine to mill, and prospector from town to claim. The Chamber of Commerce did what it could to generate support, but the real money came from the AEC, as it was called, funneled through the VCA. As one resident truthfully wrote, "There is an awful lot of gossip around here [1949] that AEC (who seems to have worlds of money) can be persuaded to tie these three points [Durango, Naturita, and Monticello, Utah] together with good highways, since there are no railroads in this area." Better roads were a boon to Durango's economy in many ways, especially to tourism.

Continual improvement of the milling operation (VCA had purchased the plant in 1953) kept Durango in the forefront of the industry, and when the Naturita plant closed in 1957, part of its equipment was moved there. All things come to an end, however, and the emphasis of the cold war soon shifted. When America had stockpiled ample supplies of uranium and bombs, the excitement and pressing necessity evaporated. In 1962 the VCA's contract with the AEC expired; there was little public demand for uranium—the AEC had furnished everything, from the money for exploration to a market. As a result, the Vanadium Corporation closed its Durango plant early in 1963 and transferred its milling operations to Shiprock, New Mexico, closer to some of the still producing mines.

Overall, the fifteen-year stay of the VCA had proven a decided advantage. Few would dispute that the jobs and economic stimulus it provided benefited the community and the region. Nevertheless, there had been a few tender spots, and some unresolved questions persisted as the company pulled out for greener mining pastures.

Labor unrest, involving union representation, dogged the operation in the 1950s. Although repeated elections failed to satisfy all parties, the labor violence of earlier years did not reappear. Even at this early time, there was concern about employees' exposure to radioactive materials. The Durango plant was one of several cited by the government for possible violations of safety measures. Within the realm of knowledge for that day, the VCA did try to provide safe working conditions. The tailings pile changed, too, with the addition of slightly radioactive material. This danger, like more direct exposure to radiation, was not immediately perceived. Fortunately, except for where it blew, the waste was not distributed around town for use as land fill or in some other capacity, as in Grand Junction where it contaminated homes, schools, and other buildings. When the danger was finally recognized, an attempt was made to stabilize the tailings by growing vegetation on them. This cut the blowing dust somewhat but left Durango with one of the few radioactive vistas in America.

The VCA, like the AS&R before it, came and went, leaving a void in the economy. Luckily, the impact of its departing was not so calamitous. Although the mill propelled Durango's economic growth in the late 1940s, its total significance had declined, because another benefactor had finally gushed into prominence—oil and natural gas. For sixty-seven of Durango's eighty-three years, milling/smelting had undergirded its economy; now it was gone for good.

Oil was something that had been around nearly as long as the mill. Production statistics do not begin to tell the entire story, when at long last profitable oil and gas fields were found in La Plata County. Colorado enjoyed almost statewide oil prosperity in the fifties, setting all-time production and drilling records, and La Plata County marched right in step. Indeed, La Plata was hailed as the state's outstanding county for natural gas production by mid-decade.

All this benefited Durango's economy, but the impact of oil and gas went far beyond that. Assessed property values in the county leaped from twelve to forty-two million dollars in the 1950s, and the city's population to 10,530 (up 41 percent). The whole pattern of life changed. Some important decisions had to be made that would alter Durango's destiny.

For the moment only one of those decisions will be examined. Durango lay on the edge of oil and gas fields, which stretched west and south. Both Farmington and Durango stood to gain from their development, and the leadership of each community possessed some latitude in choosing the direction of their involvement. Durango, as merchant Gardenswartz pointed out, "could have been the hub of the Basin as Farmington is today, but we wanted the white collar instead of the laboring class of people in here. So we went more or less for the white collar town. . . . " Thus Durango attracted company headquarters, managers, professional engineers, and geologists, bringing in highly educated and generally well-paid people. The companies, for their part, did not hesitate to take advantage of Durango's climate and scenery. Farmington, on the other hand, secured mostly the crews, equipment and repair firms, and the support operations needed to maintain the fields. This division was logical; Farmington was surrounded by wells, and economics dictated operation from that point. There are, however, many more "roughnecks" and support personnel than exploration teams and engineers, so as Durango jumped, Farmington vaulted, from 3,637 to 23,786 people in the decade. The whole San Juan Basin concept changed from Durango's viewpoint.

The sudden influx of outside capital brought with it more outside control and leadership. No Durango individual or financial institution possessed the resources needed for extensive development. The Durango Natural Gas Company was bought out by Southern Union Gas of Dallas, Texas, which underwrote exploration of local oil and gas fields and improved service into town. Natural gas had grown exceedingly popular after its introduction in 1929; in fact, after the war, local sources failed to meet the demand. By 1947 shortages of gas forced the company to discontinue supplying the Western Colorado Power Company during peak use periods, in order to keep gas flowing to local homes. Southern Union could easily tap outside gas from interstate pipe lines; service improved at the expense of local dominance. It all came about so painlessly that few comprehended the loss of control. It was simply one of the prices that had to be paid for the unprecedented boom.

Never before in Durango's history had it been so caught up in a mineral excitement. Oil and gas drilling rigs and producing wells dotted the southern and western portions of the county. They produced more than just the frustration of earlier efforts. Although petroleum reached only the $70,000 production range, gas topped $5 million. As late as 1969, when major exploration and development had ended, the county still produced $4.6 million worth of natural gas.

Unfortunately, no other areas of mining were stimulated by these developments. In the same year, 1969, no precious metals were reported, and only $117,000 worth of coal was mined. Sand and gravel quarried from pits along the Animas River more than doubled the total value of mined coal, so far had that old standby slipped.

There had been a few other slight mining rumblings in the previous years. Revival of the Neglected or the possibility of a new vein in the Bessie G out in the La Platas provided subjects for discussion and debate over a cup of coffee. One small gold dredge on the Animas, north of town, actually tried in the 1960s to recover the placer gold thought to be in the riverbed. That venture dispelled yet another myth, that the Animas harbored rich placer gravels. The dredge did little but dig into stockholders' pockets and turn up some sand and gravel. Some people still blamed poor roads for retarding development in the La Plata and Needle mountains. There just had to be gold and silver there!

Coal, at least historically, offered better potential for success, though once mining gets into one's blood, rational behavior is often driven out and all prospects look glittering. A little coal mining kept that industry barely alive. The booster edition of the *Herald-News*, May 1953, put out especially for visitors, asserted that enough coal existed in the San Juan Basin to supply the United States for 337 years. Impressive! The promoters of 1880 would have been proud of the writer. In his or her defense, it should be pointed out that huge coal reserves do underlie parts of the county, a fact known since the 1870s. If coal demands had never increased over 1952 levels (a great natural gas and oil period), the estimated reserves would have lasted that long, provided they could be mined economically. Those "ifs" scuttled exploitation for the next two decades. Neither demands nor production costs permitted the predicted coal age to desecrate a large part of the region.

The article's tone showed that expectations had not changed much over the past seventy-five years. Nor had the idea that the promised land languished just a step away. The article went on to say that Durango's coal was going begging for want of a broad-gauge railroad to take it to market. Sound familiar? Back in 1947 promoters had dusted off the hoary southern outlet scheme, which promptly died again. While gas, oil, and the smelter prospered, agriculture declined, or at least failed to keep pace. Its relative economic significance and its importance to Durango diminished. One of the first signs of the change was the construction of homes on what were once ranching and farming lands in the beautiful Animas Valley north of town. Comparison of a 1940 photograph with one a quarter century later is startling. As the idea of living in the country, yet near town, caught on, the farmer/rancher found it easier and more profitable to sell than to continue the struggle.

Times were hard for the farm and ranch, and not just in La Plata County. After the war-induced boom, agriculture again experienced an unpredictable, often depressed, market, a woe compounded by rising taxes and operational costs. Government regulation played a role, too; open sheep-grazing land in the mountains became limited by permit and recreation. Durangoans did not rise to the sheepherders' defense; perhaps they did not relish the thought of the extra flavor all those grazing woolly creatures might be contributing to their water. Before long, sheepherding, once a major factor in local agriculture, had all but disappeared.

The farmer and rancher did not threaten to follow their sheepherding comrades into oblivion. But the cards appeared to be stacked against them. The gap between town and country, which had narrowed so dramatically in the previous generation, reversed its direction. During these years the attractions of the city far outweighed those of the farm, even for people who moved to the country. They took with them all the comforts and benefits of city life that they possibly could and vainly hoped to leave its problems behind. In the end the popularity of the move spoiled the attraction, and the Animas Valley became less a thing of beauty and more an urban sprawl.

In other ways, too, rural life changed. The car had already passed judgment on crossroads stores, which hung on in some places by the narrowest of margins. School consolidation doomed the one-room neighborhood school and replaced it with busing, which meant long-distance rides for some children. The larger school district included several rural elementary schools, but for high school everyone came to Durango. The cowboys, "stompers," or whatever name they were called, often found themselves at odds with their more "sophisticated" city brethren. The political clout of rural La Plata County declined sharply, as Durango's voting block, if it could be marshaled on an issue, easily outvoted the rest. In a sense, Durango played in La Plata County the same role Denver played in the state—the urban power in a rural setting. Those people who moved into the county did not help the political balance either; they were simply transplanted urbanites who often failed to understand their neighbors' attitudes.

To make matters worse, federal and state governments never developed a successful plan to boost agriculture's declining profits or mitigate its rising expenses. By the end of the sixties, it was prohibitively expensive for the newcomer to start farming. Figures like $200,000 to $250,000 were casually suggested as the amount needed. Weighed against expected profits, it was enough to scare out even the most determined.

Farmers could not control the weather and faced the same problems as their forebears. Water still flowed past their fields on its way to New Mexico or the lower Colorado basin, while they suffered shortages. The interstate compacts seemed designed to inhibit La Plata County, and the promise of its own Animas–La Plata Project, with storage dams and irrigation systems, remained on paper. The small but vocal group of environmentalists who opposed the idea were met with consternation and antagonism. Water projects had helped southwestern agriculture bloom. Why would anyone want to deny La Plata County its share?

Lemon Dam and Reservoir were completed as part of the Colorado Basin concept. Though smaller than neighboring Vallecito, this project irrigated land on the Florida Mesa and in the Florida River Valley. Storage began in mid-1963, and the mountain-enclosed reservoir soon became a favorite fishing and vacation spot. While helping agriculture and tourism, Lemon also encouraged more growth by providing the prerequisite water.

Even the railroad appeared to be against agriculture; it retrenched operations, finally willing to admit that freight and passengers were going elsewhere, leaving it only with losses. Passenger service between Alamosa and Durango went first, in January 1951. Opponents of this retrenchment rose up in righteous anger, hastening over the mountains to the hearings to argue their case. According to tradition, the railroad's lawyer asked the representatives how they got there and they sheepishly admitted by auto. That damaged their case and emphasized exactly what the Rio Grande wanted to demonstrate. As far away as New York, where the *Times*, March 4, said it marked the "end of a chapter in American railroading," people bemoaned this closing of the last regularly scheduled narrow-gauge passenger train. Then came the final run of the Rio Grande Southern in December 1951, a bad year for railroad buffs. The railroad's pruning policy was a response to financial reality. "You can't run a railroad on sentiment," contended the Rio Grande. The Rio Grande Southern never did live up to Mears's or Durango's expectations, born a day late and a dollar short. It expired a decade away from becoming perhaps a prime railroad attraction; its lumbering, rickety "galloping goose" would undoubtedly have attracted riders.

Within seventeen years (1968), the Durango-to-Farmington and Alamosa routes went the way of the Southern. Farmers and city dwellers now stood as much at the mercy of truckers as they had once of the Rio Grande. For Durango, an epochal link with its past had been broken.

But the break was not complete; left behind was the Durango-Silverton narrow-gauge line. Isolated from all other railroads, it survived solely as a tourist attraction and devoted supporters stubbornly fought to retain it. Private individuals published, and the Chamber republished, a pamphlet to stimulate interest in the train. Nationwide circulation brought people in droves to ride the "little train." The Rio Grande wanted to sell even this profitable bit of nostalgia, if only a buyer could be found. Passionate steam-railroad buffs could not understand why; more hard-headed railroad men knew. Slide or flood damage and extensive equipment replacement could put the line quickly into the red, and the Rio Grande did not consider itself to be in the entertainment business. A 1959 attempt to sell to a nonprofit organization failed amid commotion over the possible loss of county taxes and other pressures. Other efforts (one in 1960) followed suit. What the Rio Grande finally achieved was a ruling from the Interstate Commerce Commission that it need not operate from October until the start of the next tourist season, and it no longer had to carry freight. Not that there was much need anyway, truncated as it was. Durangoans, though, kept a wary eye on the Rio Grande, in case it attempted to abandon this line.

What started out as a small operation grew from a few thousand enthusiasts taking the "trip into yesterday" to nearly a hundred thousand by the end of the sixties. Tourism had turned into a major industry. Overshadowed still by oil and milling, it grew steadily, helping to end agricultural dominance. As the other declined or leveled off, tourism picked up the slack, preventing what might have been a sharp local recession in the early 1960s. Durango could count its blessings.

Mesa Verde showed a similar increase, and became the other major attraction upon which the tourist industry flourished. The surrounding mountain scenery, Vallecito and

Lemon reservoirs, and the now crumbling remains of nineteenth-century mining attracted their share of visitors, too, and then came the startling increase in skiing. The development of the Purgatory Ski Area in the 1960s, if it did not exactly place Durango in a class with Aspen, at least put it squarely in the picture.

All these things poured money into the economy, created jobs, and gave rise to a swarm of new businesses. Motel operator Art Wyatt expressed what happened in this fashion: "Tourists just exploded all over this western country. . . . Poured in here, [we] couldn't accommodate them. . . . The result was that many of these people moved here, came and liked this country." Unlike the prewar, two-and-a-half-month season, he could rent to transients all year; people got into a vacation habit, he explained, and discovered this country to be "a vacation paradise." It was still primarily seasonal, however; the big rush came in the summer months—skiing was as yet unable to fill the winter gap. This made Durango a federally designated "depressed area," with many unskilled and semiskilled workers unemployed half the year.

This kind of vulnerable economy kept wages down, a fact that bothered employers—who only fattened their profits—not at all. Salaries paid by the oil companies helped somewhat and caused mumbling on Main Avenue about the unfairness of such competition. No union organization marched to the defense of local workers, except in the transportation and building crafts. Setting and climate continued to attract more and more people, producing a labor surplus willing to work for less and making it harder to achieve a higher wage scale. Local leadership realized the need for year-round employment, but, except for a sawmill and a few smaller shops, Durango attracted no industry. When it tried to do so, it ran up against the traditional problems of isolation and poor transportation. By the end of the sixties, the question of attracting industry was being weighed against the industrial impact on the environment. No pulp mills or smelters need apply.

Hence Durango's economy, which hummed during these years, failed to hit upon a permanent solution to a perplexing problem. Neither the smelter nor the oil/gas boom lasted out these entire twenty-three years; only tourism emerged as a mainstay, along with Fort Lewis College, which moved into town from the old site near Hesperus. Tourism supplied a clean industry, which contributed increasing profits; its only weakness was its failure to overcome the seasonal nature. The college furnished a limited number of local openings, a steady, slow growth, and, best of all, pumped new vigor into cultural life, money into the economy, and provided an added promotional vehicle. Former City Councilman Ned Wallace, a man of many hats at Fort Lewis, aptly described its significance:

> The one thing that had the greatest impact in the shortest period of time would be the college. The greatest impact in the long period of time, say my twenty-six years, would be the mobile public, the tourist industry. But these dollars are elusive and hard to measure, whereas the college impact between 1956 and now, just twenty years later, is measurable.

Durango's leadership struggled to match the challenges, most often adequately, sometimes with outstanding success, and occasionally with far less. The sudden growth, the complexity of problems, and the diversity of the people crowding into town left little time for extensive contemplation. The days of the Parsons Coffee Club's influence and others like it were numbered. Time-in-residence and inherited wealth no longer wielded the influence they once had; home-bred wealth paled before the oil money gushing into town.

The sale of the First National Bank and the retirement of A. M. Camp in 1955 symbolically broke another bond to yesteryear. The Camps, father and son, had been influential since Durango's founding—through their bank, in behind-the-scenes leadership, and in community activities. Neil Camp, praised as a bridge between the old and new after the war, now was gone, his bank purchased by William M. White from Pueblo, a further example of outside money coming in to replace local.

The leadership now combined old and new. The new leaders were the oil people, who had fewer ties to Durango's past and to local agriculture. The rapid change fostered strains within the structure when old and new conflicted, neither at times grasping the extent of problems facing the city. When they could get together, it was reminiscent of the days of Porter and Graden. As oil's influence waned, other groups, such as the college and business newcomers, stepped in to take their places. The establishment splintered into cliques, and the control exercised by older Main Avenue merchants diminished. As the days of a monolithic leadership, dominated by a few families, had passed into history, so now did control by a select group of merchants. For a while the old power elite ostracized the upstarts. C. R. Ellsworth, who moved to Durango in 1968, felt the friction even then, a problem he would face when he became head of the Chamber of Commerce. "There was a lack of wanting to see any change, I think, in the business community." Money and progress won out in the end, as both adjusted and pulled together on common concerns.

One thing they agreed on, the importance of air transportation to Durango. Despite promises by Western Air Lines and others, Monarch was the first line to fly in with regular service. Organized in 1946, it soon landed DC-3's at the local field. Three years later Monarch merged with two other companies to become Frontier. It did not take long for the field on top of the mesa, with its limited runways, to become outdated. The airport was moved southeast of town to the Florida Mesa and, with several enlargements and modernization, is the present La Plata Field. Here was shown the leadership and the Chamber at their best, as they saw a need and worked to solve it.

Not everything worked out so well. The changing 1950s forced reconsideration of the San Juan Basin concept and its eventual abandonment. Farmington's sudden expansion challenged and demolished Durango's pretention to sole Basin leadership. This ensued partly from the choice made earlier by local leaders regarding oil developments and the kind of population they wanted for Durango. Whether it was actually they or the oil companies who made the choice is open to debate; however, its ramifications possibly caught Durango off guard. The depression, New Deal, World War II, and changing economy forced Durango out of its insular isolation and introduced new challenges. In the end, the Basin concept gradually faded into oblivion, still heard occasionally although lacking the vigor and confidence of pre-1941.

On another issue the leaders used a speck of deviousness to net what they thought best for their town. At least one irate resident denounced the city council for underhandedly fluoridating Durango's water supply without public approval. Councilman Fred Kroeger placed it in a different perspective. After the State Health Department recommended it be done, the council "just voted on it, not behind closed doors or anything and that was it. Nobody was aware of it." When it finally became known, there was some objection to the "poison," but such sentiment faded away, as so many other issues have done.

The steady growth already threatened to cause water shortages, and in the late 1950s summer rationing went into effect. Then, Mayor Kroeger vividly remembers, "we ran out of water." The water came from the Florida River, and the city actually had to sandbag the river to build up enough of a supply to divert the entire meager flow. A new reservoir and filtration plant helped, so did Lemon Dam, but the problem would not go away. This seemed incomprehensible to residents who saw water flowing continually in the Animas River.

This same growth also reactivated that almost constant Durango plague, a housing shortage. It hit right after the war, accelerating when the oil people moved in. As a result, subdivisions opened in both the Crestview and Riverview sections of town and others followed. A construction boom, which has hardly abated to this day, began then and with it came higher priced land and homes. Another favorite Durango enterprise, land profiteering, revived after a hiatus caused by the depression. People with a little money, foresight, and a penchant for speculating stood to profit, just as they had in 1880–81.

A new development, mobile home parks, not temporary tourist courts, mushroomed around Durango's fringes. The high cost of land and housing forced alternatives, and the threat of "ticky-tacky" urban sprawl grew ever more real. Former motel owner Art Wyatt, reflecting on a subsequent extensive state legislative career, recognized the threat and spoke of one of his political disappointments:

> I wanted to see the county zone the valley areas way back in the fifties, and that would have preserved it, but they couldn't see it. They have ruined the valley now. . . . I was talking to one man and he said, "You know, I remember when you said we ought to be zoning this county and be very strict how we developed it. I thought you were crazy, and I voted against it, but what fools we were for not listening."

Zoning efforts by both county and city languished. Durango's quality of life was threatened, but there were few Paul Reveres to cry a warning.

One that did was the *Basin Star*, which was started in March 1959; it promised to present both sides of controversial subjects. A month later the *Star* lauded the La Plata County Commissioners for creating a county planning and zoning commission. This would prevent a crazy-quilt pattern of growth, the editor fancied. Had actions followed words, it might have. Within three years, the *Star* was no more, and the zoning controversy had reached a stalemate. A golden opportunity had been lost.

Back in town, the city manager-council government struggled with all the problems associated with a boom situation. They had no luck with zoning, nor better than average success with building and repairing roads, extending services, and trying to keep pace with growth. Residents and council clashed over every imaginable issue, and the council itself was not always unified. As in earlier days, many of the power elite chose not to run for office, preferring to remain behind the scenes to exercise their leadership.

One accomplishment of this period was long overdue. After all those years, Durango and Animas City finally agreed to merge in 1947. Animas City bowed to the inevitable before being completely swallowed. Durango's northward growth moved the two closer together, and Animas City could not keep ahead of its neighbor. Thus ended the controversy that had begun back in the winter of 1879–80 between the town and railroad.

Even at this late date jealousy persisted. Rich Macomb commented that Animas City did not want to be annexed: "They kind of put up a scrap on that a bit. They kind of wanted to maintain their own deal out there."

Short of money, limping along as a renter on Durango's water system, and faced with mounting sewer, water, and street demands, Animas City needed to merge, and the councils sat down to serious negotiations. On October 28, 1947, both communities overwhelmingly voted to unite. Only 40 percent of Durango's eligible voters bothered to cast a ballot, while 72 percent of Animas City's did, which probably reflected accurately their needs and interest. City Manager Jim Wigglesworth promptly pledged to start urgent street projects, and Mayor Tom Kimball, a little pompously, called this the greatest day in the histories of the two towns. He did welcome the new Durangoans with "untold pleasure."

Change was the theme of the postwar years. The Durango of 1969 hardly resembled the one of 1946. "There was a big change. Oh, yes and awful," perceived Dave and Gertrude Warlick, who left in 1948 and returned in 1969. "It was built up and the tourists were everywhere. There were so many fences and roads, we didn't know where we were."

Neil Camp saw it coming and that was one reason he decided to sell, concluded the bank's lawyer Fred Emigh. "He could see that after the war this whole complexion of business in the San Juan Basin was changing." Camp proved to be one of the farsighted ones; others fought and resisted the threat to the Durango they had known. And this too emerged as a theme in the fifties and sixties.

13. A Hell of a Place to Make a Movie

Durango in 1945, a three-score and five-year-old community just recovering from the depression, was mired in a generation-old semistagnation. The next twenty-five years brought great transformation. First came the oil people.

They created an immediate impact, sending ripples throughout the community. Lester Gardenswartz, who had seen it all since the days of the twenties, called attention to an obvious consequence: "The purchasing power in Durango changed when the oil people came in 1951. We had a group of people, instead of making $4,000 or $5,000 a year, were making $8,000, $10,000 and $15,000. So they had new purchasing power, greater purchasing power." Main Avenue merchants knew what this meant; they grumbled about the high wage scale of these outsiders and what it would do to Durango. Unlike the smelter, which employed mostly locals at prevailing wages, the oil companies hired at wages paid elsewhere and brought in large staffs.

Leo Lloyd, a young doctor anxious to build Durango, felt "the community was backward and not very foresighted. They didn't want things to change too much." Native-born Leonard Glazer recalled the growth and sensed a difference in the population. Oilman Walt Osterhoudt, one of those who stayed, pointed to the community improvements and the new homes that came with the oil companies. Some of their men ran for city council and, like outspoken, impatient Harry Miller, crashed right into the "old Durango city people." Sparks resulted, but so did paved streets, an improved golf course, a city recreation director, and a mosquito control district. That last brings to mind the mosquito hordes in the valley. "When we [Osterhoudts] moved here, we couldn't work outdoors from four o'clock until dark because the mosquitoes swarmed so bad. And it wasn't just the stinging, you couldn't breathe. They'd stick in your nostrils and you'd think, well, I need some air, so you'd open your mouth and you'd swallow the darn things." Oilmen also served on city planning committees and other commissions and promoted the Four Corners Geological Society.

Their wives proved to be just as active and civic-minded, and added new luster to the social scene. Through the AAUW and other organizations they became involved in a number of movements, joining with the core of Durango women already laboring in the vineyard. The Petrol Club, an organization of oilmen's wives, created the Mercy Hospital Auxiliary in June 1959. Others taught and substituted in the schools; "very well qualified people, during a time . . . when teachers were very scarce," said Osterhoudt.

In the end everyone benefited. Durango could be thankful in many ways for this influx, which covered a little more than ten years. Most of the individual families, though, did not stay that long. Oil people's careers are transitory; John and Ann Hultman, for instance, came near the end of the era in 1964 and left as it closed in 1967. They remembered their years here with nostalgia. For them it had been a good life. Osterhoudt concurred and summarized for all: "Whether they were here a year or two years or five years they enjoyed living here. They enjoyed the small city life with its country attractions."

"It was kind of a blow when they started leaving. Lucky they didn't all leave at once, they started leaving gradually," noted realtor John Newton. In the years since, a few have returned to retire, hoping to recapture the charm of those earlier years. Fortunately for the city, which could not live on sentiment, the withdrawal symptoms were not severe. Again turning to Newton's observations: "But surprising enough, they [oil and VCA people leaving] were not the tremendous impact that they could have been, because people were moving in here and coming to live in Durango almost as fast as people were moving out."

A look back at the postwar years reveals one event that stands out as a milestone in Durango's evolution—the move of Fort Lewis College from the Hesperus campus into town. As mentioned in the previous chapter, the college transfused fresh blood into the local economy and enriched the cultural life. It encouraged Durango in other ways as well and may truthfully be said to have been the most significant development since the turn of the century.

Not everyone saw the move as an advantage, though, and opposition formed quickly. The Reverend Alfred Carlyon, who moved to Durango in 1953 to start a fifteen-year pastorate at the Methodist Church, recalled, "There were some opposed to it, but it didn't come to any knock down and drag out." Maybe not, but close enough.

It started when the college's president, Charles Dale Rea, concluded in 1952 that the institution had no future at the old fort site. Burdened with a small, declining enrollment and situated in rural isolation, the little junior college was dying on the agricultural vine. Rea initially moved to establish a branch campus in Durango, an idea supported by the governing State Board of Agriculture. Almost immediately opponents voiced disapproval. Opposition centered with the ranchers and farmers, who feared the college would lose its agricultural tradition. Also, why move, they argued, from such a beautiful, partly new campus? The debate's deep bitterness was shown in an after-the-fact letter from a Hesperus woman published in the *Herald-News*, March 20, 1955. Part of it stated,

A good many taxpayers feel we are being taken for a ride by the State Ag Board, our legislators and a small group of local citizens—perhaps within the law—never the less in an underhand way. . . . Finally patrons of Ft. Lewis

College would much prefer someone else as President of our college over a model from Esquire Magazine.

This faction gained support from some townspeople troubled about the changes that might occur in Durango and the expense involved.

The basic attack centered on the wasteful, impractical nature of the move and such peripheral arguments as how to get water on the mesa above town, the chosen site for the campus. Conveniently forgotten was the fact that the city's reservoir was already there. Like a miniature civil war, the controversy split families. Fred Kroeger supported the move; his father and brother did not. But the town's guiding forces rallied behind the idea, and on several occasions lobbyists hustled off to Denver to convince state legislators. In the end, the move-favoring faction won out; in March 1955, Governor Ed Johnson signed the bill authorizing construction of the new campus.

A rear guard, bitter-ender attempt to thwart the land purchase had failed previously, and with that the opposition melted away. Much of the credit for the move must be given to President Rea, a controversial figure. Dr. Lloyd commented, "Dale was the roughest character that has ever lived with the legislature. He just did everything that almost nobody would have courage enough to do to finally hold onto the thing long enough, until we got it brought here." There was no question that some individuals opposed the move simply because they did not like egotistical Rea. Abrasive, stubborn, domineering, Rea had a knack for rubbing people the wrong way, alienating even his supporters. And when he resigned in December 1961, his demerits outweighed his credits in a good many eyes. As one of the city councilmen remarked, "Ol' Dale gave us constant troubles."

Rea must be given his due, however, for his driving singlemindedness and his farsighted realization that a move had to be risked to save the college. In this he was joined by a cross-section of the community, including Dr. Lloyd, bankers Camp and Nick Turner, merchants Kroeger and Jackson Clark, newspaperman Arthur Ballantine, lawyer William Eakes, and a legion of determined others. Representative Wyatt emotionally forsook life-long Republican loyalty to cross party lines and support the Democrats to vote for Fort Lewis. The battle was won; the college had come to stay.

Durango benefited immediately when construction started in 1955, and permanently when the partly finished campus opened for the fall term in September 1957. Since then, the college financial inflow, talent, and educational atmosphere have permeated the community, and the student body has added a certain zest, not always appreciated. As historian Robert Delaney wrote in his recent book on the centennial of the fort and college, benefits went both ways: "The move into Durango proved to be the salvation of Fort Lewis as an institution of higher learning." Facts support his assertion. The fluctuating small enrollment stabilized and tripled within six years of the move. Better faculty recruitment improved course offerings and enhanced the college's professional image. Fort Lewis was on its way.

The next result, beginning with the desires of a few and soon becoming the wish of many, was to convert the college into a four-year degree-granting school. Planning commenced as early as 1958. Again the Chamber and others rallied to the college's aid, pressuring and going to Denver to lobby. William Eakes chaired a group that supported the four-year status, raising $10,000 for lobbying purposes. Clark and Turner resided in Denver temporarily to lobby, and others joined them as needed. This time they corralled more general local and state support, thanks primarily to some adept trade-offs involving eastern Colorado water needs. In 1962 success rewarded their efforts. The timing was perfect; it might not have been approved later, as state education needs and plans changed. Since then, few have regretted the upgrading.

There existed, to be frank, a nagging so-called town-gown split, friction between students and townspeople, and between professors and townspeople. It has not disappeared and probably never will, flaring up particularly when a different life-style, new issue, or controversial personality perpetrates a scuffle.

As the sixties moved along, the marijuana issue was one that aroused animosity, particularly after it was rumored that a college professor was holding "pot parties" in a local park with his students. Such shenanigans were looked upon with disfavor by the majority of citizens, bound as they were by the moral strictures and attitudes of a different generation. The townspeople suffered through a generation gap, as did the rest of the country. Drug-related matters were not new; those earlier opium dens had been conveniently forgotten. And the students voiced their own complaints—the "rip off" in high rents for poor housing was high on the list.

Less reaction was noted among local college students to the spreading inflammatory Vietnam issue. Student protests, antiwar rallies, and violence seen elsewhere in the United States largely bypassed Fort Lewis. What little reaction there was paled into insignificance, much to the relief of college and town. Why this issue failed to generate more emotion cannot be explained except to point out the relatively conservative, rural, or small-town background of the student body. Perhaps Durango was too remote for even instant TV coverage of the war to inspire physical protests. Nor did small, still basically rural Fort Lewis College attract a faculty likely to rush to the barricades on every political, social, or economic issue that came down the pike. For better or worse, the community's environment has a way of calming the agitated and softening issues that seem distant and unrelated.

Sam Day, pastor of the United Methodist Church, 1968–72, put his finger on the symptom. He explained his first impression of the town, "I got the feeling it was kind of nestled there in the mountains. They had their own life there and they enjoyed it, and in a way it could have been a community that kind of escapes from what is going on in the rest of the world." Four years later he felt the same way. Durango was a very easy place to hide out in, with a pleasant life-style. Like it or not, Day's view hit the target.

It should not be construed that the mountain-ringed valley was truly shielded from the rest of the world. The *Herald* offered unusually good coverage for a small-town newspaper of what was transpiring, particularly in Vietnam. Its editorials, at their best, dealt sharply and incisively with local, national, and international issues. Water problems were a recurring theme, and on July 3, 1967, the *Herald* prophetically forecast, "The longer they [Animas–La Plata and Dolores projects] wait, the less likely their chance of being built." Occasionally, too, the outside world dropped into Durango.

A reporter described his visit (October 13, 1969) to a "hippie" bus stalled in town on the way to a California rally. The "dirty, shaggy haired, filthy" occupants evoked this bit of journalism: "In the hour and a half I spent with them, I ruined my appetite for several weeks, I think. . . . "

The progressiveness of the college's move did not set a precedent for these years. There resided in Durango a group referred to as the "aginners," described this way: "No matter what issue came up, they were against any progress in the community because they were a very conservative group that was dead set against anything that [might involve] tax money." Although they fought the college issue to a loss, they won the day in an earlier fight over a community building/tourist center.

Al Ruland, a leader in the attempt to build the center, remembered it well:

That was back in 1952—we had no facilities in Durango to handle conventions, and a lot of us thought conventions would be very important to the economy [impressed by the Lamar Community Building]. . . . We had no facility like that around here. So a bunch of us were sitting around one day and we said, "Dammit, let's do it."

Working hard to arouse community interest, they convinced the city and county together to underwrite it partially and guarantee payments. A private nonprofit organization would build and operate it. The versatile building's primary purpose was to lure smaller conventions, in the 500–700 range. The center was to be multipurpose, paid for by municipal bonds. The auditorium could be converted for recreational ice skating, basketball games, and community concerts. When the bonds were retired, ownership would continue to be in private hands, with control held by a board of private, city, and county appointees.

Enter now the "aginners," headed by lawyer Lewis M. Perkins. "They started raising hell about it," Ruland commented, directing their ire especially at the public financing. A decidedly favorable vote on a bond issue in no way suppressed their efforts as they took the issue into court. Undaunted by a defeat at the district court level, the "aginners" took the battle to the state Supreme Court. To the stunned dismay of the center's backers, the court struck down the funding plan as a "nefarious scheme" of "dangling plums" in front of the public. The bitterness of this struggle endured for years, compounded by the fact that the justice who wrote the majority opinion happened to be a friend of Perkins. The words he used were burned deeply into the memories of center supporters—they just happened to be the same ones used by Perkins in a letter to the local newspapers.

The community building concept died, though not from lack of support or need. A small group frustrated the will of the community leaders, and of the rank and file as well. This was not a case of the old guard fighting upstart newcomers. "Aginners" drew their hardcore support from across these lines. Their numbers rose and fell according to the issue. One thing was certain. They could be counted on to make a heated protest when their interests were threatened.

Some of their objections were based upon a conservative attitude toward financial issues; some on a desire to keep Durango as it was, an early indication of the subsequently characterized "last settler syndrome," where the door is slammed to newcomers to maintain a community status quo; some on a political "down east" conservatism; and some, without question, on a dislike for change, compounded by a flood of fears as to what changes might mean to each individual. However they might be analyzed, the "aginners" evolved into a force to be reckoned with in the years after 1945. One of their favorite vehicles of protest came to be letters to the editor, which, if some future writer decided to use them as a sampling of public opinion, would produce a warped view of the community.

Nothing was new in this. Since the days of 1880 people with similar attitudes and fears had resided here. It was just that change had rushed in so fast after the war that these individuals found more common concerns and were agitated into action. The pace did not slacken in the 1970s.

For all their postulating, the "aginners" raised a serious, fundamental question: was change, equated with growth, good for Durango? As the 1960s passed, a small number of individuals mulled over that very issue. Long unchallenged, almost an eleventh commandment, growth received its first thoughtful questioning. Timidly at first, questions were raised about the impact growth might have on the quality of life. Was change good? Were the very things people sought to find in Durango, and conversely to escape from by coming to the community, being lost because so many people were coming? The evidence for answers was starting to accumulate, but the sixties produced no answers, simple or complex. Much that mattered to Durango and Durangoans rode on the outcome of this discussion, and the situation deteriorated as the deliberations wore on.

Although the tourist center may have lost out, tourism continued to thrive, as we have seen. It is not the increased employment opportunities or profits that are of interest here, rather the image Durango projected to visitors. After years of trying to eradicate the traces of the frontier years, the tide turned in the 1930s—suddenly the Old West heritage was salable. The change was evident in advertising, parade floats, mounting interest in the train, and by the reincarnation of the maligned saloon, best typified by the Diamond Belle in the Strater. Tourists ate it up. After several generations of the "gunsmoke and gallop" frontier, Americans came to believe that the fictional Hollywood West was the real thing. They expected to see it, and businessmen and the Chamber showed no hesitancy to oblige them.

The eminent western historian Walter Prescott Webb hit the mark when he observed that the Western allows the reader to dream about what he would like to do and then watch it acted out in a legendary setting. Durango's frontier past was not too far removed, certainly not yet lost. Infatuated railroader Lucius Beebe, on one of his jaunts, saw in the Durango of 1946 that "tough, rough, rugged nature" of the American West, including numerous saloons catering to "universal" drinking habits. Though his was a shallow impression focusing only on the facade, Beebe had emphasized just what the tourist wanted to see. As the frontier faded beyond memory, romanticism blurred reality.

Durango attempted to live off a legend, a legend that never actually existed. The gunfights, the glamorous red-light district, the heroic cowboys, and the days of simple rights and wrongs lived only in imagination, a glory that never was. In a sense, the community sought to manufacture a heritage and, in doing so, was derailed. Truth was replaced by legend and the potential for profit. This aberrance would undoubtedly have brought grimaces to the faces of the Graden, Camp, Porter crowd. In all probability, though, they would have understood. The profit motive reigns universal throughout Durango's story.

Durango, the city of the silver San Juan, had come full circle. When it finally stopped trying to imitate the East, it found its western heritage. After erasing the memory of less refined days, it suddenly rediscovered in them something glamorous. Of course, in so doing, it cleaned, polished, and molded those days into the image they "should" have had.

As tourists found Durango a scenic place, so did Hollywood. Even the name *Durango* was immediately recognizable as western. Before Hollywood ever appeared on location, the name lit up marquees: *Durango Valley Raiders* (1938) *The Durango Kid* (1940), and *The Return of the Durango Kid* (1945). Horse-oaters to the final gunfight, they captivated Saturday matinee youngsters and Western-loving adults. The good guy always triumphed and was even allowed to kiss the heroine on rare occasions.

From the late 1940s through the mid-1950s, Hollywood came to Durango, not for its name but for its scenery. A succession of films was partially or totally shot in the area, providing local stagestruck hams with the opportunity to indulge their dramatic proclivities as extras. *Across the Wide Missouri* brought that handsomest of leading men, Clark Gable, to the Molas Lake region (he loved the local fishing). *Night Passage* starred Jimmy Stewart and included Colorado Senator Ed Johnson, re-creating his one-time occupation as a telegrapher. The cast of *Around the World in 80 Days* briefly jumped aboard the Silverton train. In 1950 the personnel involved in *Ticket to Tomahawk* spent "eight long weeks" in Durango, according to bored star Anne Baxter. A then unknown bit player, Marilyn Monroe, who, in Baxter's words, "was eminently braless," attracted a lot of local attention. The movie was shot on the mesa where the college now stands and in Silverton.

Hollywood came and left, just as the oil and smelter people had done. Why? The spectacular scenery, with its endless possibilities for western movie settings, remained. Baxter's acid comments on the community provide insight: "All of us lived in Durango at the Royal Motel, a euphemism, and ate at the local greasy spoon called the Chief Diner." Tourists in Silverton interfered with production and stared at the actors as if they were lodged in a zoo. Leading man Dan Dailey loathed it and was finally provoked into a fit of rage. "Suddenly, Dan danced up to a cluster, shoved his face viciously forward like a striking snake and hissed, 'They feed us at four!' "

Some local merchants earned a reputation for charging all the market would bear. Not until the 1970s did Hollywood come back. By that time national motel chains, which would not arbitrarily raise prices, were on the scene to provide recognized accommodations. Better airline connections also alleviated the old bedeviler, isolation, which frustrated even Hollywood. Durango's ambition to become a second Hollywood withered. Not so the name, which reemerged in 1957 in *Decision at Durango* and *Gun Duel in Durango*, thereby keeping the town's name, if not its location, before the public.

The town, simply unready to cope with Hollywood's demands, had itself partly to blame; greed proved decisively shortsighted. Although the alliance was broken, each side had gained something. Hollywood profited from the films, several of which were carried by the scenery, not the story. Durango received publicity, some profit, and a strengthening of the western legend, which enhanced tourism.

All of these—oil, Hollywood, tourism, college, scenery—brought more people to Durango, an urbanized oasis in rural southwestern Colorado. As a result, it continued to be second in size only to Grand Junction on the Western Slope, though both communities lagged far behind the Eastern Slope leaders.

Trappings of mid-twentieth-century urban America arrived with increased urbanization. Like them or not, there was no avoiding them. Main Avenue's tinseled tawdry strip, after it passed beyond the old Fassbinder Addition, grew into a neon, plastic, sign-polluted midway by the end of the sixties, as motels, restaurants, and service stations scrambled to cash in on the tourist dollar. Traffic, which once had been heavy (relatively speaking) only after the train chugged in, now could be found lined up behind the traffic lights that were sprinkled along both Main Avenue and Sixth Street. New subdivisions—Crestview, Riverview, and Animas Heights—covered hills where sagebrush and scrub oak had once been king and sheep had grazed. Home-owned stores found themselves hard pushed to compete with national chain motels, quick order restaurants, groceries, and retail stores. The small corner grocery all but disappeared; the Circle K and 7-2-11 stores that replaced them offered little of the personality of their predecessors. If you walked through one, you knew them all. Durango was taking on the appearance of hundreds of other tourist-oriented towns, particularly for the tourists who stayed only for one night. Only the surrounding mountains and the meandering Animas River distinguished the town from the other stops along their route.

Crime advanced slowly during these years. The earlier custom of leaving one's house unlocked followed the horse and buggy into oblivion, as the population ballooned and community cohesiveness fractured. Old-time neighborliness in a Durango of 3,000 to 4,000 residents became rarer. Residents of Animas Heights did not often drop over for an evening's chat with those on Fifth Avenue and were separated from Crestview by the river and valley.

The population increase and the transitory residence of many of the new Durangoans fragmented society more than ever before. Ned Wallace commented, "[The influx of oil people] changed . . . the total social, economic, political description of Durango rather rapidly." The "select" group shifted just as rapidly, as new groups and institutions came and went. As long as the oil people were here, the Petroleum Club at the Strater held sway, for example. Even the churches were affected, if such a thing is possible in religion. For instance, into the late 1960s, according to one Durangoan, the Presbyterian was the "in" church. The trend of change, noticeable a generation before, reached full flower and swept away remnants of the nineteenth century, including such physical survivals as the old county courthouse. It came crashing down in the name of progress, mourned by a small (but vocal) minority. In its place rose a hybrid elongated box.

Costs of city government escalated, as more streets, sewers, water mains, and services were added. And new city hall and fire/police buildings showed Durango had come of age. The school system creaked under the weight of an exploding population and was saved when voters in 1954 and 1957 approved school construction bonds for $1,500,000. Miller Junior High and Riverview and Needham elementaries met the needs of the new subdivisions. The oil people had an impact here, too. Walt Mason, principal at Needham, commented, "They were outstanding people, and I probably had one of the best student bodies of an elementary school. . . . They just had advantages that other kids did not have because they had traveled, a lot of them extensively. They were well acquainted with books." The need for a new high school confronted divided opinions, and there the matter rested as the sixties closed.

To live in this "paradise" was becoming more costly each year; taxes moved upward, as did the cost of living and of real estate. Some people went to Farmington to shop, claiming the reduced prices more than compensated for the extra travel expenses. Isolation and high shipping costs were blamed for Durango's plight, a charge now nearly as old as the hills. A whispering campaign tried to lay the blame on profiteering merchants. The charges brought no change.

Growth, higher crime, increased living costs, Durango experienced them all, just as other similarly developing American communities did. Meanwhile, the promotional beat went on, increasing in tempo. "Come to Play, You'll Want to Stay," rhymed the Chamber in 1954. "Anyone willing to work can make a living here," sang out the First National Bank two years before. Easy, ideal, fun—what more could a potential resident ask? Surrounding photographs of the train, Diamond Circle Theatre, and an overview of the town was this 1964 slogan, "A Wonderful Place to Visit—A *Better* Place to Live." And the *Herald* published an annual booster edition that exuded local pride and advertised attractions. Perhaps it was best summed up by Chamber of Commerce publicity of 1969: "We think Durango has great potential. . . . In short, Durango is a city just beginning to move. This is your opportunity to get in on what is developing into a dynamic city, which is part of a dynamic region and state."

The campaign succeeded so well that the seeds it sowed threatened an underlying theme of the boosterism, Durango's long cherished quality of life. The definition of quality of life had evolved over the years and still obviously depended on individual perception, but certain characteristics gave it meaning. To a large degree, middle-class norms and fads defined its shape. Outdoor and recreational activities jumped tremendously in the 1960s: skiing, for example, and the city recreational programs. Much of the credit for the latter goes to the first director, "a one-man band," Dolph Kuss, and to innovative Leon Burrows, who enlarged the program to the point that it became one of the best in the country for a town of Durango's size. Where once a community center had been planned, a city/county swimming pool appeared. Fort Lewis College sponsored plays, concerts, lectures, and other programs that provided a broader and richer cultural experience than had been known before. Opportunities and facilities had improved dramatically since 1945, and all served to raise the quality of life.

With the construction of the Community Hospital and complete remodeling and enlargement of Mercy, Durango took a giant step medically. For a town of its size it was well supplied with doctors, dentists, and other medical personnel. It was also "well churched." After a lull of several decades, the churches regained some of their strength and community importance, following a nationwide trend. The school system, too, was good from elementary through high school, and beyond for those who decided to venture up the hill to continue their education. Somehow it seemed more adventuresome to go elsewhere, and many a local high school student tried his luck some place else before returning to the Fort.

However, other aspects had deteriorated since World War II. Durango was becoming crowded, and physical decline threatened some of the older sections, both commercial and residential. Available land, suitable for homes, in the river plain was all but gone, and development started to creep up the hillsides and beyond. What happened to the Animas Valley is already known. Each new construction altered the view and threatened the ecology just a little bit more.

The small-town feeling, good or bad, perished under the oil and tourist crush. Durangoans sought something to take its place. The multitude of problems discussed in this and the preceding chapters chiseled away at the quality of life, making it not quite so pleasant to live in this oasis of southwestern Colorado. And over all hung the threat of potential water shortages.

If the quality of life had its ups and downs for the dominant white middle class, what about minorities, primarily the Mexican-American community? Race relations improved after the war. Ken Periman, Gilbert Lujan, and Max Gomez agreed that the change came with the return of the veterans and a more open feeling generated by the war. Little things started to make a difference, like a voluntary boycott of bars that refused to serve Mexican Americans, instigated by vets at the old Fort Lewis campus. "The situation," Periman laughed, "certainly got better very rapidly." Lujan went further. Attitudes changed when the children of the 1930s and 1940s grew up. "They [older people] just didn't understand each other but as we grew up we saw how each other lived and there wasn't that much difference. . . . Sports helped. . . . Main thing was people didn't understand each other; it was strange." Arthur Ballantine, who had been observing changes from his *Herald* desk since 1952, concurred: "I've seen a notable improvement over the last twenty years [to 1974] in Durango's attitude towards the Spanish."

Most people showed signs of increased sensitivity. The *Herald-News* and KIUP sponsored a contest to choose a new name for Mexican Flats, a "hideous term," as banker Camp said. It was symbolic of the whole problem, however, that the name selected, El Patio, soon dropped out of use, just as the whole question of subsistence-level housing was purged from the minds of many. Santa Rita became the label for the territory south of town—a rural slum by any other name still existed.

Art Gomez, who moved to Durango in 1956, was most impressed by the openness of the people, especially the children. Yet he found racism, if not overt, still there. "You don't know where it's coming from. You don't know who it is, specifically; all you know is it happened." Ballantine called it an "unconscious prejudice." With a tinge of bitterness, Gomez saw it surface in the high school athletic teams. Relations made progress during the postwar generation, and from the Anglo view they seemed ideal. The Mexican Americans saw roads that still needed to be traveled. One disturbing statistic was the tendency of the latter group to drop out of school before graduation. Legislation could not solve this problem. Solutions had to be found in human nature, individually, and if past experience taught anything, they would not be easy.

The other numerically significant racial minority, the neighboring Southern Utes, drifted out of the picture. An Aspen man who played the piano in a local bar, recalled Durango in the 1950s as being full of Indians with plenty of money. One 300-pound Ute woman enjoyed hearing the "Banks of Minnetonka," a request "you don't refuse," he said with a chuckle. They came by the pickup load for the weekend, bought plenty of whiskey, and often slept off a binge on the flatcars standing on the railroad siding. This reminiscence was not what Durangoans wanted to remember.

But a cultural change was not long in coming. The Utes regained tribal pride and started to focus more of their life around Ignacio, a tricultural community. The growth of this village also kept them home for their entertainment and shopping. Over the years, too, they adopted more modern dress, looking less like tourist-imagined Indians and therefore blending into the Main Avenue crowd. By the end of the sixties the Utes resembled most other Durango visitors, and more were enrolling in Fort Lewis College.

By 1969, Durango, going on ninety years old, was a pretty spry four-score and ten. Tourism thrived, the college was growing, construction hummed, and satisfaction seemed to permeate every corner. Considering that this was a decade of national turbulence, such tranquility was remarkable. Most likely, it reflected the national norm more than did the upheavals featured on the TV news, which grabbed attention in Durango and the rest of the country. Nonetheless, much had changed recently, and an undercurrent of uneasiness about the future lay just beneath the surface of the "dynamic city."

A strange mixture it was—of old and new, of change, and of trying to recapture the lost. Durango had not been remade in an entirely new image, but just as certainly it was not the town of 1945.

PART FIVE

Where There Is No Vision
1970-1979

Where there is no vision, the people perish: . . .

Proverbs 29:18

14. Crossroads of Dissent

Durango in the 1970s approached a crossroad in its community journey. The changes of the past twenty years had hastened the approach, but few were sure just where the town was going. And change still came. So, too, came reaction and dissent, which whirled around like a dust devil, touching individuals and groups here and there. They responded and tempers often rose. It seemed that few were satisfied in what only recently had been described as a near Eden in southwestern Colorado.

The city finally had to face the problems of growth. Durango had caught up with the majority of urban America. But the supposed lack of growth could still cause grief—a humorous predicament in some ways. Horror of horrors, the census bureau reported after the 1970 count that 197 fewer people resided here than a decade earlier! Growth advocates and boosters were stunned. How could such a thing have happened when there were more telephones, toilets, electrical outlets, and who knows what all to show that blessed growth had not stopped? The furor subsided after self-righteous rationalizations "proved" that the census was in error. Then, in 1978, La Plata County was selected for a trial run for the 1980 census. It happened again! This time moans were heard, not because growth had not occurred but because it did not look like enough. City officials and others insisted major mistakes had been made. The comedy of errors showed that the persistent "grow or die" philosophy had not perished. To love Durango meant to love growth, according to a particular segment of the population.

Perhaps the census bureau made mistakes on both occasions, yet that was not the real question. The issue was fairly drawn between those who insisted that growth held the key to the future and those who wanted to preserve some of the qualities that made the community a pleasant place in which to live.

Each side had its points; this was not a clear-cut, black-and-white issue. Growth would supply more permanent jobs, a larger tax base. It also would provide, as the *Today*, July 12, 1978, explained, more federal aid, especially revenue sharing, and make it easier to attract industry. Hence the emotional interest in those census figures. Anything that could do these things would be beneficial; anything less might mean recession in an area that already had its depressed pockets.

Arthur Ballantine, in a 1974 interview, presented the argument for "controlled" growth. He was not one of those who wanted Durango to stay "as it has always been." "I think we need growth. It's got to be the right kind of growth, controlled growth, but unless Durango goes ahead to grow there's not going to be a sufficient economic basis to support the people who want to live here." Ballantine saw young people being attracted to other places because of limited opportunities. That had caused consternation for years.

Opponents were not at all convinced. To them the very nature of the Durango they had grown to love was in danger of disappearing forever under an avalanche of growth. The echo of earlier protests can be heard clearly through the din. Only the times and people changed. Little common ground was found between the two factions.

Much more emotional, more controversial, was the split over zoning, which involved the same question of the future. The lines of battle crossed urban and rural ones. No simple characterizations can be drawn. People who considered growth good thought that zoning was the answer to keeping it in check. Those who presumed growth to be harmful believed that zoning deprived individuals of their freedom.

Both county and city formed planning groups or hired agencies. Public meetings generated controversy and few resolved anything. Planning took a back seat to bickering. Tragically, the fate of the future ran last in the race for individualism, emotionalism, and profit.

Moreover, town and county could not agree; zoning sundered their relationship. But that was not all. They argued over local control, bond issues, taxation, and the future. For the rural spokesmen it was a discouraging fight; Durango and the city-oriented county residents could outvote them with ease, if necessary. Indicative of this trend was the vote on the airport bond issue; county residents voted "no," only to be swamped by the urbanites. Actually, La Plata County was much more rural than the state average; statistics, however, can be misleading. People were moving to the county in increasing numbers, showing where the population that Durango thought it should have probably went.

In reality, for all their hate-love feuding, La Plata County and Durango were becoming one and the same. The county commissioners and city council showed commendable foresight in working together on some common problems. Many of their constituents did not march to the same beat. Until the two groups could sit down and hammer out agreeable solutions to their interlocking problems, the course of the relationship promised to be rocky. Old-time bromides about rugged frontier individualism, bucolic rural and decadent urban America had to be discarded; they should have gone with the horse and buggy.

The issues proved as complex as the emotions generated: individual rights vs. community rights; government "red tape" regulation vs. private enterprise; urban vs. rural; planning vs. chaos; and, from the developers' view, higher costs vs. economy. Heated exchanges, "screaming meetings," as one participant described them, were the outcome. Two letters, among many, to the *Herald* illustrate the depth of feeling:

> Outside planners who plan the use of private property, even though they are
> paid for this activity from tax monies, and other individuals who attempt to

subject the use of private property to consensus decisions are engaged in an illegitimate activity. . . . (Dec. 23, 1977)

Land use regulation is nothing more than an attempt by the majority of Americans [urban] to draw the line on subsidies to a vocal and demanding minority [rural]. . . . Land use regulations will always be flawed and unjust. . . . [County Commissioners] deserve a great deal of credit for their efforts to assure that local land use regulations are as fair and as uncomplicated as possible. (Dec. 29, 1977)

The struggle went on and on. Over it all presided a regional planning agency, damned if it did, damned if it didn't. Exasperated by the intolerable situation, planner Lynn Vandegrift resigned in July 1977, with parting shots at "vocal groups," too-hasty action, and lip service to planning. His successors made little more headway. In an interview in November, Vandegrift dissected the problem. La Plata County displayed a classic Colorado pattern of development with too little effort toward real planning until it was too late. Then came the frantic effort to correct what had already been done wrong, while many resisted planning in the name of private enterprise. The area, he feared, would pay the price and someday look just like sprawling Boulder or Fort Collins.

Still the cry went on for growth and more growth. Both sides had their heroes and villains, developers perhaps being painted in the darkest hues. Once hailed as prophets of prosperity, they now were vilified as land-grabbing, greedy, self-centered materialists, who raped the land, made their profits, and ran. There were just enough shoddy, if not actually crooked, practitioners in the business to give substance to the charges. To them, in town and county, zoning was anathema.

Angry residents tried to forestall some of the unlicensed excesses, with mixed results. The fight over the Hill Top View Estates was one example. In 1976 and 1977 the developer fought through a series of bitter hearings with alarmed nearby residents of Animas Heights before finally obtaining permission to level a small neighborhood hill. Brought into sharp focus were county and city subdivision regulations, land-use concepts, and growth philosophies. Unfortunately for the residents, the zoning laws proved inadequate to prevent the rape; and the added cost and delay ruined the developer. Nobody won, everybody lost, notably the land and environment, which were being continually modified and pressured by actions such as these.

These fights had been long in coming, and now the city suffered the results of its earlier ostrichlike stands. More surprising were the hassles involving the school board, administrators, teachers, and public. Contested board elections and debates over policies and construction were not unknown in the past. They were not like those of the 1970s, however. Teachers found themselves at odds with the board on several occasions over such issues as dismissals and recognition of the Durango Education Association as a bargaining agency. Threats of a strike, when salary negotiations stalled, lost the teachers some of their public support and changed attitudes toward the profession. Attendance policies and other issues put the public, administrators, and the board at odds, even relegating the zoning fights to a back page on occasion. The intensity of feeling was shown by a landslide rejection of a 1976 mill levy for school district funding.

Studies and reports attempted to find solutions, an emotional task. At the least, they kept communication channels open and offered hope for better relations in the future.

Downtown, the Heritage for Tomorrow Committee examined ideas to preserve the architectural style and business nature of the area before it went the way of many other central business districts. The group formulated plans, held hearings (Durangoans seemed to hold meetings at the slightest provocation, frequently with the slightest results), and generated controversy of its own. What it promised was to lead, not to dictate, as had been so often charged of those agencies promoting zoning. The plans were promising, the idea sound, but no groundswell supported adoption.

Such concern came none too soon. Durango retained a magnificent Victorian business and residential area, which it could have lost to development, as had Denver and so many other cities. The Heritage for Tomorrow Committee achieved one goal—awareness—and that was good. They were actively supported in creating interest by the La Plata County Historical Society and local people who gave talks and slide shows on history and architecture. Ned Wallace explained his concern: "That's one of the reasons I was so strong for a central business district plan. To make every attempt not only to preserve it physically, but to preserve it as the economic center of this immediate area. . . ." He worried about the typical suburb-shopping-center pattern emerging. Everybody worried about lack of parking.

Wallace's concern proved timely. Already the movement for decentralization was starting, and shopping centers were rumored for outlying areas. The United Methodist Church moved from Third Avenue to Animas Heights, and only at the last moment was the old church building not sold for a commercial enterprise. If other Third Avenue churches followed suit, but ended up selling their holdings, much of the charm of the old avenue would be dissipated. Architecturally, Main looks much as it did seventy years ago, a fragile appearance that a few glass and metal concoctions would ruin. The turning point came perhaps in 1974 with the fire and the building of the Main Mall in the same general architectural style. The site could have gone the way of parking lots or a modern out-of-character building. One need only contemplate the government office building on Camino del Rio to shudder at what might have happened.

The August 1974 fire, the most costly since 1889, destroyed much of the west side of Main's 800 block and claimed the lives of a fireman and a policeman; it resulted from arson. Instrumental in the rebuilding effort was Lester Gardenswartz. He had this to say about why he did it. Unintentionally, perhaps, he said much about the spirit that made Durango.

> Well, because I love my town. That's the main reason. I'm not saying it is my town, but I love it here. It's been my home. Durango has been good to us. . . .

> It is a beautiful mall—it's well done—it looks like it has been there for a hundred years. . . . I think it saved downtown Durango.

> There will always be a Main Street in Durango because of the way the river splits the town. There will always be a downtown Durango; there may

be one or two shopping centers on the outskirts, but there will always be a downtown.

As an illustration of what can be done with a little foresight and consideration, the Main Mall stands nearly alone in recent years. Located in the heart of downtown, it just may have saved the area, as Gardenswartz claimed.

Meanwhile, at city hall, City Manager Robert Rank, who came to that office in 1960, assumed the role of community lightning rod for the various public outbursts. Rank became a scapegoat for much of the discontent over the policies and actions of city government. A center of controversy in the mid-seventies, he stayed on. Malcontents found in the city charter that they had the right to recall the city manager. Recall petitions forced a 1977 election, which Rank survived by a substantial margin.

His problems reflected those of the city government and council. As the community grew, so did its problems. Zoning, the site of the city dump, water, street maintenance, recreation, water meters, crime, taxes—the list goes on. Citizens brought their complaints to meetings, and the harassed council members reacted as they thought best. Their reactions did not satisfy everybody, and sometimes nobody. As Mayor Maxine Peterson noted, "The council needs to develop its own goals. We need a better picture of what we want so we can make sure it happens, rather than just reacting." Each individual resident seemed to have his own idea of how that should be done.

Sometimes, scathing comments were couched in humor, as illustrated by this "Ode to a Durango Spring," which appeared in the *Herald*, April 2, 1978:

> I guess potholes are here to stay
> I doubt they'll ever go away.
> It matters not how large or small,
> My vehicle seems drawn to all.

The author, Mary Downey, called attention to a decades-old problem, which had grieved her predecessors almost from Durango's beginnings. It just seemed worse now. More serious were the hotly contested council elections during the seventies. Challengers came forth who wanted to test their ideas in the caldron of council sessions.

In town, out of town—Durangoans had their pick of burning issues. Some of them were upset at the idea of having a regional airport to serve Farmington, Durango, and Cortez; when this plan was scuttled, some others became agitated over the cost, necessity, and importance of enlarging La Plata Field. Voters finally approved a bond issue to remodel it into a jetport, which opened in November 1977. The renovation did not improve service, and Frontier Airlines was raked unmercifully by irate customers for poor or nonexistent service.

Discontent and dissent were evident in a multitude of other causes, some of which involved only a few Durangoans, others a majority of them. Unionization of workers at Mercy Hospital fueled a fire and prompted several employees' elections. Creation of a paving district to improve streets and alleys incited some land owners to petition and speak strongly against it in mid-1978. Their objections dwelled on the cost to individuals, not on the value of improvements. The new high school finally was constructed after an emotionally charged debate over abandonment of the older building and the suitability of the new site. The rising price of land and homes brought joy to realtors and sellers, dismay and disappointment to buyers. Leadership or lack of it raised hackles, one person hissing the epithet "Mainstreet Barricudas" when referring to who ran the town. In the end, the controversies were bound to rub Durangoans raw, as would a sandstorm, and so they did. Complex problems do not lend themselves generally to simple solutions. And as the going got harder, so did the choices. The gusts buffeted the community.

What about Durango and its people? All life did not pivot around dissent and issue-oriented matters. One noticeable trait was that most people remained remarkably tranquil and conciliatory in the face of so much controversy. No one took to the streets, and almost invariably (once the race had been decided) they could get back together on other issues.

The census of 1970 found that among those residents it tabulated, 93 percent were of native American parentage, over half of them born in Colorado. Less than half had lived in the same residence five years before, indicating the transitory nature of the population. The largest minority group, some 18 percent of the population, were those identified as Spanish-surnamed. They, too, showed the same mobile tendencies and an even higher percentage of native born. Homogeneity seemed to have arrived.

In the last few years Durango has witnessed an influx of a younger, perhaps more idealistic, group of settlers, one reason, surely, for the clashes over environment and zoning. Young vs. old, old-timer vs. newcomer, idealism vs. materialism—the points of conflict are many. They settled in town and in the county and the least that may be said is that they rocked the establishment. Not all were satisfied, and some moved on. Don Hughes departed with this blast in a letter to the *Herald*, February 26, 1978. Among the things that angered him: "Housing that cannot be afforded; high prices; surly clerks; 'fellowship' instead of leadership; and most of all, I am tired of a town of loners."

That last accusation was interesting. Durango has always prided itself as a friendly community. With increased size, however, the old-time neighborliness became endangered. Durango, as local writer Sandy Thompson observed, was really a series of communities, each one tied together by its common interests—professional, college, business, poor, middle-income, employed, unemployed, retired, and property owners. All of these elements resulted in fragmentation, and as Thompson sagely noted, "make us very much urban" in the modern American sense. Apparently Hughes, as an example, did not feel that he belonged.

Another factor in the decline of neighborliness was the increase of crime. It shot up rapidly in the late sixties and increased through the next decade. After a particularly gruesome murder of a young woman, a long time resident said, "We once were a nice little city, now that can be shortened to little city." The statement said a lot about what had happened to Durango.

Perhaps it would be fairer to say that communitywide neighborliness changed, to be replaced, at least in some sectors, by a block or street neighborhood. Donna Jones and her husband were attracted to Durango in 1967 because the scenery and the "small town nature" appealed to them. For her at least, the "neighborhood spirit," a "closeness," continues to exist in her portion of Third Avenue. Interestingly, this is precisely what the area south of Sixth Street once offered earlier arrivals. It is not unreasonable to project that this type of smaller neighborhood will become the core of personal relationships, rather than larger Durango. In this, it would be following an urban American pattern.

One interesting deviation from the usual urban western pattern for cities of similar size was the extraordinarily large number of professional people who settled here. This trend, noted earlier, became more pronounced, probably for the same reasons that the predecessors of these professionals were attracted. Durango was endowed with an outstanding medical and dental community; and they were augmented by lawyers, teachers, engineers, and professional people of all kinds. This population made itself felt subtly in voting patterns, community involvement, and cultural activities. They were better educated, higher paid, and more involved than the average person. They stood in the forefront of many of the fights described earlier and worked behind the scenes elsewhere. Despite some grumblings and inevitable jealousy, Durango has been fortunate to secure such a talented group.

In contrast, one factor that became less noticeable in the 1970s was poverty. It did not go away. It was just that urban renewal, aided by arsonists, extinguished the Santa Rita section once and for all. Its residents were scattered into several areas of town, and low-cost apartments were built to provide residences for them. The area beyond Sixth Street still retained its reputation for being a lower income district, but the stigma of earlier times disappeared; and the line, which one group or another previously did not cross without courting trouble, vanished. Though poverty remained, it lacked its prior visibility. For some people this meant that it had gone away and no longer needed to be a concern.

Leonel Silva, who did much to develop the Durango Housing Corporation and its apartment house complexes, believed that the racial situation improved on all fronts in the seventies. Realistically, he conceded there was bound to be a certain percentage of prejudice against Blacks, women, Spanish-surnamed, or whatever group challenged, or seemed to threaten, the dominant majority. Prejudice did not come totally from without; it emanated from within these groups themselves as well. Silva saw more educational and economic discrimination, rather than purely racial or cultural. Durango was a very good town to raise a family in, he concluded, an ideal environment. Just the fact that he could make such a statement showed how far the community attitude toward minorities had matured.

Many things remained the same. Some jobs stayed seasonal, unskilled, and low paid. Efforts to attract light, nonpolluting industry failed to have an impact on broadening the employment market. One of the largest employers was the federal government, by virtue of the multitude of agencies created since World War II. Unions made no more inroads than they ever had in this primarily nonunion town. The energy scare of the early seventies renewed interest in local low-grade coal deposits, which started just beyond the city limits and extended to Gallup, New Mexico. What potential for strip mining! Rumors, investigation, and a couple of small underground operations kept the industry alive. Expectations of exploitation were reminiscent of turn-of-the-century days. Only time and the worsening national energy problems might possibly tell, maybe even dictate, what would happen locally.

Tourists drove on their merry way, in spite of gas shortages and price hikes. The charm, family-oriented activities, scenery, and "old-timey town" feeling appealed to the Jack Eberls of Escondido, California, and hundreds of thousands of others. And it was well that it did, geared as the community was toward this now year-round business. In 1970 Durango had forty-four hotels and motels, plus restaurants, gas stations, tourist shops, and the train, all of which relied largely, if not exclusively, on visitors for a living. By the late seventies, over 120,000 people were riding the D&RGW to Silverton, and more went to Mesa Verde. Isolation no longer stood as a barrier. The car, bus, plane, motorcycle, bike, and foot overcame it for those determined to reach Durango.

Purgatory grew steadily to become the major ski resort in southwestern Colorado. The enlargement of the airport promised even more skiers, as did the improvement of motel and hotel accommodations in town and at Purgatory, including condominiums. The construction of the exclusive resort, Tamarron, north of town on the way to the ski area, opened new vistas. Looking back over the years since Tamarron's opening in December 1974, one of its planners and builders, Stan Wadsworth, said much about tourism and its future.

> Well, we liked it very much when we were here [previous visits], number one, and number two, the more we began to think about it, we thought there were a lot of possibilities in building a resort that had both the summer and winter season, to make as much of a twelve-month season as you could possibly get. . . .

> Durango is one of the largest, if not the most successful tourist areas in the state of Colorado, summer I'm talking about. . . . Then it had Purgatory in the winter.

> The more we looked at the property the more we were convinced that was what we had to have to build. To do anything that wouldn't lend itself to that land would be a crime, really. . . . We spent a great deal of time and effort planning Tamarron so that it would fit into the property as best as it can. That's a big project.

That *was* a big project, and thanks to an awareness of the environment and quality of life, this major development did blend into the site and met its developers' goals.

The airport, Purgatory, and Tamarron all interrelated in the plan to promote Durango as a tourist area and give support to the industry as a year-round business. Although business was still slower in winter than in summer, a much better balance was achieved than ever before.

These improvements did not guarantee refinement of the image the visitor might receive. This gem of misinformation appeared in an article about Tamarron in the June 1976, issue of *Travel:* "Finally, we entered the town of Durango, once an Indian trading

center, then a wild boom town supported by the many silver mines in the area. . . . "
Either the writer with the overly active imagination or the informant ought to have
been lynched on the spot.

In the meantime, the Denver and Rio Grande was entertaining inquiries about
selling its narrow-gauge line. Claiming still that "we don't belong in the entertainment
business," president Gale Aydelott called attention to the investment and expenses for
upkeep, insurance, and the like, which exceeded income. Few Durangoans seriously
considered the possible ramifications if the train ownership changed or if it quit
operating.

Voters rocked no political boats (See Table 2). Louis Newell, in a *Herald* editorial,

Table 2

VOTING PATTERNS IN LA PLATA COUNTY, PRESIDENTIAL ELECTIONS, 1884–1976

	Democrats	Republicans	
*1884	44%	51%	
1888	47%	51%	
1892		34%	66% (Populist)
1896	96%	3%	
1900	81%	17%	
1904	43%	51%	
1908	53%	37%	9% (Socialist)
1912	50%	19%	18% (Bull Moose) 10% (Socialist)
1916	68%	27%	
1920	44%	50%	
1924	39%	38%	24% (Progressive)
1928	39%	60%	
1932	57%	38%	
1936	55%	42%	
1940	42%	57%	
1944	40%	60%	
1948	47%	51%	
1952	33%	66%	
1956	33%	67%	
1960	41%	59%	
1964	55%	44%	
1968	34%	57%	9% (American Independent)
1972	31%	62%	
1976	36%	59%	

*1884 was the first year Durangoans voted in a presidential election; the county vote jumped 2⅓ times over the 1880 total. No third party totals are given unless they received 8% of the vote. Percentages have been rounded to the nearest tenth. La Plata election data, except for 1976, were made available by the Inter-University Consortium for Political and Social Research.

As the dominant vote bloc in rural La Plata County, Durango's voting patterns are clearly reflected in these totals. Few third parties have made much impression since 1924, except for conservative votes in the past decade. No victories have been as decisive as Bryan's 1896 and 1900 sweeps, which mirrored the Colorado mining attitudes of the day. Durango shows primarily a middle-of-the-road, slightly conservative voting preference.

April 7, 1977, pretty well summarized the situation when commenting on the recent city election in which only 35 percent of the eligible voters turned out:

> Most of the people just don't care. Political Dullsville. Durango has a good city government. It is not as good as Bob Rank would have you think it is but it is still better than 65 percent of the voters deserve, the 65 percent who don't care how the city of Durango operates.

The business community, joined by the college-related people, dominated the council in the 1970s. Generally the business moved along routinely, although an emotional issue could keep the council in turmoil for several sessions. For a community of this size, the members provided conservative, competent, "safe" leadership, only rarely showing flashes of the brilliance needed to cut through the hoary traditions of the community and their office. Is this bad? Apparently not. Voters got the type of leadership they wanted from their elected officials. If it had not been for some emotional issues in the election Newell described, the vote percentage might have been lower. Unless the boat was rocked too much, Durangoans tolerated their city leadership and went about their business. The question might be fairly asked, why would anyone want to put up with the time demands and personality clashes that harassed council members' days and heckled their meetings? The office generated little enough respect or reward.

Table 3

POPULATION OF DURANGO AND ENVIRONS

Durango		Animas City	
1880	2,000 (December, estimated)	1880	286
1885	2,254 (Colorado census)	1885	83 (Colorado census)
1890	2,726	1890	180
1900	3,317	1900	154
1910	4,686	1910	200
1920	4,116	1920	250
1930	5,400	1930	457
1940	5,887	1940	712
1950	7,459		
1960	10,530		
1970	10,333		
1978	13,500 (estimated)		

Perins		Porter	
1910	80	1895	144 (estimated)
1913	200 (estimated)	1900	50 (estimated)
1920	137	1908	100 (estimated)
1926	150 (estimated)		

Population statistics are from the federal census unless otherwise indicated. The estimates for Porter and Perins were found in business directories. Porter was never reported as an individual community, only as a precinct.

Durango, with two exceptions, has shown growth in every census year. Postwar periods especially have been years of growth, with the greatest spurt in the fifteen years after World War II. The 1970s have the potential for the greatest numerical increase ever recorded for Durango.

Just who were the town leaders? C. R. Ellsworth, then head of the Chamber of Commerce, considered that question one October afternoon in 1976 with the author. He concluded that they came from various elements of the community and pointed out that a cross-section of banking and business people had joined to promote and develop the industrial park south of town. Others interviewed were not so sure just who was in control. Leadership generally seemed to be by committee. The fragmentation noticeable earlier now reached full flower. Several names were mentioned, usually ones connected with business and/or money, but no one appeared to be carrying the ball alone.

It was more fun to be one of the "grabbers or clutchers," as they might be defined, either on the prowl to gain something or protect what they had already gathered in the corral. This old struggle had continued unabated since 1880, with only new faces and new methods. Much of what has been previously discussed may be traced to this conflict, but Durango endured, a pawn in the outcome.

The quality of life advanced and retreated in the hands of the concerned or the unmindful. A clearer definition started to emerge, if not a consensus. For Durangoans, the quality of life included the natural environment, neighborliness of the people, cultural opportunities, recreation, "casual" pace of life, modern conveniences, and a safe place to live, with no overcrowding. A box score would show some gains made, more than balanced by regressions in other areas.

Here were the crucial questions as Durango's first century neared an end; they were a heritage of the past as surely as the railroad, Strater Hotel, and Carnegie's remodeled library. For a community simply to reach its centennial was not the salient point. What had been accomplished in those five score years was the important thing. Equally significant was where it might be headed in its second century.

15. Durango, Yesterday and Tomorrow: A Personal View

September 1978 came and went. Ninety-eight-year-old Durango slid past yet another birthday without the slightest notice. Amid the uproar of the seventies, maybe it did not seem important to remember times gone by. People did not notice as their town entered its ninety-ninth year, diverted as they were by a heated election campaign, name-calling over land-use planning, another familiar community fight (this time about the proposed Ninth Street bridge), continued abuse of elected officials, and mounting criticism of the Animas–La Plata Project. For all the bickering, the city remained a spry and lively near-centenarian. No one evidenced fear of decline or stabilization, only concern about where the future would lead the community.

One-hundred-thirty-five inches of snow later, the winter of 1978–79 finally loosed its snowy grip. A fifty-year-old snowfall record lay shattered; accurate records went back no farther. The new record may even have rivaled the one of 1883–84, which the *Southwest* called a "winter in 400 years." As the May sun brought flowers and grass back to life, the decade of the seventies was racing to its end. Concrete plans for two outlying shopping centers greeted the warm days, along with continued inflation and sharply rising gasoline prices. The tourist industry worried about possible impacts of the gas shortage and what the future might hold with the sale of the Denver and Rio Grande's narrow gauge line, now that a buyer seemed to have been found. It was a season of uncertainty; only the Purgatory ski area, which had just completed a record year, could momentarily breathe a sigh of relief.

Durango, like much of America, had reached a watershed in its political life. For the better part of a decade the community had been rent by divisiveness—shouting, bitterness, and a proclivity for treating questions as simple black-and-white issues, agitated by an "I'm right, you're wrong" philosophy. The common reaction had become, "if the elected officials do not think my way, recall them." Single-issue champions galloped forth to tilt with the establishment, clothed in their own righteousness of narrow-mindedness, convinced that if the cause were resolved their way, everything would be set right. The Ninth Street bridge debate, petitions against water meters, and the zoning arguments illustrated this attitude as it ripped Durango.

Whatever happened to the old "give and take" philosophy of democracy, the ability to listen, to compromise and to grant willingly that the other side might have merit to its position? Respect, too, was lacking; each side glared at the other, hurling reckless epithets and accusations.

This was not the democratic system. Thoughtful people here and elsewhere wondered if government could survive such an ordeal. Colorado's Senator Gary Hart, on a visit, October 24, 1978, called attention to that very issue several times. Referring to its harmfulness to the country, state, and community, Hart pleaded for an end to the selfishness and divisiveness, for a reconciliation, and a rediscovery of Americans' ability to talk to each other and work for the common good. Whether his plea would be heard and heeded would tell much about the early years of Durango's second century.

Such a contentious situation defies easy analysis. Contemporaneousness and personal involvement preclude time-refined objectivity. Superficial blame can be laid on Watergate and the mistrust of government and officials which that tragedy bred. Farther back, the Vietnam war created ill will and reinforced the American trait of seeking a simple solution to the country's complex woes. When the going gets tough, Americans like to find a scapegoat, which, when eliminated, promises to solve nearly everything; hence agitation over slavery, prohibition, and communism. Change, much of it rapid, affected everything in the sixties and seventies and created an edginess, a fear of the unknown, a desire to strike out against those things that produced change. Elected officials became an easily visible target. The age-old resentments of the "haves" by the "have-nots," and an underlying feeling that elected officials become power hungry and corrupt in office, stoked the fire further.

Durango also now reflected American attitudes more quickly than ever before, thanks to instant communication. What was taking place here was happening elsewhere; the site provided no isolated shelter against storms of controversy. Perhaps Americans felt frustrated in a growingly impersonal world, where the worth of the individual appeared to be declining and his voice lost in the babble. These proved to be frustrating, trying years for everyone. "We can't go on this way," Hart observed. "We can't run the government nor expect democracy to function responsively" under such pressures. As the centennial closed, no easily implemented solutions presented themselves. No greater challenge had arisen in the past 100 years.

Debate over the Animas–La Plata Project grew to a bitter crescendo, all the way from Durango to Washington. One of the victims of President Jimmy Carter's infamous "hit list," its worth, along with other western water projects, was being severely questioned in the East. Challenges, too, came from local residents who insisted that the Animas–La Plata boded ill for them or their community.

Neither side recruited a monolithic army ready to do battle; a wide range of opinions rested under each banner. Opposition to the project ranged from those upset because of threatened land condemnation, not the project's concept, to die-hards opposed to any governmental effort. Regrettably, a strong current of antiintellectualism marred their presentation. Questions were raised about eventual payment, water rights, who really benefited, growth, energy waste, wildlife dislocation, and a basic one about the economic logic of the whole project in remote southwestern Colorado. Some of the accusations were more emotionally ignited than logically thought out, but the sincerity of most of the participants could not be doubted. Without question, various government agencies, state and federal, had played into the hands of the opposition by their own arrogance and bumbling. Allegations of secret meetings, changing positions, lack of information, refusals to listen, and threats were leveled by embittered opponents, who provided facts to back up their complaints.

Those in favor of the project marshaled their charts and facts and joined the battle. They spoke of agricultural, recreational, municipal, and industrial benefits and promised twenty million dollars in annual benefits. They discussed, not expenses, but investments, a wise step in a day of tax-payer revolts. Only 3 percent, they estimated, of the eventual cost would be nonreimbursable for a project that would take ten years and millions of dollars to complete. Like their opponents, they, too, fell to arguing among themselves over land exchange and wildlife habitat modification.

After a series of local meetings, Senator Hart pointed to the two major concerns as he saw them: first, the merits of the project, which, even after the hearings and years of planning, still seemed vague; and, second, how the project was put together, who benefited, and who was hurt. On this second concern Animas–La Plata opponents scored some points as they hammered at the threatened bureaucratic condemnation of land, seizure of water rights, and insensitivity to local worries and attitudes.

Neither side sallied forth wrapped in a banner of all good or all bad. To get them together to find the answers, without emotional arguments, rhetoric, and mistrust, might call for a Solomon, yet it had to be accomplished for the future of the Animas–La Plata and Durango.

Democrats and Republicans fought the good fight in 1978. When the last speech was given, the final advertisement purchased, and the last vote tabulated, Coloradans in La Plata County and throughout the state had once again proven to be maverick voters. Party loyalty or political philosophy appeared to govern little of their voting. Issues and personalities tipped the scale time after time. Trying to analyze such an illogical pattern was nearly impossible and gave political forecasters and party leaders sour dispositions. In part, the pattern reflected the constantly shifting and mobile electorate, continually transfused with new voters, and partly a disaffection for politicians, combined with a dash of the traditional American political philosophy of "turning the rascals out."

La Plata County clearly showed these attitudes. The voters generally followed their conservative ways, but overwhelmingly rejected an amendment to limit state spending. The Democratic candidate for county sheriff won a substantial victory, while the Republican county commissioner candidate came in first in the most bitter of local races, caused by personality clashes and the old bugaboo of land-use regulations. Durango, which had once dominated the county, found itself in a stand-off as rural voters turned out in large numbers. The trend toward country living was never more clearly shown. The authentic rural precincts, however, did not show great increases in voters, just those that were becoming semiurbanized through subdivision.

The race between Governor Dick Lamm and Republican challenger Ted Strickland illustrated the voting patterns as clearly as any. Lamm captured 55 percent of Durango's vote, only to lose by nine votes in the total county returns. Statewide, he won with a landslide 60 percent vote, showing that La Plata County marched out of step with much of the rest of Colorado. The Democrats' traditional alliance of minorities and urbanites (labor was and is an insignificant factor) held, as the party carried the two minority-dominated precincts (one of them in the county) and the city. This majority failed to withstand the Republicans' rural strength, supported by the small county villages. Actually, Lamm did better than any other statewide Democratic candidate, as his party again took a local beating. Minority candidates made little headway, although sixteen voters supported the slate of Sal A. Mander and G. "Turkey" Murphy, Aspen's contribution to political lunacy.

So La Plata County and its county seat continued to go their own way with little impact on the statewide results. It was evident that voters throughout the state continued to be independent in their attitudes, unfettered by party loyalties, and determined to vote for whom they pleased. Neither of the major parties was as strong nor as active as a decade before. Independent voters held the balance of power.

The dissent that had torn county and city for the past decade clearly affected the vitriolic county commissioner race. Articulate incumbent Gilbert Slade, who advocated planning and an activist-responsible government, found himself locked in an angry fight with rural landowners and others opposed to his ideas and activities. Forecasters predicted a county/urban fight, with the outcome pivoting on Durango's vote. Slade carried nine of the ten city precincts, but by a much smaller margin than he needed. Even before most of the county returns began to come in, he had lost, eventually with only 45 percent of the vote. The mandate, if such a thing were possible, called for less planning and government involvement in individual lives. The immediate legacy produced more bitterness, a further cleavage between the town and the surrounding county, and some soul-searching about what the future might bring.

Politics aside, the community's future was clouded in other respects. It was still "Bound to Boom," and therein lurked the murkiest of all problems. Growth would bring change, a disturbing, unknown probability. That fear underlay the zoning fights, sanctified by the hallowed belief that land ownership rested on the divine right to do as one pleased. Those who felt that land was a stewardship to be held in trust for future generations lost the battle in 1978, not the war. The self-serving, greedy beat hammered on—sell, develop the land for profit—and the future be damned. No wonder conscientious Durangoans looked ahead uneasily. A self-centered individualism, not the self-reliant individualism of western lore, had snared too many people.

The trait is easy to see. One of the facts of local economic life has been the propensity for several similar enterprises to cut into the profits of the one already prospering there. Thus, a couple of fast-food-type restaurants do not satisfy; the town must have half a dozen, with the number constantly growing. If several small souvenir shops can make a profit, why not a score? And then there are the real estate firms, and agents, which seem to be spawned with each new moon. Although this may be shrewd business practice, it has led to numerous closings and business transfers.

In the postwar years, Durangoans have been an increasingly transitory lot. A prewar, rural-oriented class has changed into a well-educated, professional, urban-oriented one. This is evident, for instance, in the county fair, which exists more as a relic of the past than a viable community celebration. Less attachment to the town and a lack of deep roots in the area have diminished community spirit and backing for the fair.

The old spirit has faltered elsewhere as well. After two losing football seasons, support for the high school team slumped. While this illustrates Americans' penchant for winners and the transitoriness of the population, it also shows a waning of community involvement and a change in attitude from the days when the local high school or similar institution was a rallying point. Great pride is taken in local cultural attainments, yet relatively few people bother to attend such events. Probably fewer than 200 people saw the opera *Susannah*, put on by an affiliate of the San Francisco Opera in March 1978, and the community concert series rarely draws a full house.

Residents have likewise, on occasion, shown an alarming lack of interest in their present and future. Only about 250 took the time to participate in a series of workshops, which extended over thirteen days and evenings, on open space and planning. Even fewer attended lectures on solar heating a little later in the fall of 1978. Nor have they displayed a bulldog tenacity for problem solving. The initial excited outburst and shock over some particular issue is likely to result in a good turnout at meetings and letters to the newspaper—for a while. If the issue persists and no immediate solution emerges, the numbers dwindle. Interest wanes only slightly less quickly than it rose with the initial disclosures. The majority rules in name only. Basically passive, its members allow the minority to govern, choosing instead not to be involved unless the matter in question directly affects them. Lack of interest, poor attendance, short attention span are time bombs planted for the future.

Hard feelings and bitter intolerance permeate the town, perhaps reflecting more the times than the community. It brings back memories of the 1920s and the Klan; only the organization died, not the sickness that gave it birth. Examples, unfortunately, are many as the ranting and raving go on. The attempt to smear Judge William Eakes on the eve of the 1978 election, leaving little chance for rebuttal, by a group interestingly called "People Against Injustice," comes to mind. The "zanies" on both ends of the political spectrum who indulge in name calling and inflexible thinking produce more than their share of dissent. The *Harmony Valley* play written by some opposed to the Animas–La Plata Project displayed neither good satire nor a shred of respect for those in favor of the project. And still, after all these years, racial intolerance remains, though not as openly. This list could be extended, but to little purpose. Senator Hart's call for listening to one another and constructive discussions fell on deaf ears, and his later observation, "It's tragic to see [Durango, La Plata County, and Colorado] torn apart by people who cannot get along," hits home.

The greed for profit that nearly monthly has driven real estate and land prices to new highs threatens to turn Durango into a town for the wealthy. Perhaps its destiny is to emerge as the "Aspen of Southwest Colorado." A study by Fort Lewis College Professor Barney Anderson indicated that the trend was already being established. "Bayfield is a prime growth area because of lower land and housing costs. [Its] growth rate already exceeds Durango," he wrote. Many people complained about the high cost of living, but did nothing about it. A disgusted potential resident, Mary Olsen, wrote the *Herald*, September 5, 1978: "The practice of pushing the prices of housing, food and clothing as far as the traffic will bear is not only despicable, it's unethical and inflationary."

Speaking of inflation, an ever-present concern, the city government budget for 1979 topped four million dollars. Yet few people troubled themselves to attend one of the budget hearings to see why and how it would be spent. There were those who argued it was not a bargain at any price. Opposition to the installation of water meters was not only based on its being too costly to the individual, but also on the fact that the city seemed unable to repair the leaks in the reservoir, which lost an estimated seventy-five thousand gallons of water per day through seepage.

All is not dismaying, short-sighted, and self-interested. Those qualities that served Durango so well over the past century are still in evidence, perhaps about to stage a renaissance. A positive citizen concern about local government was shown by the commission that revised the city charter and that document's subsequent strong approval by voters in November 1978. The 1978 charter, in the words of the commission, "is designed to encourage citizen involvement and participation in matters of local government. We believe that when citizens are active participants in government, it best insures the protection of the public interest." This mature attitude has been needed sorely in the 1970s.

City Council members have shown a growing willingness to listen to concerned citizens, even if some of those citizens doubt the council's intent to follow the advice so freely given. A long overdue step was taken with the appointment of a Parks and Recreation Board. Few cities have so much to lose by a failure to plan for open space and parks and so much to gain by doing it—parks for all people from the walker to the softball player, from the youngster to the senior citizen.

The recent blood drive showed that community spirit has not expired, as record numbers turned out to donate. And planning, though not in good graces with some, is not dead. There is increasing concern that something needs to be done. Not last-resort zoning, but planning, planning that is not outdated before it can be implemented. Planning must involve everybody; planning for someone else's property and welfare without his agreement and help solves nothing. People are realizing that they cannot have their cake and eat it, too, when it comes to Durango's environment.

Even some of those tenacious tenets, such as the benefits of tourism, are being reconsidered. Is tourism, which brings in all that money from the 120,000 train riders, 190,000 skiers, and thousands of other visitors, being challenged? It is, and not just by some visionary, but by Main Avenue merchants. One commented that perhaps the time has come to cut back on Chamber of Commerce tourist advertising. The sheer numbers of tourists is becoming threatening, he argued, and it is not the "clean" industry that it has been claimed to be for so long. Durangoans are concerned about the future and its quality.

The ever-present isolation has been steadily overcome since 1945. Now the airport is served by two airlines (a third one operated briefly in 1978–79), and another smaller private field nearer town is operating. Wolf Creek Pass is multilaned and hardly deserves the treacherous reputation it has acquired. The small-town atmosphere that so many cherished, though eroded, has not disappeared and it can still be felt in so many ways. A day or two in Denver will convince anyone that Durango has its attributes.

Two noteworthy points about the future emerge. First, the old Durango is gone, even that town I first knew in 1964. It can be recaptured about as easily as yesterday's fleeting sunset. Second, in the words of Robert Redford at an August 1978 symposium in Vail, "It's insane to assume that we can go forward without development. We are a development-oriented society." The community needs to plan for tomorrow in order to provide an orderly development and to control growth while protecting the environment. Failure to do this yields the frightening alternative of uncontrolled urban sprawl, traffic congestion, despoliation of the scenic beauty, pollution of the air and water, and the collapse of all that has made the community a memorable place to live. Durangoans need only to look to some appalling examples elsewhere in Colorado to realize what could be in store for them.

Durango's second century promises new problems and a continuation of familiar ones; it offers challenges and opportunities and does not promise an easy road to the good life. A large measure of successes and failures, joys and disappointments will mark that path, and unless the present generation dares to face its obligations, it will be cursed more than praised by future ones. Pessimists would say that about summarizes the future, but Durangoans over the years have shown more resiliency, optimism, and faith than that. The future will be challenging. At the same time, it will be exciting and rewarding. The late Milford Shields composed a short poem entitled, "Durango, Colorado," which summarizes his home pretty well:

> As long as men shall seek the better way
> Shall they come here and, finding it, shall stay;
> A virile city in a rugged land,
> While stand these mountains shall Durango stand.

Caroline Romney, John Porter, and the others would understand; they had been there before.

Epilogue

The valley of the river of lost souls is lonely no more. The river still curves through this oasis in southwestern Colorado as it has for eons. Its waters now wash business block and home yard, a few discarded junk car bodies, and the litter of a throw-away civilization. Meanwhile, the city of Durango keeps growing.

Through the Animas Valley has marched the saga of western settlement and man's struggle with the mountains. The Anasazi and Ute passed here, some calling it home. Only slightly disturbing the land, they left merely a trace of their habitation in the ruins of their homes and campsites.

Eventually Spaniards journeyed through in search of trade, gold, and lost souls to save. They left but legends and a name behind. A wandering trapper or two traveled this way, seeking beaver in the mountain streams and the freedom of a fast vanishing way of life. Army patrols and an occasional Indian agent, too, rode by, sensing the quiet of the valley. And still the Animas rolled on undisturbed.

Not until 1860, with civil war menacing the states back east, did the miner and promoter make their way here, seeking not quiet but a dream, a dream of wealth and growth. Then the valley began to change. The first wave of settlers ebbed, driven back by isolation, lack of gold, and the Utes. Others came to take their places and the quiet solitude gave way to the rancher, farmer, carpenter, and merchant. Within ten years ranch and farm homes and a little hamlet dotted the valley, and would-be coal miners were digging away. A second stage of development was under way.

Soon roads replaced trails and steam power superseded horses. Iron rail and telegraph wire intruded into centuries-old seclusion. Visitor and settler found it easy to reach the valley of the Animas. Over it all watched Durango's founder and promoter, organizer and developer, the Denver and Rio Grande. Nearly singlehandedly it guided the community's early years, yet its day passed rapidly. Within a generation, the first automobile and airplane arrived and the train was no longer unchallenged king. The very success of the city it had brought up diminished the railroad's role.

Transformation came rapidly. Electric lights, the telephone, movies, the radio, the automobile, and television altered ways of life beyond recall. Isolation no longer presented a problem. The world was brought to the Animas Valley, and with it came growing numbers of people, each with a dream about the valley's promise. From a few hundred to a few thousand, to a projected thirty-four thousand or more by the century's end, the city grew and the valley changed—it, too, beyond recall.

And the Animas nurtures its valley yet, unperturbed by the changes that crowd its banks. Each of the waves of settlement left a mark on the valley, relics of a passing existence; some are called history, others litter. Durangoans have marred, scraped, dug, and moved the land, while the river rolls on. James Grafton Rogers, writing about his mountain valley where Georgetown nestles in its corner of the Colorado Rockies, said, "Our valley is a palimpsest, a parchment written upon, erased and written over again." He could have been describing the valley of the river of lost souls.

Into the Second Century

Durango, now nearly six years into its second century, confronts some of the same problems it faced a hundred years ago, and a multitude of new ones. The one factor that has remained constant is change.

Durango's growth did not equal earlier projections; in 1980 census takers counted 11,649 residents. La Plata County grew much more rapidly during the 1970s, surpassing even the state average, and Durango's percentage of the total county population slipped to 42%. Expansion slowed for both as they passed the mid-1980s mark. These trends produced new problems and challenges for county and city.

Change was a primary theme for the city's outstanding centennial celebration in 1980-81. Durangoans celebrated for a full year with events designed to suit everyone's tastes: for example, historical lectures, dances, an old-time community Christmas, dedication of Pioneer Park, art fair, film festival of Hollywood movies shot locally, commissioned symphony and concert, dedication of the Animas School Museum, and reinactment of the driving of the silver railroad spike on a hot August 1981 day. Honored guests and speakers included former President and Mrs. Gerald Ford, Governor Richard Lamm, and Louis L'Amour.

The centennial celebration took a look at both the past and the future, with discussions of where the community had been and where it might be headed. By the end of the year Durangoans had a much better appreciation of their heritage and an awareness of their future. Heightened historical perception became evident when both Main Avenue and Third Avenue were designated as historic districts, helping to preserve one of Durango's greatest attractions — its architectural heritage.

A major change, anticipated for some time, came during the centennial year. The Denver and Rio Grande sold its Durango-to-Silverton narrow gauge line on March 25, 1981 to Florida businessman Charles Bradshaw, who promptly pledged to bring improvements while maintaining the train's nineteenth-century charm. The most visible innovations since that time include year-round operation (only to the Cascade Canyon Wye and back in winter), four trains daily during the summer season, and increased promotion. The result has been a steady rise in the number of passengers (177,000 during the 1985-86 train year) and improved community relations at both ends of the line.

Although the railroad no longer ties Durango to the rest of the state, airlines and highways do. An ongoing issue has been the question of whether the local airport should be enlarged. Hot words have been exchanged between the county commission and the city council over ways in which to develop a plan and find funding.

The airport has also seen a dramatic change in the airlines that use it. When Frontier Airlines pulled out in October 1984 as part of a general reorganization, thirty-seven years of service to Durango came to an end. Other smaller lines moved in and out, most unable to find enough passengers to sustain profitable service.

Highways, always the essential ingredient in promoting tourism, Durango's primary economic pillar, became especially important with expansion of the Purgatory ski area and the railroad. The tourist industry acquired a firm, year-round basis. That old standby, Mesa Verde National Park, continued to register increasing numbers, even when national hard times slowed tourist travel elsewhere. Few areas of Colorado could rival Durango for the variety of attractions offered.

Even with these blessings, all was not well with Main Avenue merchants and Main Avenue's motel row. The recession that hit the United States for several years finally affected the community in 1984-85. This delayed reaction reinforced the general Durango economic pattern, always somewhat behind overall national trends. The winter of 1985-86 found more store and office vacancies than at any other time in memory.

Making matters worse, franchised motels and restaurants moved in and threatened to dominate the local scene. Two shopping malls built south of town brought Durango in line with the rest of the country but cut into local businesses even more. The potential threat of the Purgatory complex to Durango business caused concern, because the former had rooms, food, and stores to offer in competition with the latter. The business community remains in a state of flux with an unknown future.

The county and city governments have not escaped their share of dissension. More than ever in 1983-85 they feuded on issues that ranged from the airport to the library, to the humane society. Money caused most of the grief. Federal government cutbacks increased competition for funding, and neither entity relished the thought of raising local taxes.

The changing nature of city and county relationships generated more controversy. As satellite subdivisions mushroomed around mountain-locked Durango, the county grew more urbanized. Demands for and the cost of county services rose at the same time funds declined. Meanwhile, the agriculturalists of the county found themselves enduring the same hard times faced by their counterparts throughout the country. They could ill afford to see their taxes raised. And agriculture was playing a diminishing role — only 93,000 acres of cropland and 193,000 acres of pastureland remained in 1982-83, compared to 397,000 acres in 1964.

All these changes resulted in inter-governmental disputes over expenses and needs, the classic rural-urban fight. No easy answers came to the rescue. The fact that county residents continued to be more conservative in their voting pattern than Durangoans, who had a higher average income, widened the gap between the two elements.

The same pattern could be discerned in that on-going debate over the Animas-La Plata Project. It refused to go away, and the issue was not satisfactorily resolved.

Opponents and proponents marshaled their facts and figures and attempted to out-letter-write and out-shout each other, while the majority of people sat on the sidelines as spectators. Funding, environmental impact, feasibility, need, Indian water rights — all the old familiar battle grounds were revisited.

On a more upbeat note, the Bodo Industrial Park developed into a resounding success, even though the variety of industry needed to balance the economy did not come with it. Durango's isolation and transportation problems continued to hex efforts to attract it, as they had for over a century.

Durango has always been an attractive place to live, provided a livable income can be earned. Sometimes that can be a difficult proposition, as many individuals continued to discover. The mere desire to live in such a pleasant environment rarely turned hope into reality. The pioneers of the 1880s could have told their descendants about this oft-shattered dream.

Many of those who wanted to settle here were once students at Fort Lewis College, which grew steadily during a time when higher education in the state faced declining enrollments. A fight over governance of the college in 1984-85 produced more heat than light but did help to unify local support behind the institution. Despite lingering town/gown suspicion, the college bestowed much of value on Durango, not the least of which was its economic and cultural blessings.

That elusive term "quality of life" was, and will be, an issue crucial to Durango. Progress has been made toward retaining some of it. A 1981 Tree City USA award symbolized the community's continuing effort to expand and maintain one of its major assets, an urban forest. Surpassing any effort of previous decades, a monumental parks development program over the past eight years has preserved this generation's greatest legacy for the future. From Gateway Park at the city's entrance, through the beautiful riverfront sequence, to the recreational complex at the college, new parks beckon all ages. These efforts will be expanded in the years ahead, it is hoped, to provide a lasting heritage of open space for generations to come.

But because the "rape and run" mentality endures, threats to Durango's natural beauty and quality of life persist. Planning and zoning arouse fears and belligerence among those who refuse to realize that they are stewards of the land, not owners in perpetuity. The consequences of unbridled growth stagger the imagination — and should be stirring the soul.

Another ghost from the past continues to haunt the town into the '80s — the uranium tailings pile across the river. Even after myriad meetings, studies, and reports, it still sits there in 1986, six years after the formation of a local task force to coordinate removal action, and eight years after Congress passed legislation to that end. The required federal, state, and local plans have not been fully developed, although some progress has been made. One of the surprises this ghost disclosed — tailings had been used as fill under the city/county swimming pool. They were removed.

Lest recent years seem to have been all gloom and doom, here is a look at a few of the more humorous incidents. The *New York Times* created a row when it described Durango in a travel article as a "cowpoke town." Many Durangoans arose in righteous anger over that "slander." Decrying that description, Durango's mayor, Ian Thompson, leaped to his community's defense in a rebuttal letter to the metropolitan journal, thus quieting the issue in the "Big Apple" and saving Durango's honor.

Then came a test (Feb., 1985) by United Bank of its burglary system with a mock robbery. When bank officials neglected to notify local law enforcement officers, the "robbery" brought immediate response by armed police and alarmed Durangoans. Redfaced bankers were forced to do some fast explaining.

There are encouraging and discouraging signs for Durango as 1986 fast becomes history. One could become despondent about the future, but none of the problems appear to be unsolvable; their like has been seen before. Some will require only patience and time; others need a willingness to tackle the difficult solutions and make them work.

For starters, the city and county must work together. They are not two different entities living in two different worlds. Urban and rural dwellers have to come to a mutual understanding as well, and realize that tourism, the college, and agriculture can lie down together for the betterment of all. Without question, all need to see that times do change and the old solutions and old ways are not going to serve for tomorrow.

"Where there is no vision, the people perish," wrote a Jewish writer in Proverbs. That bit of wisdom is as relevant for the people crowded into the Animas Valley as it was for those long ago along the Jordan River.

On Searching for Durango's Past
A Bibliographical Essay

"History," Henry Ford said, "is bunk," a sentiment undoubtedly echoed by others. Or they might agree with George Eliot that "the happiest women, like the happiest nations, have no history." It is hoped that the reader of this volume will not agree with either. A writer or teacher may be dull, but not history itself.

The heart of Durango's history is her people, the who, not the where and when. The people interviewed by the author are listed in another section. The Civil Works Administration interviewed old-timers during the 1930s, and those reminiscences are found in the La Plata County section. The four volumes of *Pioneers of the San Juan Country* (Colorado Springs; Durango; Denver: 1942–61), sponsored by Durango's Sarah Platt Decker Chapter of the DAR, have many firsthand stories and interviews. Beyond these, the newspapers are the best source, dating from 1881 to the present. Newspapers obviously contain a bonanza of all types of Durango information and those used are listed at the end of this essay.

While it is impossible to review each source examined, those that provided the most help follow. The dustbin of history is a fascinating place in which to grope around, and many are the rare finds that await persistence. Traps that need to be avoided constantly are the antiquarianism and parochialism so frequently the refuge of the writer of this genre of history.

No book-length study of Durango has been written and only a few pamphlets on varied aspects of it. Although their authors fall into the trap just mentioned, Marion Jarvis, *The Strater Hotel Story* (Durango: n.p., 1963) and *Come on In Dearie* (Durango: Herald, 1976) and Retha Luzar, *The Animas City Story* (Durango: Herald, 1978) offer some facts, some legends, and some misinformation. The *Colorado Magazine* has a few references to Durango, including Mary Ayres's article "The Founding of Durango, Colorado in 1880" in the May 1930 issue. The same is true of the collections of the Denver Public Library, Colorado Historical Society (Durango Trust, Land & Coal Company, and Bell Papers), and Western Historical Collections of the University of

Colorado. The single and multivolume Colorado histories all mention Durango and are invaluable for placing the community within the larger state framework.

Books that touch upon Durango and/or subjects related to the community are a varied lot. Robert G. Athearn's *Rebel of the Rockies* (New Haven: Yale University Press, 1962) remains the place to start on the D&RG. From here one can follow the company and the narrow-gauge train in pamphlet and specialized studies. Thomas Baker, an early Durango superintendent of schools, offers surprisingly little on the town in his *Thomas Orville Baker: An Autobiography* (privately printed c. 1942). Robert Delaney, *Blue Coats, Red Skins and Black Gowns: 100 Years of Fort Lewis* (Durango: Herald, 1977), Horace Hale, *Education in Colorado* (Denver: News, 1885), and Cecil McKinley, "A History of the Public Schools of Durango, Colorado" (M.A. Thesis, University of New Mexico, 1944), are much better. Anne Baxter's comments were included earlier; however, for those who seek further elaboration, *Intermission* (New York: G. P. Putnam's Sons, 1976) has them and more. *A Frontier Army Surgeon* (New York: Exposition Press, 1962) by Barnard Byrne tells of Durango in the 1880s, but uses conversations and appears to remember a bit too clearly for the time that passed between the events and the writing. *Colorado: A Guide to the Highest State* (New York: Hastings House, 1945 & 1970) gives a few odds and ends and some legends.

Various of the Colorado mining directories and John Canfield's *Mines and Mining Men of Colorado* (Denver: Carson, 1893) present insights into that local industry. The numerous Colorado business directories have brief discussions of the town, list people, and display ads of the business community. Promotional books such as George Crofutt's *Crofutt's Grip-Sack Guide to the Highest State* (Omaha: Overland, 1885) have Durango sections, but should be used with care. A local endeavor of the same type, full of information, is Richard McCloud *Durango as It Is* (Durango: Board of Trade, 1892). *Durango* (Durango: Herald, 1883), *Durango Directory for the Year 1892* (Trinidad: Bensel, 1892), R. C. Rohrabacher, *The Great San Juan of Colorado and New Mexico* (Durango: Democrat, 1901), *Durango and La Plata County Colorado* (Durango: Democrat, 1909), *The San Juan Basin* (Denver: Carson, c. 1911), and *A Story Told in Brief of Durango and La Plata County* (Durango: Democrat, 1909) do the same thing.

A few people who have lived here have written books. Fred Girard, *Durango: The End of the Trail* (Santa Fe: Sleeping Fox, 1975), tells a personal story of the era starting with the late 1920s; Robert McConnell, *The Autobiography of Robert Earll McConnell* (New York: Cross, 1966) describes Durango of the 1890s and turn of the century; and one of the strangest a reader will encounter is Ruth Starr's *Wonders from the Heavens: How the UFOs Rocked the Town of Durango, Colorado* (Hicksville, N.Y.: Exposition Press, 1977). (According to Starr they were supposed to have landed in 1961.) For Animas City see Robert Athearn (ed.) "Major Hough's March into Southern Ute Country, 1879," *Colorado Magazine*, May 1948.

On the social circuit, *The First 50 Years of the Electra Sporting Club* (Durango: n.p., 1960) by long-time club secretary James Noland offers a personal view. *Prominents or the Social Record and Club Annual* (Denver: Empire, 1911) covers the whole state, allotting three pages to Durango. A few visitors have left their impressions: Ernest Ingersoll, *The Crest of the Continent* (Chicago: Donnelley, 1885) is especially good, while Lucius Beebe's *Mixed Train Daily* (Berkeley: Howell-North, 1961 reprint) is indeed mixed. The same can be said for Sandra Dallas's *No More than Five in a Bed* (Norman: University of Oklahoma Press, 1967).

In Roger Lauen's "Community Change" (Ph.D. dissertation, University of Colorado, 1973), Durango, a "mountain town," is the subject of a sociological study. The high school yearbook, *The Toltec*, started out as a newspaper and has some interesting insights. Bernard Anderson's economic feasibility study (June 1976) of the Bayfield area has much in it for Durango's consideration. Densil Cummins's thick tome, "Social and Economic History of Southwestern Colorado, 1860–1948" (Ph.D. dissertation, University of Texas, 1951), contains some information on the town and county. Helen Daniels, *Adventures with the Anasazi of Falls Creek* (Durango: Center of Southwest Studies, 1976) recounts her work, and Florence and Robert Lister's *Earl Morris and Southwestern Archaeology* (Albuquerque: University of New Mexico Press, 1968), tells the larger story.

Locally there are several depositories that contain a wealth of information. The Center of Southwest Studies at Fort Lewis College (especially its collection of the Western Colorado Power Company Records) and the Durango Public Library offer a potpourri of materials, and the First National Bank holds its banking records since the 1880s. The District Court has records, as do La Plata County and the city. Durango's ordinance and council minute books are prime sources. State and federal publications furnish information, for example, the coal inspectors' reports. By far the most important, however, are the federal and state censuses. The original returns for 1880, 1885 (state), and 1900 provide all kinds of surprises.

The backbone of this study has been the newspapers, of which Durango has had many. Some proved extremely helpful, others only muddled the picture. Their value depended on the editors' and reporters' skill and ambition. Only the names and years used will be given, with no effort to evaluate them beyond that already indicated in the text.

The Basin Star	1959
The Daily Idea	1888
Daily Southwest	1893
Denver Tribune	1882
Durango Daily Morning Herald	1887, 1889
Durango Democrat	1926
Durango Evening Herald	1898, 1924
Durango Examiner	1888, 1891
Durango Exchange News	1928
Durango Herald (daily)	1892, 1894, 1896, 1899, 1964–79
Durango Herald (weekly)	1881–83, 1888–91, 1895–97
Durango Herald-News	1955
Durango News	1933–36, 1947
Durango Record	1881–82
Durango Semi-Weekly Herald	1899, 1901–05, 1917
Durango Weekly Democrat	1900, 1906–12, 1915–21, 1925

Durango Weekly Herald	1913–16, 1919–20, 1923, 1929–31, 1935, 1937, 1940–45
Durango Weekly Tribune	1891
Field and Farm (Denver)	1899
Great Southwest	1892
The Idea	1885–86
La Plata Miner (Silverton)	1879–81
Morning Democrat	1897
New York Times	scattered issues
Rocky Mountain News (Denver)	scattered issues
Solid Muldoon	1893–94
The Southwest	1883–84
Today	1976–79
Weekly Republican (Denver)	1899

I am sincerely indebted to the people who graciously offered their time and memories; without them much of the richness of the history would have been lost. Many were interviewed more than once in the period from 1976 through 1978. They came from all walks of life—carpenter, minister, postman, banker, housewife, farmer, businessman, fireman, newspaperman, doctor—and gave a multifaceted view of Durango, dating from the 1880s. If I did not conduct the interview, the name of the interviewer is included. The date beside the name indicates when that person was born in or came to Durango.

Ballantine, Arthur (1952); interviewer, David McComb, Colorado Historical Soc.
Bonavida, Anna (1920)
Bryce, John (1891)
Carlyon, Alfred and Yvonne (1953)
Dale, Mabel (1916)
Camp, A. M. (1884); interviewer, Earl Barker, Jr.
Cantrell, Marguerite (1892)
Daniels, Helen (1899)
Day, Samuel (1968)
Dorsett, Alton (1945)
Eakes, William (1946)
Eberl, Jack and Kay (tourists)
Ellsworth, C. R. (1968)
Emigh, Fred (1921)
Finegan, Bessie (1906)
Flora, Zeke (1933)
Gardenswartz, Lester (1916)

Glaser, Leonard (1910)
Gomez, Art (1956)
Gomez, Max and Anne (1916)
Helton, Mrs. Vernon (1896)
Jones, Donna (1967)
Kroeger, Fred (1918)
Lloyd, Leo (1936)
Lujan, Gilbert (1932)
Macomb, Richard (1905)
McCulloch, Mary (1900)
McDaniel, Ed (1899) and Zipporah (1895)
Mason, Walt (1920)
Murray, Helen (1896)
Nelson, Ethel (1906)
Newton, John (1950)
O'Connell, Mamie (1886)
Osterhoudt, Walt (1951); interviewer, Bruce Heller
Parker, Schuyler (1925)
Periman, Ken (1938)

Petty, Mary (1916)
Root, Homer and Wilma (1930)
Rowe, Minnie (1894)
Ruland, Al and Lilian (1938)
Sartoris, James (1936)
Sawyer, Robert (1953)
Short, Alva (1902)
Shry, Angela (1909)
Silva, Leonel (1964)

Smiley, Mrs. Emory (1904)
Smith, Louis (1891)
Smith, Violet (1929)
Sponsel, Josephine (1907)
Wadsworth, Stan (1974)
Wallace, Ned (1950)
Warlick, Dave (1916) and Gertrude (1907)
Wyatt, Arthur (1929)

Index